Pronunciation Matters

Pronunciation Matters

Communicative, Story-Based Activities
for Mastering the Sounds of
North American English

Lynn E. Henrichsen, Brent A. Green,
Atsuko Nishitani, and Carol Lynne Bagley

Illustrations by
Lynn E. Henrichsen and Atsuko Nishitani

Ann Arbor
THE UNIVERSITY OF MICHIGAN PRESS

To J. Donald Bowen (1922–89), who inspired us and many others.

Preface

Pronunciation Matters is a pronunciation improvement book for intermediate and advanced learners of English as a second or foreign language. It provides meaningful, communicative, and motivating practice activities leading to mastery of targeted sound contrasts in North American English.

Pronunciation Matters contains 186 focused, independent instructional units that help English language learners recognize and overcome their pronunciation difficulties. These units address a wide variety of areas that experienced ESL/EFL teachers around the world have noted as problematic for learners of English. The units are organized in eight sections—vowels, consonants, consonant clusters, reduction and blending, word stress, sentence stress, intonation, and segmentation.

Before using these instructional units, individual learners' particular pronunciation difficulties are identified using the diagnostic procedures and materials in Section 1. Then learners and their teachers can quickly turn to the appropriate units and find a wealth of ready-to-use instructional materials focusing on those difficulties.

The recommended procedures for using the instructional units employ a story-based, contextualized approach that has proven to be effective, enjoyable, and easy to use. Each unit begins with an engaging story that illustrates the communicative importance of the particular sound targets and lays the foundation for a variety of follow-up practice activities. These activities progress through various modes—imitative, rehearsed, and extemporaneous. Working in large and small groups, learners have fun in a variety of natural and game-like practice situations that reduce stress and build confidence. Phonological explanations, diagrams, and hints provide backup support for learners and teachers. In all these practice activities, learners need to pay attention to meaning while maintaining communicatively correct pronunciation, just as second language speakers must do in order to communicate successfully in real-life contexts.

Acknowledgments

A large number of colleagues and students, who were most generous with their time and talents, contributed to the development of *Pronunciation Matters* in various ways. First of all, we would like to thank the many trial users who piloted *Pronunciation Matters* units in their classes: Lauri Arrington, Brigham Young University; Jamie Baker, Minico High School; Robyn Campbell, Brigham Young University; Anita Wai Fong Chan, Brigham Young University; Carol Cini, United States Information Service, Hungary; David Christiansen, Brigham Young University; Jamie Cluff, Brigham Young University; Becky Donaldson, Brigham Young University; Paul Garver, InterNexus Center for Language Studies; Jeri Wyn Gillie, Brigham Young University; Arien Hamblin, Brigham Young University; Debra A. Larsen, Hillcrest High School; Judi Lin, Columbia University; Peggy Lindstrom, Colorado State University; Mary Livingston, Arizona State University; Leona Marsh, New York University; Pam Mooney, Colorado Springs, Colorado; Marshall Murray, Excellence in Education; Judi Pemán, Truman College; Beatriz R. Prezenszky e Silva, Evoluta Language Center; Marguerite Shaddy, Kansai Gaidai University; Marilyn Sturm, Doorways English School for International Women; Noriko Takahashi, Ichimura Gakuen Junior College; Priscilla Taylor, California State University, Los Angeles; Olga Troyachenko, Kazakstan; Karol L. Walchak, University of Nevada, Reno; and Cathy Young, Syracuse University. These people and their students provided us with valuable feedback that we used to improve the materials and procedures in *Pronunciation Matters*.

In addition, we would like to thank various people at Brigham Young University, including the administrators in the College of Humanities and Department of Linguistics for their staunch support of our efforts during the years *Pronunciation Matters* was being developed. We also owe a special debt of gratitude to Gwyn Williams (Thammasat University, Bangkok, Thailand), Judi Pemán (Truman College, Chicago, Illinois), and many TESL-L subscribers for lesson ideas. In addition, we acknowledge David Baker's help with the articulatory explanations, and we thank Diane Strong-Krause and the students in her ESL 302 classes for their generous sharing of their class time.

A number of other individuals have provided invaluable guidance during the production and publication phase: Tim Stookesberry; Susan Maguire; Kelly Sippell, acquisitions editor at the University of Michigan Press, and several reviewers.

Contents

Detailed Listing of Instructional Units and Peer-Tutoring Practice Cards

Note: The letter-number combinations (e.g., V1, V2, etc.) in the first column label the particular contrastive sound targets in English that are written in phonetic symbols and/or described directly below them. These targets are the focus of the instructional units and practice cards listed in the center column. (Capital letters in the final part of each letter-number combination indicate complete instructional units; lowercase letters indicate peer-tutoring practice cards. The masters for those cards are found in the teacher's manual.) The numbers in the right column show the pages on which the corresponding instructional units and phonological explanations are found.

SECTION 3. CONSONANTS (C)

Note: Consonant sounds tend to vary according to their position in a word or syllable. Therefore, in the units in this section, an extra, lowercase letter *i, m,* or *f* is added to the label (e.g., C1*i*-A/a) to indicate the location of the target sound within the contrasting words. These letters stand for *initial* (at the start of the syllable or word), *medial* (somewhere in the middle), and *final* (at the end).

SECTION 4. CONSONANT CLUSTERS (CC)

SECTION 6. WORD STRESS (WS)

Note: In the phonological representations in the left column, the symbol [S] stands for *syllable.*

Pages

To the Learner

Each unit in *Pronunciation Matters* focuses on a particular pronunciation contrast in English that causes difficulty for some ESL/EFL learners. When using this book, you should not work through all the units in order from beginning to end. The units you need will depend on your particular pronunciation difficulties. For example, if you have no trouble distinguishing between "lock" and "rock" you should not do C14 ([l]-[r]). If, however, you have trouble pronouncing or hearing the difference between the consonants in "ice" and "eyes" you should work on C15 ([s]-[z]).

Before you start working on the units, you should go through Section 1, "Diagnosing Your Pronunciation Difficulties." It will help you identify your particular pronunciation difficulties in English and decide which problems to work on first. It will also refer you to the particular *Pronunciation Matters* units that will help you with these difficulties.

Each instructional unit is based on a story context, illustrated with pictures. Although these stories were written especially for *Pronunciation Matters,* many of them are based on real-life incidents. As you may already know from your own experience, the pronunciation problems they illustrate and the confusion these problems cause are real.

Each story is designed so that a particular sound contrast makes a difference in meaning. Of course, in some real-life situations you may be able to communicate your intended meaning through nonvocal means—using gestures, pictures, etc.—or the situation itself may clarify the meaning. Nevertheless, since the purpose of *Pronunciation Matters* is to help you communicate as proficient native speakers of English do, try to avoid using nonvocal signals when you do the practice activities.

Detailed instructions for the various learning activities for each unit are provided in the first unit in each series (the one whose identifying number ends in A). Abbreviated instructions are provided in the other units (the ones whose identifying numbers end in B, C, etc.). If you are working on one of those units and can't remember what to do, just go to unit A in that series and look at the instructions or come back to this page and the explanation below.

All the different learning activities explained in "To the Teacher" can be used with every *Pronunciation Matters* unit. Briefly, here is what you should do with each one.

Story Listening. Listen to the story as your teacher tells it (and/or listen to it on the audiotape/CD). Make sure that you get the main ideas even if you don't understand every word. If there are new words or parts you don't understand, try to figure them out from the story context first.

Contrasting Sentences—Listening. Write the appropriate key word in the blank in each of the contrasting sentences. Then, when your teacher says one of the contrasting sentences from the story, respond correctly by marking the box in front of it, pointing to the right picture, making the corresponding gesture, or saying the appropriate rejoinder.

Contrasting Sentences—Speaking. Choose and say one of the contrasting sentences (to a partner or the whole class, as directed by your teacher) so that your listener(s) can respond correctly. Your teacher may suggest several ways of doing this.

Phonological Explanations. If you wish, check the explanations and diagrams (in Section 10, toward the back of the book) for your target sounds. Try following the hints to make sure your pronunciation is correct.

Other Words. See if you can find the listed words in the printed story. (In Sections 5, 7, 8, and 9, the examples may be phrases or sentences.) If you can't find them, don't worry. All of them may not be in every story. Often, however, a listed word or phrase will appear in a story several times. Also there may be additional words/phrases in the story that contain or use the target sounds. When you find these words/phrases, circle or underline them. Then say each marked word or phrase aloud—individually and then in its entire sentence. Finally, look for additional words in the story that use the target sounds. Mark and say them also.

In some units (those in Sections 2 and 6), you will need to sort the listed words into two groups according to the sound the boldface letters represent. Write the words in the spaces provided.

Cards—Listening. Find someone who has already mastered the target sounds you are working on. Then get a set of peer-practice cards for those target sounds. Follow the procedure your teacher demonstrates and work with your partner until you can point to the right card every time. Continue until you have earned all the cards in the stack.

Cards—Speaking. Find someone who has already mastered the target sounds you are working on. Then get a set of peer-practice cards for those target sounds. Follow the procedure your teacher demonstrates and work with your partner until you can say the target words so accurately that your partner points to the right card every time. Continue until you have given away all the cards in the stack.

Story Reading. On your own, practice reading the story in your chosen unit until you feel confident enough to read it aloud to a partner or your whole class. Record it on tape and listen to it (and/or play the tape to your partner or the whole class). When you listen to your classmates' readings, respond with a smile, buzz, or hmmm as explained by your teacher.

Story Dictation. Close your book and get out a blank sheet of paper. Then as your teacher (or a classmate) reads the story aloud, write it down, sentence by sentence. When you are finished, you may open your book and check what you wrote.

Cloze Reading. Go through the printed story and black out key words or phrases of your choice with a pencil or pen. Then, read the story again and let your mind tell you what the blacked out words are. Say them aloud even if they're blacked out. Do this several times. Every time you read the story, black out a few more words. Continue until most of the story is blacked out and you can tell it to a partner without looking at the page very often. When you listen to your partner's reading, respond with a smile, buzz, or hmmm as explained by your teacher.

Story Retelling from Outline. Black out all the remaining words in the story except those that you need to remind you of the story line. Or else make a quick outline of the story on a blank sheet of paper. Tell the story to your partner and/or class using just this skeleton or outline. When you listen to your partner's reading, respond with a smile, buzz, or hmmm as explained by your teacher.

Free Story-Telling. Tell the whole story without looking at your book or any paper. You can use your own words and even shorten the story, as long as you keep the main target sentences right. When you listen to your partner telling the story this way, respond with a smile, buzz, or hmmm.

Parallel Story. Create your own story similar to the one you have been reading and telling. It might have different characters, a different situation, or a different story line, but it should use many of the example words and others that use the target sounds of your unit. When you listen to your partner's story, respond with a smile, buzz, or hmmm.

Mini-drama. Get with some classmates and make up a skit or do a role play based on the story. Keep the target sounds and contrasting sentences from the original story as much as possible but feel free to be creative with everything else. Present your mini-drama to the whole class.

Do the activities that your teacher suggests, or if you are working independently, do all the ones that work for you. For some of them you will need a partner, and for others you will need the peer-tutoring pronunciation cards that can be made from the masters in the teacher's manual. Initial or check off each activity as you complete it so you can keep track of your progress.

A set of audio recordings (on cassette tape or compact disk) accompanies *Pronunciation Matters*. You will find these recordings helpful as they provide a model of correct pronunciation. Sometimes, the recorded pronunciation will be slightly different from your teacher's pronunciation due to dialect differences. Don't worry too much about that. Just choose the model that you desire.

As you go through each unit, don't forget to consult the pronunciation hints and the "Phonological Explanations" Section (Section 10) at the end of the book. Sometimes imitation alone may not be enough to enable you to produce the target sounds properly. The hints and explanations will give you information that will help you make sure you are pronouncing a sound correctly.

If you are looking for a particular story or unit and can only remember one of the main words that is contrasted in that unit, use the key-word index at the back of the book.

To the Teacher

Teachers of English to speakers of other languages are acutely aware of the need for better methods and materials for improving their students' pronunciation. In response to this need, *Pronunciation Matters* provides a wealth of instructional activities and materials that are effective in improving students' pronunciation yet easy for classroom teachers to use. These activities are also varied, flexible, and adaptable. Lessons can be focused and short, or they can fill an entire class hour without boring students. For these reasons, *Pronunciation Matters* units can form an entire pronunciation course for intermediate–advanced students focusing on microlevel skills, or they can fit into almost any ESL/EFL curriculum on an ad hoc basis when an emphasis on pronunciation is desired.

The accompanying teacher's manual is an essential resource for teachers using *Pronunciation Matters.* Be sure to get a copy and use it. The teacher's manual not only explains important *Pronunciation Matters* features and principles but also goes through the many recommended instructional procedures and variations in great detail. In addition, it provides a sample teaching plan outline for a *Pronunciation Matters* lesson—in skeleton form and with a complete teacher script. Last, but certainly not least, the teacher's manual contains the reproducible masters for the peer-tutoring pair-practice cards that are a key element in the pronunciation practice and improvement process.

In brief, the recommended instructional procedures and variations for a complete *Pronunciation Matters* lesson include the following.

Diagnosis of Students' Difficulties

Follow the procedures described in Section 1 of *Pronunciation Matters* and use the diagnostic materials provided there.

Initial Presentation and Practice

1. Select appropriate units.
2. Announce that you are going to tell a short story.
3. Tell (or play) the story.
4. Draw pictures.
5. Convey meaning and model pronunciation.

6. Continue.
7. Present and focus on contrasting sentences.
8. Provide varied contrastive listening practice.
9. Move on to speaking practice.
    a. Reverse roles.
    b. Have one student be the "teacher."
    c. Arrange student-to-student practice with audience involvement.
    d. Set up a communicative "information gap" situation.
    e. Reverse the procedure.
    f. Provide phonological explanations.
    g. Practice with the "Other Words" or "Other Examples" exercises.
10. Go on to peer-practice card activities, to storytelling practice, or to another story/lesson.

Peer-Practice Card Activities

1. Assign students to "strong-weak" pairs.
2. Choose a particular sound contrast for each pair to work on.
3. The "strong" student takes the role of "tutor." The other is the learner.
4. Two different cards from the set are placed face up between the students.
5. The "tutor" shuffles the rest of the cards in the set, holds them in his or her hand, takes the top card, looks at it, and says the sentence it represents.
6. The learner listens carefully and then points to the teaching card that corresponds to the sentence that he or she just heard.
7. The tutor then shows the practice card to the learner.
    a. If it matches, then the tutor gives it to the learner.
    b. If the two cards do not match, the tutor puts it back in the stack of practice cards to be used again.
8. The listening stage ends when the tutor has given all the practice cards to the learner.
9. The two students may then go on to another sound contrast, or they may go on to the speaking stage with the same contrast.
10. In the speaking stage, the learner holds the practice cards and says the appropriate sentences to the tutor (listener), who then points to the teaching card that corresponds to what the learner said. The "game" is finished when the learner has given away all the cards.

Story Reading and Retelling Practice

After they have mastered the pronunciation of the contrasting sentences, students may practice reading or retelling the entire story. This storytelling practice may also take several forms.

1. Reading practice
2. In-class readings
3. Practice with recordings
4. Student-made recordings
5. Story dictation
6. Cloze reading
7. Story retelling from a skeleton/outline
8. Free story retelling
9. Parallel story creation
10. Skits and/or role plays

Once again, extensive, detailed instructions for all these (and other) activities, as well as reproducible masters for the peer-practice cards, are provided in the teacher's manual.

Section 1

Diagnosing
Your Pronunciation
Difficulties

For the Teacher

Diagnosis may be done informally, by simply listening to students as they speak English, or more formally, by going through the procedures outlined below. Regardless of the approach you take, the following guidelines may be helpful.

- As it is usually difficult to hear and remember everything a student needs to work on from just one exposure to that student's pronunciation, making audio recordings of students as they speak is recommended. You may then listen to these recordings later and analyze them carefully so as to arrive at a more accurate and complete diagnosis of which sounds in which positions are difficult for each student. (*Note:* After adequate instruction and practice have been provided and students have mastered their pronunciation difficulties, these "before" recordings also provide dramatic evidence of students' improvement.)

- If the number of students you work with or the speech sample you take from them is large, do not attempt to carry out a detailed microanalysis. Such an analysis is tedious and time consuming for you, and the results are often overwhelming for the students. A wiser and more practical course is to identify a few of your students' most prominent pronunciation difficulties and then work on them. As you do this, don't forget reduction and blending, word and sentence stress, intonation, and pausing. These pronunciation features are not always represented by letters of the alphabet, but they are still very important to natural- sounding speech.

- Since students are often already aware of many of their own pronunciation difficulties, an alternative diagnostic method is to simply ask them what aspects of English pronunciation they want or need help with. For a more detailed and thorough self-analysis, have students go through the procedures outlined below.

- A similar approach is a guided self-analysis in which, under your direction, students work individually or with their class-mates and decide what their major difficulties in English pro-nunciation are.

Note: This approach has several advantages: (1) It takes less time than interviewing each student individually. (2) It generally results in greater motivation on the part of the students. (3) In addition, it recognizes and emphasizes students' own responsibility for improving their pronunciation. The greatest disadvantage of self-analysis is that students are sometimes not aware of their own problems relative to the English sound system. In such cases, your guidance (and diagnosis) plays an important part in arriving at a correct analysis of students' difficulties.

In either case, the diagnostic materials that follow will be helpful. They can be used by students identifying their own difficulties, or by you, their teacher, as you help them discover and prioritize their pronunciation problems.

Diagnostic Forms for Student
(or Teacher) Use

Name _____ Date _____

Diagnosing Your Pronunciation Difficulties

The purpose of this section is to help you and your teacher identify your particular pronunciation difficulties in English. This diagnosis provides the basis for deciding which *Pronunciation Matters* units you should work on and which instructional activities will help you the most. It can also help you and your teacher decide which of your difficulties with English pronunciation are the most important for you to overcome. For these reasons, it is important to take the time to do this diagnosis well. It consists of three parts: (1) Self-Analysis, (2) Storytelling and Story Retelling, and (3) Free Speaking.

1. Self-Analysis

You are probably already aware of most of the difficulties you have in pronouncing English. If not, think about particular words or phrases you have trouble saying. Write them down. Has there ever been a time when someone misunderstood you or you were embarrassed because of a mispronunciation in English? Write a few notes about the problem.

How about listening in English? Do you sometimes get confused because of similar-sounding words or phrases? Are there some English sounds that seem the same to you or that you just can't hear? Write down some notes about these particular difficulties also.

Now that you have thought about these things and made notes on them, go through the checklists below.

- As you do so, you may want to listen to the audio recording of the words and sentences on the checklist or have a proficient speaker of English read them aloud to you.
- If you would like to see the checklist words in larger, full-sentence contexts, or if you wish to see more examples of the target sounds, just look at the listings presented by units in pages xi–xviii.

- In the first column in the checklist, every pair of items (words, phrases, or sentences) represents a particular pronunciation difficulty in English. In each pair, the letters representing the key sounds are in boldface type. (Please note that a few of the pronunciations are spelled in nonstandard ways.)
- If you normally have difficulty *hearing* the difference between the two key sounds when they are spoken, make a check mark (✓) to the right of the pair in the column labeled "Listen."
- If you normally have difficulty *pronouncing* the correct distinction between the two key sounds, put a check mark (✓) in the column labeled "Speak."
- If you have trouble *hearing and pronouncing* the difference, put check marks in both columns. For example, if you have trouble both hearing and pronouncing the difference between words like *heat* and *hit* you should put a check mark in the two columns to the right of "sleep—slip."
- If you don't understand the difference between the two items, write a question mark (?) by the items. To really make sure, turn to the corresponding *Pronunciation Matters* unit and read the contrasting sentences or even the entire story.

The information in the column labeled "Unit" refers to the *Pronunciation Matters* unit that focuses on this difficulty.

Difficult Sounds

I. Vowels

	Listen	Speak	Unit
sleep—slip			V1
bitter—better			V2
taste—test			V3
pen—pan			V4
axe—ox			V5
shock—shark			V6
boss—bus			V7
clock—cloak			V8
bud—bird			V9
bucks—books			V10
stood—stewed			V11

II. Consonants

	Listen	Speak	Unit
pill—bill			C1i
rapid—rabid			C1m
cap—cab			C1f
pan—fan			C2i
lapping—laughing			C2m
cup—cuff			C2f
vote—boat			C3i
calves—cabs			C3m
curve—curb			C3f
worse—verse			C4i
rowing—roving			C4m
fan—van			C5i
shuffle—shovel			C5m

	Listen	Speak	Unit
safe—save			C5f
fought—thought			C6i
roofless—ruthless			C6m
reef—wreath			C6f
thigh—thy			C7i
ether—either			C7m
teeth—teethe			C7f
thought—taught			C8i
rethread—retread			C8m
myth—mitt			C8f
think—sink			C9i
mouthy—mousy			C9m
faith—face			C9f
they—day			C10i
father—fodder			C10m
loathe—load			C10f
then—Zen			C11i
teething—teasing			C11m
tithe—ties			C11f
cart—card			C12f
nap—lap			C13i
snob—slob			C13m
bone—bowl			C13f
long—wrong			C14i
collect—correct			C14m
file—fire			C14f
sip—zip			C15i
racer—razor			C15m
ice—eyes			C15f
sip—ship			C16i

	Listen	Speak	Unit
classes—clashes			C16m
lease—leash			C16f
dilution—delusion			C17m
shin—chin			C18i
washes—watches			C18m
lash—latch			C18f
choking—joking			C19i
etching—edging			C19m
batch—badge			C19f
Jell-o—yellow			C20i
yeast—east			C21i
coat—goat			C22i
picky—piggy			C22m
tack—tag			C22f

III. Consonant Clusters

	Listen	Speak	Unit
glass—grass			CC1
spouse—espouse			CC2
state—estate			CC3
scape—escape			CC4
strange—estrange			CC5
thing—think			CC6
fort—force			CC7
pass—passed			CC8
fail—failed			CC9
beast—beasts			CC10
dog—dogs			CC11
code—cold			CC12
train—terrain			CC13

IV. Reduction and Blending

	Listen	Speak	Unit
Sarah saw **her** yesterday.—Sarah saw **'er** yesterday			RB1
She **can** tell jokes well.—She **can't** tell jokes well.			RB2
It is time for dinner.—**It's** time for dinner.			RB3
I **want to** go home.—I **wanna** go home.			RB4
I **don't know** what to do.—I **dunno** what to do.			RB5
What do you want?—**Whaddaya** want?			RB6
What are you doing?—**Whatcha** doing?			RB7
Did you ever hear . . . ?—**Didja** ever hear . . . ?			RB8
I **guess you're** happy now.—I **guesshur** happy now.			RB9
Do you think they**'ll** do that?—Do you think they**'d** do that?			RB10
They**'ve** eaten all their dinner.—They**'d** eaten all their dinner.			RB11
Where**'d** you run to?—Where**'ve** you run to?			RB12
Where**'d** you run to?—Where**'ll** you run to?			RB13

V. Word Stress

	Listen	Speak	Unit
Peter loved the désert.—Peter loved the dessért.			WS1
Beverly was part of the cómedy.—Beverly was part of the commíttee.			WS2
They're going to **ré-léase** the film.—They're going to re**léase** the film.			WS3
My uncle has a **hót** dog.—My uncle has a hot **dóg.**			WS4
I saw a little **béar** hunting in Alaska.— . . . a little bear **húnt**ing in Alaska.			WS5

VI. Sentence Stress

	Listen	Speak	Unit
We ordered **twó** hamburgers.—We ordered two **hám**burgers.			SS1
He **hád** studied for the test.—He had **stúd**ied for the test.			SS2

VII. Intonation

	Listen	Speak	Unit
It's **dark already.**—It's **dark already?**			I1
I'm reading a good book. **What?** ↗ —**What?** ↘			I2
He won't jump, **will he?** ↗ —He won't jump, **will he?** ↘			I3
What are you doing? **Studying?**—What are you doing? **Studying.**			I4
I'll have fried rice and **cashew chicken . . .** — . . . and **cashew chicken.**			I5
Should I use a **pen, or a pencil?**—Should I use a **pen or a pencil?**			I6
Would you like the **soup 'r salad?**— . . . like the **Super Salad?**			I7
The lady had lots of **golden jewelry.**— . . . lots of **gold 'n' jewelry.**			I8

VIII. Segmentation

	Listen	Speak	Unit
"Elizabeth," said John, "was late."—**Elizabeth** said, **"John** was late."			S1
Make sure to **wash, Suzy.**—Make sure to **wash Suzy.**			S2
Have we **met, Mr. Smith?**—Have we **met Mr. Smith?**			S3
What's **two plus four,** times three?—What's **two,** plus four times three?			S4

Other pronunciation difficulties (not noted on the checklist)

	Listen	Speak	Unit

Now, after you have marked the items that are difficult for you with a check mark (✓), go back and write an asterisk (✻) by the marked areas that you think are *important* for you to master. You may even want to put a double asterisk (✻✻) by the things that are *most important* for you.

2. Story Reading and Retelling

The purpose of this section is to help you and your teacher identify particular aspects of your English pronunciation that need modification. You may have already identified many of these features in the preceding self-analysis section. The two activities in this section will confirm that analysis and perhaps help your teacher identify additional areas where you can improve your pronunciation.

2A. In the first activity, you will simply read aloud the story that starts at the bottom of this page. If you wish, you may read and practice it in advance—either silently or out loud. (The story is recorded on the accompanying tape/CD if you wish to listen to it first.)

2B. In the second activity, you will retell the same story in your own words. (Do *not* try to memorize it word for word!) As you retell the story, you may look at the skeleton/outline provided, or you may make your own outline and notes. You should *not*, however, look at the story text that you read in the first activity. If you (or your teacher) prefer a free speaking activity instead of this story retelling, go directly to Activity 3 on page 10.

As you read and then retell the story (and/or speak spontaneously in Activity three), it is usually best to record your speech on an audiocassette. Then you and your teacher can listen to it several times. Doing so will allow a more careful analysis of your speech. It will also make your pronunciation improvement over time easier to notice. However, if no cassette recorder is available, you may do the reading and retelling "live," with your teacher listening and taking notes as you speak.

If you listen to your own voice on the tape after you have recorded it, try to be objective in your analysis of the pronunciation problems. Pretend that you are listening to someone else. Try to figure out what areas of English pronunciation that person needs to work on. Then mark them on the checklist.

Be sure to give your marked self-analysis pages to your teacher along with your recorded cassette. (If you are doing these activities live, give your marked self-analysis pages to your teacher before you start speaking.) Your teacher will use this same sheet to note any additional areas where your pronunciation seems to need modification.

2A. Story

"Jen, turn off that loud music! I'm going crazy!" shouted Jennifer's mother.

"You're going crazy?" thought sixteen-year-old Jennifer. "I can't even listen to a little music without hearing complaints.

And without music, this place is so quiet that I can hardly stand it."

"Turn it off! Are you doing homework or partying? How can you concentrate with all that noise?"

"Mom, you may not believe this," Jennifer replied, "but music actually helps me study. When it's too quiet, I can't think. Every little sound distracts me."

"Well, then why don't you play some decent music? Something classical, like Brahms or Mozart. Just try it. I'm sure you'll like it."

"Brahms? You've got to be kidding! I'd rather die. You're forgetting—I have tried classical music, and I just don't like it."

Jennifer and her mother, Sue, frequently disagreed about music. Mom liked quiet, soothing melodies, and Jennifer liked her music loud and lively. One day, Jennifer's father, Tom, heard them arguing and tried to help. He started off with an objective, academic approach. "There are many kinds of music," he explained. "There's classical music, folk music, country music, rock music . . ."

"Oh, Dad, don't you think we know that?" interrupted Jennifer. "The problem is that we don't like the same kind. Mom likes old-fashioned music, and I like modern music."

Tom changed to a new approach—negotiating a compromise. "Jen, how about if we listen to your music for an hour, then switch to Mom's for the next hour, and so on? That would work, wouldn't it?"

At that point, Sue stopped him. "I'm sorry, Tom, but I don't think I could stand listening to Jen's music for an hour. I'd get a headache and have to leave the house. Would you like me to do that, or do you have any other ideas?"

"What'll we do? There's got to be a solution." Tom thought and thought. Desperately, he joked, "You could let me choose the music."

Sue and Jennifer didn't think that was very funny. "Golden oldies!" they screamed. "Then we'd both go crazy, wouldn't we." For once they agreed.

So the "committee" continued to brainstorm. They even thought about remodeling the house and adding a music room with soundproof walls. After about thirty minutes they finally came up with a brilliant solution. It was so very simple they wondered why they hadn't come up with it before. Earphones! Jennifer wore them while she was studying. With earphones on, she could hear her music and nothing else—not even her mother's classical music in the next room. And if Tom wanted to listen to the oldies station, he just went out in the garage, turned on the car radio, and sang along. Out there, even if he sang off key, no one complained.

2B. Story Skeleton/Outline

(*Note:* The purpose of this skeleton/outline is to help you remember the main events of the story as you retell it. You may find that your own outline, or some other device, helps you remember even better. If so, use it. Just remember to retell the story in your own words.)

Jennifer's mother: "Turn off loud music! . . . going crazy!"
Jennifer: "You? . . . can't listen . . . without complaints.
    Without music . . . so quiet . . . can hardly stand it."
Mom: "Off! . . . homework or partying? How can . . . concentrate?"
Jen: "Music helps study. . . . Too quiet . . . can't think . . . little sound distracts."
Mom: "Why not classical? . . . Brahms or Mozart."
Jen: "Brahms? . . . kidding! . . . rather die . . . have tried . . . don't like."
Jen and Sue . . . disagreed . . . music.
    Mom . . . quiet, soothing
    Jennifer . . . loud and lively.
Jennifer's father, Tom . . . tried to help . . . academic approach.
    "Many kinds . . . classical . . . folk . . . country . . . rock."
Jen: "Problem . . . don't like same kind.
    Mom . . . old-fashioned . . . I . . . modern."
Tom . . . new approach . . . compromise.
    "Jen's music . . . an hour . . . Mom's . . . next hour? . . . work?"
Sue stopped.
    "Sorry . . . headache . . . leave. . . . other ideas?"
Tom: "What? . . . solution . . . let me choose."
Sue & Jen: "Golden oldies . . . both crazy" . . . agreed.
So . . . "committee" . . . brainstorm
    Remodel . . . music room . . . soundproof.
    Solution . . . simple . . . earphones . . . while studying.
    With earphones . . . her music . . . nothing else.
    Tom . . . oldies station . . . garage . . . car radio . . . sang along.
    Even if . . . off key.

3. Free Speaking

This activity may be done after Activity 2B (story retelling) or instead of it. Both activities usually produce similar results. For this activity, choose *any **one*** of the following topics and talk freely about it (on tape or live) for a couple of minutes. Remember to select just one topic and speak naturally. This should *not* be a prepared speech.

A. My family

B. My hometown

C. My favorite activities

D. A place I would like to visit

E. My plans for the future

F. My biggest frustration in life

G. My most embarrassing experience

H. A famous person I would like to meet

Your teacher will listen to what you say and note any additional difficulties on your self-analysis pages. *Note to teacher:* Another alternative activity is to provide students with a picture for them to describe.

Quick Unit Number Identification Grids for Vowels and Consonants

To quickly find the particular *Pronunciation Matters* unit number for a known vowel or consonant contrast, simply locate the point where the column of one of the sounds intersects with the row of the other sound. The number in the box at the horizontal-vertical intersection of the two sounds is the number of the unit(s) you are looking for. Key words for each sound are given to help identify the sounds.

For example, if you know you have trouble hearing the difference between [l] and [r], find those two consonants on the "Consonant Contrasts" grid. Go down from [l] and across from [r] and you will find the number 14. Consonant unit number 14 (C14) is the identifying number for the *Pronunciation Matters* units that focus on this contrast.

Vowel Contrasts and *Pronunciation Matters* Unit Numbers

iy   heat

| 1 | ɪ | hit |

ey   hate

| | 2 | 3 | ɛ | head |

| | | | 4 | æ | hat |

| | | | | 5 | ɑ | hot |

| | | | | 6 | ɑr | hard |

| | | | | 7 | | ə | hut |

| | | | | 9 | | ər | bird |

| | | | | 8 | | | ow | code |

| | | | | 10 | | | | ʊ | book |

| | | | | | 11 | uw | moon |

Consonant Contrasts and *Pronunciation Matters* Unit Numbers

m	men														
	p	pea													
	1	b	bee												
			w	wee											
	2			f	fee										
		3	**4**	**5**	v	very									
			6		θ	thin									
			7		ð	thy									
			8		t	tie									
				10	**12**	d	die								
						n	no								
					13	l	lie								
						14	r	run							
				9				s	sun						
				11				**15**	z	zone					
								16	ʃ	shy					
								17	ʒ	measure					
								18	tʃ	chair					
									19	dʒ	judge				
									20	y	year				
										k	key				
										22	g	go			
										21		iy	ear		

Section 2

Vowels (V)

Unit V1-A [iy] sleep—[ɪ] slip

Story

Listen to the story as your teacher reads it, or on tape, until you understand the main ideas.

Many modern ships have metal decks which can become very slippery when wet. In order to warn passengers of this danger, many cruise ships have signs which read "Slippery when Wet." They don't want anyone to (1) **slip** on the deck and get hurt.

In addition to these warning signs, other signs are placed along the deck which ask the passengers not to (2) **sleep** on the deck overnight. These signs were put up after a serious accident occurred. A passenger fell asleep on a deck chair late one evening. When he awoke early in the morning he was so disoriented in his search for his room that he fell over the side of the ship.

#1

#2

Contrasting Sentences

Listening: Write the appropriate key word in each blank. Later, as you hear each sentence, mark the box, point to the picture, make a gesture, and/or say the rejoinder. Speaking: Choose and say each sentence so that your listener(s) can respond correctly.

❑ Don't _____ on the deck. (fall asleep)

❑ Don't _____ on the deck. (slide on a wet surface)

Explanations and diagrams for this unit's target sounds are on page 331 in Section 10.

Additional Practice

Mr. Green was *beaten/bitten*. (V1-B/b), Look at Olivia's *cheek/chick*. (V1-C/c), Where's the *meat/mitt?* (V1-d), Look at the *sheep/ship*. (V1-e), That's a high *heel/hill*. (V1-f), What a *feast/fist!* (V1-g), You must *heat/hit* it. (V1-h)

Other Words

Sort the words listed below into two groups according to the sound the boldface letters represent. Write the words in the spaces provided. The first two have been done for you. Then, circle or underline these words each time they occur in the story. Say each marked word aloud. Then say the entire sentence. Look for additional words in the story that contain the target sounds. Mark and say them also.

th**e**se, h**e**, **i**n, h**i**s, ser**i**ous, **e**vening, d**e**cide, sh**i**p, th**i**s, add**i**tion

[iy] ver**y**,

[ɪ] wh**i**ch,

Other Practice Activities

❑ Partner Cards—Listening. *Practice until you can point to the right card every time.*

❑ Partner Cards—Speaking. *Practice until you can say the contrasting sentences so accurately that your partner points to the right card every time.*

❑ Story Reading. *Practice reading the story aloud. Mark any difficult words. Then record the story on tape.*

❑ Story Dictation. *Write the story as your teacher reads it or as you listen to it on the audiotape.*

❑ Cloze Reading. *Choose some key words in the story and black them out. Then read the entire story aloud. Do this several times.*

Each time black out more words. Continue until most of the story is blacked out and you can tell it without looking at the page very often.

❑ Story Retelling from Skeleton. *Black out all the remaining words except those you need in order to remind you of the story line. Then, using just this skeleton, tell the story to your partner or class.*

❑ Free Story Retelling. *Retell the whole story from memory, without looking at your book.*

❑ Parallel Story. *Create your own story similar to the one in this unit.*

❑ Mini-drama. *Make up a skit or do a role play based on the story.*

Unit V1-B [iy] beat—[ɪ] bit

Story

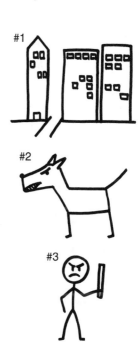

Mr. Green was walking home from work one day. He decided to take a shortcut and went (1) down a dark alley. Suddenly, a mean-looking man with a vicious dog jumped out at him.

When Mr. Green tried to run away, (2) the dog chased him and **bit** him on the leg. Mr. Green fell and couldn't get up because of the pain in his leg.

(3) The mean man then picked up a large stick, **beat** Mr. Green, and took all of his money.

When Mr. Green reported the incident to the police, they asked him what had happened. He told the officer that first the dog had bitten him and then the man had beaten him and taken all his money. Mr. Green decided he would never take that shortcut again.

Contrasting Sentences

❑ Mr. Green was _____. (by the dog)

❑ Mr. Green was _____. (with a stick)

Additional Practice

Don't *sleep/slip* on the deck. (V1-A/a), Look at Olivia's *cheek/chick*. (V1-C/c), Where's the *meat/mitt?* (V1-d), Look at the *sheep/ship*. (V1-e), That's a high *heel/hill*. (V1-f), What a *feast/fist!* (V1-g), You must *heat/hit* it. (V1-h)

Other Words

Green, him, mean, vicious, police, mister, heat, scream, with, stick

[iy] he,

[ɪ] his,

Other Practice Activities

❑ Partner Cards—Listening.
❑ Partner Cards—Speaking.
❑ Story Reading.
❑ Story Dictation.
❑ Cloze Reading.

❑ Story Retelling from Skeleton.
❑ Free Story Retelling.
❑ Parallel Story.
❑ Mini-drama.

Unit V1-C [iy] cheek—[ɪ] chick

Story

My neighbor Rick, who is quite an artist, has two young daughters—Colleen and Olivia. On special occasions or holidays, he often paints little designs on their faces. For example, on the Fourth of July, he paints small American flags on their foreheads. It's a strange custom, but they love it.

Last fall, before a big football game, Colleen came running up to me and said, "Look at Olivia's (1) **cheek**." I looked and saw that Rick had painted our team's name on one of Olivia's cheeks

The following spring, on the day before Easter, Colleen showed me a little rabbit painted on her forehead and then said, "Look at my sister's **chick**."

I replied, "Don't you mean her cheek?"

"No," she said, "her chick is on her forehead." When I looked at Olivia's face, I saw that Rick had painted (2) a little yellow baby chicken on Olivia's forehead.

#1

#2

Contrasting Sentences

❏ Look at Olivia's _____. (part of face)

❏ Look at Olivia's _____. (baby chicken)

Additional Practice

Don't *sleep*/*slip* on the deck. (V1-A/a), Mr. Green was *beaten*/*bitten*. (V1-B/b), Where's the *meat*/*mitt*? (V1-d), Look at the *sheep*/*ship*. (V1-e), That's a high *heel*/*hill*. (V1-f), What a *feast*/*fist!* (V1-g), You must *heat*/*hit* it. (V1-h)

Other Words

sister, Coll**ee**n, **i**t, Olivia, before, **i**s, r**e**ply, bab**y**, b**i**g

[iy] t**ea**m,

[ɪ] l**i**ttle,

Other Practice Activities

❏ Partner Cards—Listening.
❏ Partner Cards—Speaking.
❏ Story Reading.
❏ Story Dictation.
❏ Cloze Reading.

❏ Story Retelling from Skeleton.
❏ Free Story Retelling.
❏ Parallel Story.
❏ Mini-drama.

Unit V2-A [ɪ] bitter—[ε] better

Story

Listen to the story as your teacher reads it, or on tape, until you understand the main ideas.

My sister Ellen is not a "natural" when it comes to cooking. In fact, in order to cook a good meal, she has to practice and practice. The worst part is that she practices on us, her family.

I remember the first time that she made spaghetti sauce. It was (1) very **bitter**. I don't know what she put in it, but we couldn't even eat it. I hoped she would never cook again.

Now she has made the dish at least twenty times and it is (2) much **better**. We don't mind at all if she cooks—as long as she cooks spaghetti. The problem is that now she doesn't like to cook spaghetti. Now she is learning to cook chow mein, and we are suffering again.

#1

#2

Contrasting Sentences

Listening: Write the appropriate key word in each blank. Later, as you hear each sentence, mark the box, point to the picture, make a gesture, and/or say the rejoinder. Speaking: Choose and say each sentence so that your listener(s) can respond correctly.

❏ The spaghetti sauce is _____. (I can't eat it.)

❏ The spaghetti sauce is _____. (I like it.)

Explanations and diagrams for this unit's target sounds are on pages 331–32 in Section 10.

Additional Practice

I need a *pin/pen* for the message. (V2-B/b), Will you please pick up that *litter/letter* for me? (V2-c), They're *picking/pecking* the fruit. (V2-d)

Other Words

Sort the words listed below into two groups according to the sound the boldface letters represent. Write the words in the spaces provided. The first two have been done for you. Then, circle or underline these words each time they occur in the story. Say each marked word aloud. Then say the entire sentence. Look for additional words in the story that contain the target sounds. Mark and say them also.

ag**ai**n, **E**llen, **d**ish, rem**e**mber, th**i**s, twenty, **i**n, spa**g**hetti, **s**ister, h**i**s

[ɪ] **i**t,

[ɛ] wh**e**n,

Other Practice Activities

❑ Partner Cards—Listening. *Practice until you can point to the right card every time.*

❑ Partner Cards—Speaking. *Practice until you can say the contrasting sentences so accurately that your partner points to the right card every time.*

❑ Story Reading. *Practice reading the story aloud. Mark any difficult words. Then record the story on tape.*

❑ Story Dictation. *Write the story as your teacher reads it or as you listen to it on the audiotape.*

❑ Cloze Reading. *Choose some key words in the story and black them out. Then read the entire story aloud. Do this several times.*

Each time black out more words. Continue until most of the story is blacked out and you can tell it without looking at the page very often.

❑ Story Retelling from Skeleton. *Black out all the remaining words except those you need in order to remind you of the story line. Then, using just this skeleton, tell the story to your partner or class.*

❑ Free Story Retelling. *Retell the whole story from memory, without looking at your book.*

❑ Parallel Story. *Create your own story similar to the one in this unit.*

❑ Mini-drama. *Make up a skit or do a role play based on the story.*

Unit V2-B [ɪ] pin—[ɛ] pen

Story

#1

#2

My roommate, Kim, and I keep a (1) **pen** and a pad of paper next to our telephone so that we can take messages. If someone calls for my roommate when she's not home, I write down the message for her. Then I look around for a (2) **pin** so I can pin the message to the corkboard above the phone so Kim will see it when she returns. At least that's what I usually do.

One time I didn't. Someone phoned with an important message about a job Kim had applied for. I wrote the message down, but when I was looking for a pin in my desk drawer the doorbell rang. I put the paper down on my desk and went to answer the door. I forgot all about the message, and it got lost in my pile of school papers. I didn't find it until three days later. Because Kim didn't get the message, she didn't get the job. I felt really bad. Now I make sure there are pens and pins next to the phone.

Contrasting Sentences

❑ I need a _____. (to write this message)

❑ I need a _____. (to hang up the message)

Additional Practice

The spaghetti sauce is *bitter/better*. (V2-A/a), Will you please pick up that *litter/letter* for me? (V2-c), They're *picking/pecking* the fruit. (V2-d)

Other Words

Kim, desk, message, telephone, didn't, with, in, until, went, felt

[ɪ] will,

[ɛ] next,

Other Practice Activities

❑ Partner Cards—Listening.
❑ Partner Cards—Speaking.
❑ Story Reading.
❑ Story Dictation.
❑ Cloze Reading.

❑ Story Retelling
from Skeleton.
❑ Free Story Retelling.
❑ Parallel Story.
❑ Mini-drama.

Unit V3-A [ey] taste—[ε] test

Story

Listen to the story as your teacher reads it, or on tape, until you understand the main ideas.

Elaine loves homemade (1) chocolate cake, but she is not a good cook. She has made two chocolate cakes, and they both tasted terrible. One of the cakes had too much salt, and the other one was still gooey inside when she served it. But Elaine is determined. She has decided to try one more time.

This time, she follows the recipe carefully. When she puts the cake in the oven, she carefully sets the timer. When the bell rings, she **tests** the cake with a (2) toothpick to see if it is done. Then she cuts off a small piece of cake with a (3) fork and **tastes** it to make sure that it isn't too salty. To her relief, it tastes delicious! At last she has succeeded! Her determination has paid off.

Contrasting Sentences

Listening: Write the appropriate key word in each blank. Later, as you hear each sentence, mark the box, point to the picture, make a gesture, and / or say the rejoinder. Speaking: Choose and say each sentence so that your listener(s) can respond correctly.

❑ She _____ the cake. (with a toothpick)

❑ She _____ the cake. (with a fork)

Explanations and diagrams for this unit's target sounds are on pages 331–32 in Section 10.

Additional Practice

I'd like to *sail / sell* the boat. (V3-B/b), What is *Jane / Jen* like? (V3-C/c)

Other Words

Sort the words listed below into two groups according to the sound the boldface letters represent. Write the words in the spaces provided. The first two have been done for you. Then, circle or underline these words each time they occur in the story. Say each marked word aloud. Then say the entire sentence. Look for additional words in the story that contain the target sounds. Mark and say them also.

sets, El**ai**ne, m**a**de, **t**errible, **pai**d, when, recipe, m**a**ke, bell, **th**ey

[ey] c**a**ke,

[ε] **th**en,

Other Practice Activities

❑ Partner Cards—Listening. *Practice until you can point to the right card every time.*

❑ Partner Cards—Speaking. *Practice until you can say the contrasting sentences so accurately that your partner points to the right card every time.*

❑ Story Reading. *Practice reading the story aloud. Mark any difficult words. Then record the story on tape.*

❑ Story Dictation. *Write the story as your teacher reads it or as you listen to it on the audiotape.*

❑ Cloze Reading. *Choose some key words in the story and black them out. Then read the entire story aloud. Do this several times.*

Each time black out more words. Continue until most of the story is blacked out and you can tell it without looking at the page very often.

❑ Story Retelling from Skeleton. *Black out all the remaining words except those you need in order to remind you of the story line. Then, using just this skeleton, tell the story to your partner or class.*

❑ Free Story Retelling. *Retell the whole story from memory, without looking at your book.*

❑ Parallel Story. *Create your own story similar to the one in this unit.*

❑ Mini-drama. *Make up a skit or do a role play based on the story.*

Unit V3-B [ey] sail—[ε] sell

Story

Mel liked to go to the beach in the summer. One day he saw a man standing next to a sailboat on the shore and talked to him. "Nice boat," he said.

"Thank you," replied the man, (1) "but I'd like to **sell** this boat. I'm moving away from the ocean soon, and I won't have any use for it anymore. Besides, I need the money."

Mel answered, "Really? I wish I could buy your boat. I'd love to (2) **sail** it. That would be great fun. But I don't have any money."

The man was very nice to Mel anyway and promised that he would take him sailing the next day. Mel went home feeling very happy and could hardly sleep that night.

Contrasting Sentences

❏ I'd like to _____ the boat. (to get money)

❏ I'd like to _____ the boat. (to have fun)

Additional Practice

She *tastes/tests* the cake. (V3-A/a), What is *Jane/Jen* like? (V3-C/c)

Other Words

said, **w**ent, aw**ay**, **take**, **next**, th**ey**, **paid**, shade, Mel, very

[ey] **day**,

[ɛ] **when**,

Other Practice Activities

❏ Partner Cards—Listening.
❏ Partner Cards—Speaking.
❏ Story Reading.
❏ Story Dictation.
❏ Cloze Reading.

❏ Story Retelling
   from Skeleton.
❏ Free Story Retelling.
❏ Parallel Story.
❏ Mini-drama.

Unit V3-C [ey] Jane—[ɛ] Jen

Story

#1

Alexandra has one sister. Her sister's name is Jennifer, but Alexandra calls her **Jen**. (She calls Alexandra Alex.) Jen is (1) very tall and has long straight hair and glasses. She has a great sense of humor. Alexandra likes to spend time with her sister, Jen. They do a lot of fun things together.

Alexandra also likes to do things with her best friend, **Jane**, even though Jane is quite different from Jen. Jane has

(2) short, curly hair and wears contacts. She is serious and doesn't always understand Jen's jokes.

The amazing thing is that Alexandra, Jennifer, and Jane all get along well. The three of them are nearly inseparable.

Contrasting Sentences

❑ What is _____ like? (tall, straight hair, glasses, funny)

❑ What is _____ like? (short, curly hair, no glasses, serious)

Additional Practice

She *tastes/tests* the cake. (V3-A/a), I'd like to *sail/sell* the boat. (V3-B/b)

Other Words

together, sense, straight, **they**, friend, **hair**, amazing, make, very, spend

[ey] **day**,

[ε] **best**,

Other Practice Activities

❑ Partner Cards—Listening.
❑ Partner Cards—Speaking.
❑ Story Reading.
❑ Story Dictation.
❑ Cloze Reading.

❑ Story Retelling from Skeleton.
❑ Free Story Retelling.
❑ Parallel Story.
❑ Mini-drama.

Unit V4-A [ɛ] pen—[æ] pan

Story

Listen to the story as your teacher reads it, or on tape, until you understand the main ideas.

Ken loved to cook, but he was careless. One day he left a **pan** on the stove and forgot about it. The food inside burned to a crisp, and the pan became black and ugly. So Ken bought (1) a shiny new pan. It cost a lot, but he figured it was wise to pay extra for top quality.

The next day while Ken was boiling noodles in his new pan, he noticed that water was leaking out of it. When he looked closely, Ken was surprised to find a tiny hole in the bottom. Upset that his new pan leaked, Ken decided to write a letter of complaint to the company that made it. When he sat down to write, Ken noticed that his (2) **pen** had leaked ink all over his important papers. He was so angry about the pen and the pan that he threw them both away.

Contrasting Sentences

Listening: Write the appropriate key word in each blank. Later, as you hear each sentence, mark the box, point to the picture, make a gesture, and/or say the rejoinder. Speaking: Choose and say each sentence so that your listener(s) can respond correctly.

❏ This _____ leaks. (Don't cook with it.)

❏ This _____ leaks. (Don't write with it.)

Explanations and diagrams for this unit's target sounds are on pages 332–33 in Section 10.

Additional Practice

Where is the *letter/ladder*? (V4-B/b), They had to *pedal/paddle* the boat. (V4-C/c), He *begged/bagged* a lot. (V4-D/d), Where's the *X/axe*? (V4-e), The *men/man* will be here soon. (V4-f)

Other Words

Sort the words listed below into two groups according to the sound the boldface letters represent. Write the words in the spaces provided. The first two have been done for you. Then, circle or underline these words each time they occur in the story. Say each marked word aloud. Then say the entire sentence. Look for additional words in the story that contain the target sounds. Mark and say them also.
pl**ai**d, K**e**n, **e**xtra, **a**ngry, n**e**xt, th**a**t, l**e**tter, th**e**m, bl**a**ck, h**a**d

[ɛ] left,

[æ] sat,

Other Practice Activities

❑ Partner Cards—Listening. *Practice until you can point to the right card every time.*
❑ Partner Cards—Speaking. *Practice until you can say the contrasting sentences so accurately that your partner points to the right card every time.*
❑ Story Reading. *Practice reading the story aloud. Mark any difficult words. Then record the story on tape.*
❑ Story Dictation. *Write the story as your teacher reads it or as you listen to it on the audiotape.*
❑ Cloze Reading. *Choose some key words in the story and black them out. Then read the entire story aloud. Do this several times.*

Each time black out more words. Continue until most of the story is blacked out and you can tell it without looking at the page very often.
❑ Story Retelling from Skeleton. *Black out all the remaining words except those you need in order to remind you of the story line. Then, using just this skeleton, tell the story to your partner or class.*
❑ Free Story Retelling. *Retell the whole story from memory, without looking at your book.*
❑ Parallel Story. *Create your own story similar to the one in this unit.*
❑ Mini-drama. *Make up a skit or do a role play based on the story.*

Unit V4-B [ɛ] letter—[æ] ladder

Story

I hate it when my mother cleans up for me. She puts everything away her way, and I can never find what I need. For example, today after Mom had cleaned up the desk in my room I couldn't find an important (1) **letter**. "Mom," I asked, "where is the letter I wrote last night? I have to mail it today."

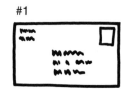

#1

She replied, "Oh, sorry. I thought that was an old letter, so I put it in the attic with your other old things when I cleaned up your room."

#2

Things got worse. I needed (2) our small **ladder** to get up in the attic, but I couldn't find it in my closet where I had left it. So I had to ask her again, "Mom, where is the ladder?"

"I think I put it away, out in the garage," she responded.

"I think I should clean up my room myself," I thought.

(*Note:* In most dialects of North American English, the [t] in *letter* and the [d] in *ladder* are pronounced as quick flaps, so they sound the same.)

Contrasting Sentences

❏ Where is the _____ ? (to mail)

❏ Where is the _____ ? (to climb)

Additional Practice

This *pen / pan* leaks. (V4-A/a), They had to *pedal / paddle* the boat. (V4-C/c), He *begged / bagged* a lot. (V4-D/d), Where's the *X / axe*? (V4-e), The *men / man* will be here soon. (V4-f)

Other Words

aft**e**r, wh**e**n, **e**xample, **e**very, d**e**sk, **a**sked, where, h**a**d, l**e**ft, that

[ɛ] st**e**p,

[æ] l**a**st,

Other Practice Activities

❏ Partner Cards—Listening.
❏ Partner Cards—Speaking.
❏ Story Reading.
❏ Story Dictation.
❏ Cloze Reading.

❏ Story Retelling from Skeleton.
❏ Free Story Retelling.
❏ Parallel Story.
❏ Mini-drama.

Unit V4-C [ɛ] pedal—[æ] paddle

Story

A few summers ago, Sally and her husband took their kids to Washington, D.C. There they saw many historical sights and had many educational experiences, but the most memorable thing they did was to rent some little boats at the tidal basin near the Jefferson Memorial.

Sally's husband and her son got a little boat and one (1) **paddle** each. They challenged Sally and her daughter to a race and thought they were going to win, but things didn't turn out that way. The boys had trouble coordinating their strokes and went around in circles a lot. After a while, they started getting blisters on their hands, so they could barely paddle at all.

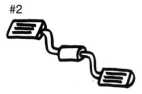

Sally and her daughter were luckier. They got a boat that operated by leg power. A set of (2) foot **pedals** near the floor in front of the seat were as easy to operate as the pedals on a bike. Their boat also had a rudder, so it was easy to steer. They never got tired of pedaling it around, and they won every race with the boys.

Contrasting Sentences

❏ They had to _____ the boat. (with their legs)

❏ They had to _____ the boat. (with their arms)

Additional Practice

This *pen*/*pan* leaks. (V4-A/a), Where is the *letter*/*ladder*? (V4-B/b), He *begged*/*bagged* a lot. (V4-D/d), Where's the *X*/*axe*? (V4-e), The *men*/*man* will be here soon. (V4-f)

Other Words

challenged, there, **every**, educational, **after**, rent, **had**, never, that, **as**

[ɛ] **leg**,

[æ] **at**,

Other Practice Activities

- ❏ Partner Cards—Listening.
- ❏ Partner Cards—Speaking.
- ❏ Story Reading.
- ❏ Story Dictation.
- ❏ Cloze Reading.
- ❏ Story Retelling from Skeleton.
- ❏ Free Story Retelling.
- ❏ Parallel Story.
- ❏ Mini-drama.

Unit V4-D [ɛ] beg—[æ] bag

Story

At a shopping center near my home, there used to be a (1) home-less man who sat on the curb or went from car to car asking people for money. Some people offered him a few coins, and others gave him food, but he didn't get much. **Begging** was a pretty miserable way to survive. Unfortunately, he didn't have any special job skills, so he didn't know what else to do.

#1

Then one day his luck changed. The manager of a grocery store in the shopping center offered him a job (2) bagging groceries. As shoppers went through the check stand to pay, he would take their groceries out of the shopping carts and put them in bags. That was something the homeless man could do. He went to work enthusiastically. **Bagging** groceries hour after hour was harder than begging, but he earned more money, and he also seemed happier with himself.

#2

Contrasting Sentences

❏ He _____ a lot. (asked for money)

❏ He _____ a lot. (put groceries in bags)

Additional Practice

This *pen / pan* leaks. (V4-A/a), Where is the *letter / ladder*? (V4-B/b), They had to *pedal / paddle* the boat. (V4-C/c), Where's the *X / axe*? (V4-e), The *men / man* will be here soon. (V4-f)

Other Words

manager, center, man, went, special, have, else, at, check, stand

[ɛ] then,

[æ] sat,

Other Practice Activities

❏ Partner Cards—Listening.
❏ Partner Cards—Speaking.
❏ Story Reading.
❏ Story Dictation.
❏ Cloze Reading.

❏ Story Retelling
  from Skeleton.
❏ Free Story Retelling.
❏ Parallel Story.
❏ Mini-drama.

Unit V5-A [æ] axe—[ɑ] ox

Story

Listen to the story as your teacher reads it, or on tape, until you understand the main ideas.

Jacob Henry was a pioneer farmer. He lived nearly two hundred years ago. His home was in the wilderness far from the nearest city, so he had to be very self-reliant. No one else was around to help him. He depended on his own strength, his tools, and his animals. One of his most important tools was his (1) **axe**. He used it for many things, like clearing land and cutting firewood. Jacob took good care of his axe. If he had ever lost or broke it, he would have been in serious trouble.

Jacob also depended heavily on his animals. His cow provided milk, and his horse was useful for traveling long distances quickly, but for heavy duty work he used his (2) **ox**. It was much larger and stronger than a horse, and he used it to plow his fields, drag logs, and pull his wagon. Without his ox, Jacob might not have been able to survive in the wilderness.

It's hard to say which was most important to Jacob Henry, his axe or his ox. He didn't try to decide. He took good care of them both.

Contrasting Sentences

Listening: Write the appropriate key word in each blank. Later, as you hear each sentence, mark the box, point to the picture, make a gesture, and/or say the rejoinder. Speaking: Choose and say each sentence so that your listener(s) can respond correctly.

❑ Jacob took good care of his _____. (tool)

❑ Jacob took good care of his _____. (animal)

Explanations and diagrams for this unit's target sounds are on page 332 in Section 10.

Additional Practice

That's my *sack / sock.* (V5-b)

For [æ]: This *pen / pan* leaks. (V4-A/a), Where is the *letter / ladder?* (V4-B/b), They had to *pedal / paddle* the boat. (V4-C/c), He *begged / bagged* a lot. (V4-D/d), Where's the *X / axe?* (V4-e), The *men / man* will be here soon. (V4-f)

For [ɑ]: It was a big *shock / shark.* (V6-A), Kevin ran after the *boss / bus.* (V7-A/a), Doug *caught / cut* the big fish. (V7-B/b), I don't like the *color / collar.* (V7-C/c), I need a *cop / cup.* (V7-d), What a *hog / hug!* (V7-e), Look at the *clock / cloak.* (V8-A/a), How did you like my *fox / folks?* (V8-B/b)

Other Words

Sort the words listed below into two groups according to the sound the boldface letters represent. Write the words in the spaces provided. The first two have been done for you. Then, circle or underline these words each time they occur in the story. Say each marked word aloud. Then say the entire sentence. Look for additional words in the story that contain the target sounds. Mark and say them also.

p**o**nd, gr**a**nd, **a**nimals, f**a**ther, n**o**t, tr**a**vel, th**a**n, w**a**gon, w**a**s, d**o**ctor

[æ] h**a**d,

[ɑ] fr**o**m,

Other Practice Activities

❑ Partner Cards—Listening. *Practice until you can point to the right card every time.*

❑ Partner Cards—Speaking. *Practice until you can say the contrasting sentences so accurately that your partner points to the right card every time.*

❑ Story Reading. *Practice reading the story aloud. Mark any difficult words. Then record the story on tape.*

❑ Story Dictation. *Write the story as your teacher reads it or as you listen to it on the audiotape.*

❑ Cloze Reading. *Choose some key words in the story and black them out. Then read the entire story aloud. Do this several times.*

Each time black out more words. Continue until most of the story is blacked out and you can tell it without looking at the page very often.

❑ Story Retelling from Skeleton. *Black out all the remaining words except those you need in order to remind you of the story line. Then, using just this skeleton, tell the story to your partner or class.*

❑ Free Story Retelling. *Retell the whole story from memory, without looking at your book.*

❑ Parallel Story. *Create your own story similar to the one in this unit.*

❑ Mini-drama. *Make up a skit or do a role play based on the story.*

Unit V6-A [ɑ] shock—[ɑr] shark

Story

Listen to the story as your teacher reads it, or on tape, until you under-stand the main ideas.

Last summer I went to Florida with my friends. First we went to a fun park. One of the hottest activities was (1) bungee jumping. My friends all did it, but I was too scared (or too smart) to try. They called me chicken, but I didn't care. Seeing them jump off a large tower was enough of a (2) **shock** for me.

Then we went scuba diving. I loved that. Deep in the ocean, everything was very beautiful. I was having a great time. All of a sudden, one of my friends signaled "Go up! Go up!" We wondered why, but when we saw his pale face we didn't question him. We all went up quickly. When we reached the surface he screamed, "I saw a big (3) **shark**! It's going to eat us!" We all started swimming back to the boat immediately without saying another word.

I was glad that none of us got killed that summer.

Contrasting Sentences

Listening: Write the appropriate key word in each blank. Later, as you hear each sentence, mark the box, point to the picture, make a gesture, and/or say the rejoinder. Speaking: Choose and say each sentence so that your listener(s) can respond correctly.

❏ It was a big _____. (to see them jump)

❏ It was a big _____. (in the ocean)

Explanations and diagrams for this unit's target sounds are on pages 332–33 in Section 10.

Additional Practice

The *gods/guards* were angry. (V6-b), Look at that *cot/cart*. (V6-c)

For [ɑ]: Jacob took good care of his *axe/ox*. (V5-A/a), Kevin ran after the *bus/boss*. (V7-A/a), Doug *caught/cut* the big fish. (V7-B/b), I don't like the *collar/color*. (V7-C/c), I need a *cop/cup*. (V7-d), What a *hog/hug!* (V7-e), Look at the *clock/cloak.* (V8-A/a), How did you like my *fox/folks?* (V8-B/b)

For [ər], a sound similar to [ɑr]: Shirley enjoys looking at the *birds/buds.* (V9-A)

Other Words

Sort the words listed below into two groups according to the sound the boldface letters represent. Write the words in the spaces provided. The first two have been done for you. Then, circle or underline these words each time they occur in the story. Say each marked word aloud. Then say the entire sentence. Look for additional words in the story that contain the target sounds. Mark and say them also.

l**a**rge, d**a**rk, h**o**ttest, w**a**s, g**o**t, f**a**ther, fr**o**m, p**ar**k, sm**ar**t, **ar**m

[ɑ] n**o**t,

[ɑr] st**ar**t,

Other Practice Activities

❏ Partner Cards—Listening. *Practice until you can point to the right card every time.*

❏ Partner Cards—Speaking. *Practice until you can say the contrasting sentences so accurately that your partner points to the right card every time.*

❏ Story Reading. *Practice reading the story aloud. Mark any difficult words. Then record the story on tape.*

❏ Story Dictation. *Write the story as your teacher reads it or as you listen to it on the audiotape.*

❏ Cloze Reading. *Choose some key words in the story and black them out. Then read the entire story aloud. Do this several times.*

Each time black out more words. Continue until most of the story is blacked out and you can tell it without looking at the page very often.

❏ Story Retelling from Skeleton. *Black out all the remaining words except those you need in order to remind you of the story line. Then, using just this skeleton, tell the story to your partner or class.*

❏ Free Story Retelling. *Retell the whole story from memory, without looking at your book.*

❏ Parallel Story. *Create your own story similar to the one in this unit.*

❏ Mini-drama. *Make up a skit or do a role play based on the story.*

Unit V7-A [ɑ] boss—[ə] bus

Story

Listen to the story as your teacher reads it, or on tape, until you understand the main ideas.

Kevin was supposed to be at work at 8:00 for an important meeting, but it was after 9:00 when he woke up. He jumped out of the bed, put on some clothes, and ran to the bus stop. While he was on the (1) **bus**, he worried about what he should say to his (2) **boss**. When the bus stopped in front of his office building, Kevin jumped off and started in. Then he noticed that he had left his briefcase on the bus. He ran after the bus, but it left him behind.

Feeling frustrated, Kevin walked into his office. The secretary told him that the boss had just left for another meeting. Kevin ran out of the office and saw the boss walking down the hallway. He ran after him to apologize, but the boss didn't notice him and went into the meeting room. Kevin felt like screaming.

Then Kevin heard a strange noise. It was his alarm clock ringing. He woke up and saw it was 7:00 A.M. "What a relief!" he said. "It was all only a dream."

(*Note:* Words such as *boss, saw, all,* and *office* are pronounced with an [ɑ] sound in some dialects of English. In other dialects, they are pronounced with an [ɔ] sound. In either case, the contrast with [ə] is important to make.)

Contrasting Sentences

Listening: Write the appropriate key word in each blank. Later, as you hear each sentence, mark the box, point to the picture, make a gesture, and/or say the rejoinder. Speaking: Choose and say each sentence so that your listener(s) can respond correctly.

❏ Kevin ran after the _____. (to get his briefcase)

❏ Kevin ran after the _____. (to apologize)

Explanations and diagrams for this unit's target sounds are on pages 332–33 in Section 10.

Additional Practice

Doug *caught/cut* the big fish. (V7-B/b), I don't like the *color/collar*. (V7-C/c), I need a *cop/cup*. (V7-d), What a *hog/hug!* (V7-e)

Other Words

Sort the words listed below into two groups according to the sound the boldface letters represent. Write the words in the spaces provided. The first two have been done for you. Then, circle or underline these words each time they occur in the story. Say each marked word aloud. Then say the entire sentence. Look for additional words in the story that contain the target sounds. Mark and say them also.
alarm, j**u**mped, wh**a**t, ap**o**logize, **a**bout, n**o**t, f**a**ther, fr**o**m, b**u**t, an**o**ther

[ɑ] st**o**p,

[ə] **u**p,

Other Practice Activities

❑ Partner Cards—Listening. *Practice until you can point to the right card every time.*
❑ Partner Cards—Speaking. *Practice until you can say the contrasting sentences so accurately that your partner points to the right card every time.*
❑ Story Reading. *Practice reading the story aloud. Mark any difficult words. Then record the story on tape.*
❑ Story Dictation. *Write the story as your teacher reads it or as you listen to it on the audiotape.*
❑ Cloze Reading. *Choose some key words in the story and black them out. Then read the entire story aloud. Do this several times.*
Each time black out more words. Continue until most of the story is blacked out and you can tell it without looking at the page very often.
❑ Story Retelling from Skeleton. *Black out all the remaining words except those you need in order to remind you of the story line. Then, using just this skeleton, tell the story to your partner or class.*
❑ Free Story Retelling. *Retell the whole story from memory, without looking at your book.*
❑ Parallel Story. *Create your own story similar to the one in this unit.*
❑ Mini-drama. *Make up a skit or do a role play based on the story.*

Unit V7-B [ɑ] caught—[ə] cut

Story

Tom and Doug were best friends, and they both loved adventures. One summer day they floated down a big river on a raft. As they were traveling, they saw a big fish swimming near their raft. They both had fishing poles, so they cast their lines in the water, and Doug (1) **caught** the fish. It was huge! Doug had never caught such a big fish before. What a thrill!

They were both hungry, so they stopped the raft, landed on the shore, and built a fire. Doug got out his knife, cleaned the fish, broiled it on a stick over the fire, and (2) **cut** it into two pieces—one for himself and one for Tom. Both Tom and Doug ate until they were full. Doug was proud that he had caught such a big fish, and Tom was happy that Doug had shared it with him.

(*Note:* Words such as *caught, water,* and *saw* are pronounced with an [ɑ] sound in some dialects of English. In other dialects, they are pronounced with an [ɔ] sound. In either case, the contrast with [ə] is important to make.)

Contrasting Sentences

❑ Doug _____ the big fish. (with a fishing pole)

❑ Doug _____ the big fish. (with a knife)

Additional Practice

Kevin ran after the *bus/boss.* (V7-A/a), I don't like the *color/collar.* (V7-C/c), I need a *cop/cup.* (V7-d), What a *hog/hug!* (V7-e)

Other Words

another, what, apologize, **a**bout, n**o**t, **fa**ther, fr**o**m, **u**p, j**u**mped, **a**larm

[ɑ] st**o**p,

[ə] b**u**t,

Other Practice Activities

❑ Partner Cards—Listening.
❑ Partner Cards—Speaking.
❑ Story Reading.
❑ Story Dictation.
❑ Cloze Reading.

❑ Story Retelling from Skeleton.
❑ Free Story Retelling.
❑ Parallel Story.
❑ Mini-drama.

Unit V7-C [ɑ] color—[ə] collar

Story

My roommate loves to go shopping for clothes, but she rarely buys anything. She is very particular about what she wears. Just last week we went to a clothing store and tried on lots of outfits, but none of them satisfied her.

I thought that one green skirt looked very good on her, but she did not agree. "I don't like the (1) **color**," she said. "It clashes with my hair and eyes."

There was also a blouse that I thought she should buy, but she didn't. "I don't like the (2) **collar**," she explained. "It makes my neck look too short."

As usual, after trying on clothes for over an hour, she left the store empty handed. I, on the other hand, bought several things that I couldn't really afford.

(*Note:* Words such as *on, also,* and *thought* are pronounced with an [ɑ] sound in some dialects of English. In other dialects, they are pronounced with an [ɔ] sound. In either case, the contrast with [ə] is important to make.)

Contrasting Sentences

❏ I don't like the _____. (It clashes with my hair and eyes.)

❏ I don't like the _____. (It makes my neck look too short.)

Additional Practice

Kevin ran after the *bus / boss.* (V7-A/a), Doug *caught / cut* the big fish. (V7-B/b), I need a *cop / cup.* (V7-d), What a *hog / hug!* (V7-e)

Other Words

one, sh**o**pping, l**o**ves, l**o**ts, **o**n, n**o**t, n**o**ne, **a**lso, **a**bout, **o**ther

   [ɑ] wh**a**t,

   [ə] b**u**t,

Other Practice Activities

- ❏ Partner Cards—Listening.
- ❏ Partner Cards—Speaking.
- ❏ Story Reading.
- ❏ Story Dictation.
- ❏ Cloze Reading.
- ❏ Story Retelling from Skeleton.
- ❏ Free Story Retelling.
- ❏ Parallel Story.
- ❏ Mini-drama.

Unit V8-A [ɑ] clock—[ow] cloak

Story

Listen to the story as your teacher reads it, or on tape, until you understand the main ideas.

Time flies when you're having fun. That's what happened when Bob and Amy went to an unusual museum. Everything on display was very big. They were surprised to see a pencil that was as tall as they were. There were large clothes, too. "Look at that (1) **cloak**!" said Amy. It was so big that they couldn't imagine who could wear it.

Bob suggested, "It must have belonged to a giant Count Dracula."

They looked at many other giant things in the museum. Then Amy said, "Look at the (2) **clock**!" "Is it as big as the moon?" asked Bob. He was disappointed when he looked where Amy was pointing. The clock was not big at all. It was just a regular clock.

Then Amy said, "Bob, it's five o'clock already! We came here at two, three hours ago. We'd better get going. I have to be to work by six."

(*Note:* Words such as *tall*, *already*, and *saw* are pronounced with an [ɑ] sound in some dialects of English. In other dialects, they are pronounced with an [ɔ] sound. In either case, the contrast with [ow] is important to make.)

Contrasting Sentences

Listening: Write the appropriate key word in each blank. Later, as you hear each sentence, mark the box, point to the picture, make a gesture, and/or say the rejoinder. Speaking: Choose and say each sentence so that your listener(s) can respond correctly.

❑ Look at the _____. (It must be Count Dracula's.)

❑ Look at the _____. (It's five o'clock already.)

Explanations and diagrams for this unit's target sounds are on pages 332–33 in Section 10.

Additional Practice

How did you like my *fox / folks?* (V8-B/b)

For [ɑ]: Jacob took good care of his *axe / ox.* (V5-A/a), It was a big *shock / shark.* (V6-A/a), The *gods / guards* were angry. (V6-b), Look at that *cot / cart.* (V6-c), Kevin ran after the *bus / boss.* (V7-A/a), Doug *caught / cut* the big fish. (V7-B/b), I don't like the *collar / color.* (V7-C/c), I need a *cop / cup.* (V7-d), What a *hog / hug!* (V7-e)

Other Words

Sort the words listed below into two groups according to the sound the boldface letters represent. Write the words in the spaces provided. The first two have been done for you. Then, circle or underline these words each time they occur in the story. Say each marked word aloud. Then say the entire sentence. Look for additional words in the story that contain the target sounds. Mark and say them also.

wh**a**t, B**o**b, g**o**ing, **o**n, ag**o**, st**o**p, o'cl**o**ck, cl**o**thes, **o**'clock, l**o**w

[ɑ] n**o**t,

[ow] s**o**,

Other Practice Activities

❑ Partner Cards—Listening. *Practice until you can point to the right card every time.*

❑ Partner Cards—Speaking. *Practice until you can say the contrasting sentences so accurately that your partner points to the right card every time.*

❑ Story Reading. *Practice reading the story aloud. Mark any difficult words. Then record the story on tape.*

❑ Story Dictation. *Write the story as your teacher reads it or as you listen to it on the audiotape.*

❑ Cloze Reading. *Choose some key words in the story and black them out. Then read the entire story aloud. Do this several times.*

Each time black out more words. Continue until most of the story is blacked out and you can tell it without looking at the page very often.

❑ Story Retelling from Skeleton. *Black out all the remaining words except those you need in order to remind you of the story line. Then, using just this skeleton, tell the story to your partner or class.*

❑ Free Story Retelling. *Retell the whole story from memory, without looking at your book.*

❑ Parallel Story. *Create your own story similar to the one in this unit.*

❑ Mini-drama. *Make up a skit or do a role play based on the story.*

Unit V8-B [ɑ] fox—[ow] folks

Story

Cindy and Julie were roommates in college. Once, Julie visited Cindy's home in the country. Cindy's family made Julie feel at home. Cindy's father and mother were always joking, and Julie laughed a lot. She told Cindy, (1) "Your **folks** are funny."

Then Cindy showed Julie a surprise—her pet (2) **fox**. When it was tiny, its mother had been killed by a car. Cindy had raised it, so it was very tame. It even wore a small collar. Julie, who had heard many children's stories about evil foxes, was surprised that it was so cute and gentle.

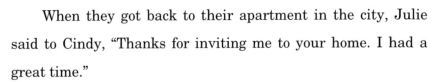

When they got back to their apartment in the city, Julie said to Cindy, "Thanks for inviting me to your home. I had a great time."

Cindy asked, "How did you like my folks?"

Julie answered, "They were very nice and funny."

"And how did you like my fox?" asked Cindy.

Julie said, "Oh, I wish I could have one, too."

(*Note:* Words such as *tall*, *already*, and *saw* are pronounced with an [ɑ] sound in some dialects of English. In other dialects, they are pronounced with an [ɔ] sound. In either case, the contrast with [ow] is important to make.)

Contrasting Sentences

❏ How did you like my _____? (They were funny.)
❏ How did you like my _____? (It was cute.)

Additional Practice

Look at the *clock / cloak*. (V8-A/a)

For [ɑ]: Jacob took good care of his *axe / ox*. (V5-A/a), It was a big *shock / shark*. (V6-A/a), The *gods / guards* were angry. (V6-b), Look at that *cot / cart*. (V6-c), Kevin ran after the *bus / boss*. (V7-A/a), Doug *caught / cut* the big fish. (V7-B/b), I don't like the *collar / color*. (V7-C/c), I need a *cop / cup*. (V7-d), What a *hog / hug!* (V7-e)

Other Words

told, lot, joking, got, collar, showed, ma, oh, pond, so

[ɑ] father,

[ow] home,

Other Practice Activities

❏ Partner Cards—Listening.
❏ Partner Cards—Speaking.
❏ Story Reading.
❏ Story Dictation.
❏ Cloze Reading.

❏ Story Retelling
   from Skeleton.
❏ Free Story Retelling.
❏ Parallel Story.
❏ Mini-drama.

Unit V9-A [ə] bud—[ər] bird

Story

Listen to the story as your teacher reads it, or on tape, until you understand the main ideas.

Shirley's favorite season is spring. She waits all winter for the snow to melt. When the (1) **birds** return and the trees start to bud, she is very happy. She knows that those (2) **buds** will soon be blossoms and leaves. She enjoys getting up early in the morning and walking in a park near her home. There, she watches the birds as they build their nests. She also likes to examine the flower buds that are getting ready to bloom. She thinks about how beautiful they will soon look. Shirley can't help telling everyone, "Spring is a wonderful time of the year!" Don't you agree?

(*Note:* Many dialects of English are "r-less." In such cases, the [ər] in *bird* is pronounced as a slightly lengthened [ə], and the vowel in *bud* may be represented with the symbol [ʌ] instead of [ə].)

Contrasting Sentences

Listening: Write the appropriate key word in each blank. Later, as you hear each sentence, mark the box, point to the picture, make a gesture, and/or say the rejoinder. Speaking: Choose and say each sentence so that your listener(s) can respond correctly.

❏ Shirley enjoys looking at the _____. (building their nests)

❏ Shirley enjoys looking at the _____. (getting ready to bloom)

Explanations and diagrams for this unit's target sounds are on pages 333–34 in Section 10.

Additional Practice

Look at the *gull / girl*. (V9-b)

For [ə]: Kevin ran after the *bus / boss*. (V-7A/a), Doug *cut / caught* the big fish. (V-7B/b), I don't like the *color / collar*. (V-7C/c), Steve needed two *bucks / books*. (V10-A/a), Jeremy *putts / puts* the golf ball. (V10-B/b)

For [ɑr], a sound similar to [ər]: It was a big *shock / shark*. (V-6A)

Other Words

Sort the words listed below into two groups according to the sound the boldface letters represent. Write the words in the spaces provided. The first two have been done for you. Then, circle or underline these words each time they occur in the story. Say each marked word aloud. Then say the entire sentence. Look for additional words in the story that contain the target sounds. Mark and say them also.

Sh**ir**ley, sea**so**n, wint**er**, ret**ur**n, flow**er**, bloss**o**m, **a**bout, ex**a**mine, beauti**fu**l, **ear**ly

[ə] **co**me,

[ər] h**er**,

Other Practice Activities

❑ Partner Cards—Listening. *Practice until you can point to the right card every time.*
❑ Partner Cards—Speaking. *Practice until you can say the contrasting sentences so accurately that your partner points to the right card every time.*
❑ Story Reading. *Practice reading the story aloud. Mark any difficult words. Then record the story on tape.*
❑ Story Dictation. *Write the story as your teacher reads it or as you listen to it on the audiotape.*
❑ Cloze Reading. *Choose some key words in the story and black them out. Then read the entire story aloud. Do this several times.*

Each time black out more words. Continue until most of the story is blacked out and you can tell it without looking at the page very often.
❑ Story Retelling from Skeleton. *Black out all the remaining words except those you need in order to remind you of the story line. Then, using just this skeleton, tell the story to your partner or class.*
❑ Free Story Retelling. *Retell the whole story from memory, without looking at your book.*
❑ Parallel Story. *Create your own story similar to the one in this unit.*
❑ Mini-drama. *Make up a skit or do a role play based on the story.*

Unit V10-A [ə] bucks—[ʊ] books

Story

Listen to the story as your teacher reads it, or on tape, until you understand the main ideas.

Steve is taking an English literature class. The teacher always gives a lot of homework. Today, she said, "Your assignment is to read (1) two **books** written by the same author and write a paper on how similar or different they are. It will be due a week from today."

Steve knew he had no time to waste, so he decided that right after class he would go to the library to find the two books. While Steve was looking for the books, he felt hungry. So, he decided to go to the snack bar to get something to eat. The hamburgers looked really good to him, but they cost (2) two **bucks** each. Steve had only one dollar, so he couldn't buy one. He just stood there feeling hungry. Luckily, his roommate came by just then, and he borrowed some money from him. He paid two bucks for the hamburger, ate it, and then went back to the library to find his books.

Contrasting Sentences

Listening: Write the appropriate key word in each blank. Later, as you hear each sentence, mark the box, point to the picture, make a gesture, and/or say the rejoinder. Speaking: Choose and say each sentence so that your listener(s) can respond correctly.

❏ Steve needed two _____. (to write his paper)

❏ Steve needed two _____. (to buy a hamburger)

Explanations and diagrams for this unit's target sounds are on pages 333 and 334 in Section 10.

Additional Practice

Jeremy *putts/puts* the golf ball. (V10-B/b)

For [ə]: Kevin ran after the *bus / boss*. (V-7A/a), Doug *cut / caught* the big fish. (V-7B/b), I don't like the *color / collar*. (V-7C/c)

For [ʊ]: Look at the *soot / suit!* (V11-A/a), Julie *stood / stewed* for a long time. (V11-B/b), I saw it in *Look / Luke*. (V11-C/c)

Other Words

Sort the words listed below into two groups according to the sound the boldface letters represent. Write the words in the spaces provided. The first two have been done for you. Then, circle or underline these words each time they occur in the story. Say each marked word aloud. Then say the entire sentence. Look for additional words in the story that contain the target sounds. Mark and say them also.

l**oo**ked, h**u**ngry, **o**ne, st**oo**d, l**u**ckily, c**ou**ldn't, j**u**st, m**o**ney, w**ou**ld, p**u**ll

[ə] s**o**me,

[ʊ] g**oo**d,

Other Practice Activities

❏ Partner Cards—Listening. *Practice until you can point to the right card every time.*
❏ Partner Cards—Speaking. *Practice until you can say the contrasting sentences so accurately that your partner points to the right card every time.*
❏ Story Reading. *Practice reading the story aloud. Mark any difficult words. Then record the story on tape.*
❏ Story Dictation. *Write the story as your teacher reads it or as you listen to it on the audiotape.*
❏ Cloze Reading. *Choose some key words in the story and black them out. Then read the entire story aloud. Do this several times.*

Each time black out more words. Continue until most of the story is blacked out and you can tell it without looking at the page very often.
❏ Story Retelling from Skeleton. *Black out all the remaining words except those you need in order to remind you of the story line. Then, using just this skeleton, tell the story to your partner or class.*
❏ Free Story Retelling. *Retell the whole story from memory, without looking at your book.*
❏ Parallel Story. *Create your own story similar to the one in this unit.*
❏ Mini-drama. *Make up a skit or do a role play based on the story.*

Unit V10-B [ə] putts—[ʊ] puts

Story

Many people love golf. They enjoy hitting a good, long drive, and some even like walking from hole to hole. Jeremy is an expert golfer, but he never hits a drive, and he walks only short distances. Why? Because he plays miniature golf.

Miniature golf can be easy, but the way Jeremy plays takes a lot of planning, concentration, and skill. Before playing a course, he studies every hole carefully. When he is ready to start, he picks up a golf ball, inspects it closely, and (1) **puts** it on the tee. He tries to concentrate in order to calculate angles and distances exactly. He pays no attention to the people who are looking at him. He holds his golf club carefully and, at just the right moment, (2) **putts** the ball. It usually bounces a few times, passes an obstacle or two, and goes straight into the cup! His fellow players are all impressed. It's not easy to get a hole in one, even in miniature golf.

Contrasting Sentences

❑ Jeremy _____ the golf ball . . . (on the ground, with his hand)
❑ Jeremy _____ the golf ball . . . (into the hole, with his golf club)

Additional Practice

Steve needed two *bucks / books*. (V10-A/a)

For [ə]: Kevin ran after the *bus / boss*. (V-7A/a), Doug *cut / caught* the big fish. (V-7B/b), I don't like the *color / collar*. (V-7C/c), Steve needed two *bucks / books*. (V10-A/a), Jeremy *putts / puts* the golf ball. (V10-B/b)

For [ʊ]: Look at the *soot / suit!* (V11-A/a), Julie *stood / stewed* for a long time. (V11-B/b), I saw it in *Look / Luke*. (V11-C/c)

Other Words

cookie, would, pull, some, distance, but, study, attention, looking, book

[ə] love,

[ʊ] good,

Other Practice Activities

❏ Partner Cards—Listening.
❏ Partner Cards—Speaking.
❏ Story Reading.
❏ Story Dictation.
❏ Cloze Reading.

❏ Story Retelling
  from Skeleton.
❏ Free Story Retelling.
❏ Parallel Story.
❏ Mini-drama.

Unit V11-A [ʊ] soot—[uw] suit

Story

Listen to the story as your teacher reads it, or on tape, until you understand the main ideas.

Ruth (1) is a good woman, but she's messy. For example, she can cook very well, but she never puts things away after she's through. She also leaves her books, papers, and clothes all over the house. When she loses or ruins something, she feels foolish and promises to improve, but she hasn't changed yet.

Not long ago she bought a new (2) **suit**. It was pink and made of wool. She was very pleased with it, and as she came in the door she exclaimed, "Look at this beautiful suit!" But after she showed it to me, she didn't put it in her closet as she should have. She just left it lying on a chair near an open window. A few days later, when she wanted to wear her new suit, it was still there.

When she picked the suit up, Ruth was very upset. There were little black particles all over it. (3) "Look at this **soot**!" she cried. She tried shaking the suit, but only a little of the soot shook off. Her new suit was dirty, and she couldn't wear it as planned. She had to take it to the cleaners instead.

Contrasting Sentences

Listening: Write the appropriate key word in each blank. Later, as you hear each sentence, mark the box, point to the picture, make a gesture, and / or say the rejoinder. Speaking: Choose and say each sentence so that your listener(s) can respond correctly.

❑ Look at this _____! (Isn't it beautiful?)

❑ Look at this _____! (Isn't it terrible?)

Explanations and diagrams for this unit's target sounds are on pages 334–35 in Section 10.

Additional Practice

Julie *stood / stewed* for a long time. (V11-B/b), I saw it in *Look / Luke.* (V11-C/c), The sign says, *"Pull / Pool."* (V11-d)

For [ʊ]: Steve needed two *bucks / books.* (V10-A/a), Jeremy *putts / puts* the golf ball. (V10-B/b)

Other Words

Sort the words listed below into two groups according to the sound the boldface letters represent. Write the words in the spaces provided. The first two have been done for you. Then, circle or underline these words each time they occur in the story. Say each marked word aloud. Then say the entire sentence. Look for additional words in the story that contain the target sounds. Mark and say them also.

r**u**ins, **R**uth, thr**ough**, w**o**man, c**oo**k, p**u**t, w**oo**l, sh**oo**k, l**o**ses, impr**o**ve

[ʊ] **goo**d,

[uw] f**oo**lish,

Other Practice Activities

❏ Partner Cards—Listening. *Practice until you can point to the right card every time.*
❏ Partner Cards—Speaking. *Practice until you can say the contrasting sentences so accurately that your partner points to the right card every time.*
❏ Story Reading. *Practice reading the story aloud. Mark any difficult words. Then record the story on tape.*
❏ Story Dictation. *Write the story as your teacher reads it or as you listen to it on the audiotape.*
❏ Cloze Reading. *Choose some key words in the story and black them out. Then read the entire story aloud. Do this several times.*

Each time black out more words. Continue until most of the story is blacked out and you can tell it without looking at the page very often.

❏ Story Retelling from Skeleton. *Black out all the remaining words except those you need in order to remind you of the story line. Then, using just this skeleton, tell the story to your partner or class.*
❏ Free Story Retelling. *Retell the whole story from memory, without looking at your book.*
❏ Parallel Story. *Create your own story similar to the one in this unit.*
❏ Mini-drama. *Make up a skit or do a role play based on the story.*

Unit V11-B [ʊ] stood—[uw] stewed

Story

Whenever a famous singer comes to town, people stand in line for hours to get tickets for the concert. Last Saturday, my friend Julie, who is a great opera fan, got up very early in the morning and went to the theater ticket sales booth. Unfortunately, she didn't get there early enough. The line was already very long, so she (1) **stood** in line most of the morning to get a ticket.

When she finally got to the front of the line, she thought her luck had changed, but it hadn't. Wouldn't you know it? The person in front of her bought the last tickets. Julie was furious. She went home and (2) **stewed** all afternoon. She was not in a good mood until the next day. Fortunately, by then she could laugh about her bad luck.

Contrasting Sentences

❏ Julie _____ for a long time. (in line)

❏ Julie _____ for a long time. (at home)

Additional Practice

Look at that *soot / suit!* (V11-A/a), I saw it in *Look / Luke.* (V11-C/c), The sign says, *"Pull / Pool."* (V11-d)

For [ʊ]: Steve needed two *bucks / books.* (V10-A/a), Jeremy *putts / puts* the golf ball. (V10-B/b)

Other Words

w**ou**ldn't, st**u**dent, l**oo**ked, c**ou**ld, ch**oo**se, st**oo**d, p**u**ll, b**oo**th, m**oo**d, j**ui**ce

[ʊ] g**oo**d,

[uw] bl**ue**,

Other Practice Activities

- Partner Cards—Listening.
- Partner Cards—Speaking.
- Story Reading.
- Story Dictation.
- Cloze Reading.

- Story Retelling from Skeleton.
- Free Story Retelling.
- Parallel Story.
- Mini-drama.

Unit V11-C [ʊ] Look—[uw] Luke

Story

(1) My grandfather has read many books and magazines.

He often remembers things he read years ago, but he can't always remember where he read them. So he tries to look them up. The other day I saw him thumbing through (2) an old Bible.

"What are you doing, Grandpa?" I asked.

"Oh, I can't remember if the story of the good Samaritan is in Matthew or **Luke**, so I'm looking it up." A few minutes later, he exclaimed happily, "Luke! It was in Luke." Then he was satisfied, and I could ask him what I had come for.

"Grandpa, do you remember anything about President Kennedy?"

"Of course I do," he replied. "In fact, I read a great summary of his presidency in a magazine once. The magazine was either *Life* or (3) *Look*. I can't remember which, but I could go to the library and look for it."

"Please don't bother," I answered. "Just tell me what you remember."

Contrasting Sentences

- I saw it in _____. (the Bible)
- I saw it in _____. (the magazine)

Additional Practice

Look at that *soot/suit!* (V11-A/a), Julie *stood/stewed* for a long time. (V11-B/b), The sign says, *"Pull/Pool."* (V11-d)

For [ʊ]: Steve needed two *bucks/books.* (V10-A/a), Jeremy *putts/puts* the golf ball. (V10-B/b)

Other Words

doing, **few**, lo**o**king, g**oo**d, c**ou**ld, t**oo**k, **to, do**, sugar, thr**ough**

[ʊ] **put**,

[uw] **you**,

Other Practice Activities

- ❏ Partner Cards—Listening.
- ❏ Partner Cards—Speaking.
- ❏ Story Reading.
- ❏ Story Dictation.
- ❏ Cloze Reading.
- ❏ Story Retelling from Skeleton.
- ❏ Free Story Retelling.
- ❏ Parallel Story.
- ❏ Mini-drama.

Section 3
Consonants (C)

Unit C1i-A [p] pill—[b] bill

Story

Listen to the story as your teacher reads it, or on tape, until you understand the main ideas.

When my sister was young, she was often sick. Sometimes her illnesses were very bad. One winter, when my mother took my sister to the doctor, we found out that she had pneumonia and strep throat. She had to take penicillin. The penicillin (1) **pills** that the doctor gave her were so large that we called them horse pills. My sister hated to take them, but she knew she had to in order to get better.

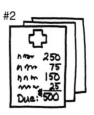

#1

Of course, medical care is not cheap, and because my sister was sick so often the doctor (2) **bills** were also very large. My mother hated receiving those big bills as much as my sister hated taking her big pills. But if we didn't pay them, the doctor might not help us the next time my sister got sick.

#2

Contrasting Sentences

Listening: Write the appropriate key word in each blank. Later, as you hear each sentence, mark the box, point to the picture, make a gesture, and/or say the rejoinder. Speaking: Choose and say each sentence so that your listener(s) can respond correctly.

❏ Those _____ are very large! (They'll be hard to swallow.)

❏ Those _____ are very large! (They'll be hard to pay.)

Explanations and diagrams for this unit's target sounds are on pages 335–36 in Section 10.

Additional Practice

Pete caught a fantastic *pass*/*bass*. (C1i-B/b), That was not a good place to *park*/*bark*. (C1i-C/c), Look at that *pear*/*bear*. (C1i-d), Here's the *pump*/*bump*. (C1i-e), What a beautiful *peach*/*beach!* (C1i-f), These *peas*/*bees* all look alike. (C1i-g), He has the *pox*/*box*. (C1i-h), *Rapid*/*Rabid* dogs are dangerous. (C1m-A/a), A robber stole my uncle's *cap*/*cab*. (C1f-A/a), I need a new *rope*/*robe*. (C1f-b)

Other Words

Many, if not all, of the words listed below are in the story. Find them and circle or underline them each time they occur. Say each marked word aloud—individually and then in its entire sentence. Look for additional words in the story that contain the target sounds. Mark and say them also.

[p] **p**enicillin, **p**ay, **p**ad, **p**ig, **p**ut

[b] **b**ad, **b**etter, **b**ecause, **b**ig, **b**ut

Other Practice Activities

❏ Partner Cards—Listening. *Practice until you can point to the right card every time.*
❏ Partner Cards—Speaking. *Practice until you can say the contrasting sentences so accurately that your partner points to the right card every time.*
❏ Story Reading. *Practice reading the story aloud. Mark any difficult words. Then record the story on tape.*
❏ Story Dictation. *Write the story as your teacher reads it or as you listen to it on the audiotape.*
❏ Cloze Reading. *Choose some key words in the story and black them out. Then read the entire story aloud. Do this several times.*

Each time black out more words. Continue until most of the story is blacked out and you can tell it without looking at the page very often.
❏ Story Retelling from Skeleton. *Black out all the remaining words except those you need in order to remind you of the story line. Then, using just this skeleton, tell the story to your partner or class.*
❏ Free Story Retelling. *Retell the whole story from memory, without looking at your book.*
❏ Parallel Story. *Create your own story similar to the one in this unit.*
❏ Mini-drama. *Make up a skit or do a role play based on the story.*

Unit C1i-B [p] pass—[b] bass

Story

Pete participates in lots of different outdoor activities and excels in all of them. In the fall, he loves to play football. He can run very fast, so he often gets past the defense, catches a (1) **pass** from his quarterback, and then runs for big yardage. In the final seconds of a game last year, he caught a fantastic pass and ran for a touchdown. The points he scored put his team ahead, so he was the hero of the game. When basketball season started, it was the same story. And baseball season brought him more glory.

But team sports are not the only activities that Pete participates in. He also loves to go boating and fishing. Trout are his favorite fish, but he catches all kinds. In fact, last year he caught a great big (2) **bass.** It almost broke the record for our state. Why do some people have all the luck?

Contrasting Sentences

❏ Pete caught a fantastic _____ . (He was the hero of the game.)

❏ Pete caught a fantastic _____ . (It was a big fish.)

Additional Practice

Those *pills / bills* are very large! (C1i-A/a), That was not a good place to *park / bark.* (C1i-C/c), Look at that *pear / bear.* (C1i-d), Here's the *pump / bump.* (C1i-e), What a beautiful *peach / beach!* (C1i-f), These *peas / bees* all look alike. (C1i-g), He has the *pox / box.* (C1i-h), *Rapid / Rabid* dogs are dangerous. (C1m-A/a), A robber stole my uncle's *cap / cab.* (C1f-A/a), I need a new *rope / robe.* (C1f-b)

Other Words

[p] **P**ete, **p**articipates, **p**ast, **p**oints, **p**ut, **p**eople

[b] **b**ig, **b**asketball, **b**aseball, **b**oating, **b**ig, **b**roke

Other Practice Activities

❏ Partner Cards—Listening.
❏ Partner Cards—Speaking.
❏ Story Reading.
❏ Story Dictation.
❏ Cloze Reading.

❏ Story Retelling from Skeleton.
❏ Free Story Retelling.
❏ Parallel Story.
❏ Mini-drama.

Unit C1i-C [p] park—[b] bark

Story

I work part-time as a private investigator. That may sound exciting, but PI work is not like what you see on television programs. In fact, it's often boring. I spend a lot of time (1) in my car just waiting for people to come out of their homes. So sometimes I take my dog along for company. If a situation gets tough, my dog can also provide some extra protection. Sometimes, however, he causes trouble.

Last week, for instance, I parked near a suspect's property just as it began to get dark. I thought that was a good place to **park,** but I was wrong. As it got darker, security lights began to shine in all directions. Then, some people walked by, and my dog began to bark at them. (2) It was not a good place (or time) to **bark.** I was afraid someone from the house was going to hear the noise, look out, and see me. I realized that I was parked too close to the house, and I couldn't make the dog stop barking, so I drove away and found a better place before I blew my cover. It was more embarrassing than exciting.

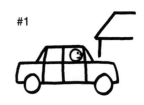

Contrasting Sentences

❏ That was not a good place to _____. (It was too close to the house.)

❏ That was not a good place to _____. (But I couldn't make my dog stop.)

Additional Practice

Those *pills/bills* are very large! (C1i-A/a), Pete caught a fantastic *pass/bass.* (C1i-B/b), Look at that *pear/bear.* (C1i-d), Here's the *pump/bump.* (C1i-e), What a beautiful *peach/beach!* (C1i-f), These *peas/bees* all look alike. (C1i-g), He has the *pox/box.* (C1i-h), *Rapid/Rabid* dogs are dangerous. (C1m-A/a), A robber stole my uncle's *cap/cab.* (C1f-A/a), I need a new *rope/robe.* (C1f-b)

Other Words

[p] **p**art, **p**rivate, **p**eople, **p**rovide, **p**rotection, **p**roperty

[b] **b**ut, **b**oring, **b**egan, **b**efore, **b**lew, **b**etter

Other Practice Activities

❏ Partner Cards—Listening.
❏ Partner Cards—Speaking.
❏ Story Reading.
❏ Story Dictation.
❏ Cloze Reading.

❏ Story Retelling
   from Skeleton.
❏ Free Story Retelling.
❏ Parallel Story.
❏ Mini-drama.

Unit C1m-A [p] rapid—[b] rabid

Story

In the countryside you have to be careful. There are plenty of hazards and wild animals. But sometimes the most dangerous animals are wandering dogs. Because many dogs run free in the country, you never know what to expect. If you don't know a dog well, you shouldn't go near it—even if it appears harmless.

Sometimes a dog is sick and looks pitiful, but even a pathetic dog can be dangerous. If it behaves strangely or foams at the mouth, (1) it might be **rabid.**

#1

Some dogs are mean, and they will chase after you, either alone or in packs. If that happens, whatever you do, don't run. Dogs naturally like to chase after things that run, (2) and dogs can run very **rapidly.** You won't be able to outrun them. It's better to face them or climb a tree, but it is best to simply stay far away from strange dogs in the first place.

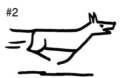

#2

Contrasting Sentences

❏ _____ dogs are dangerous. (They carry a deadly disease.)

❏ _____ dogs are dangerous. (You can't outrun them.)

Additional Practice

Those *pills/bills* are very large! (C1i-A/a), Pete caught a fantastic *pass/bass.* (C1i-B/b), That was not a good place to *park/bark.* (C1i-C/c), Look at that *pear/bear.* (C1i-d), Here's the *pump/bump.* (C1i-e), What a beautiful *peach/beach!* (C1i-f), These *peas/bees* all look alike. (C1i-g), He has the *pox/box.* (C1i-h), A robber stole my uncle's *cap/cab.* (C1f-A/a), I need a new *rope/robe.* (C1f-b)

Other Words

[p] a**pp**ears, u**pp**er, sim**p**ly, a**pp**ly, sta**p**le, crum**p**le

[b] pro**b**ably, ru**bb**er, cra**bb**y, am**b**le, sta**b**le, crum**b**le

Other Practice Activities

❏ Partner Cards—Listening.
❏ Partner Cards—Speaking.
❏ Story Reading.
❏ Story Dictation.
❏ Cloze Reading.

❏ Story Retelling from Skeleton.
❏ Free Story Retelling.
❏ Parallel Story.
❏ Mini-drama.

Unit C1f-A [p] cap—[b] cab

Story

My uncle drives for a cab company in a big city. There is a lot of crime in big cities, so all the drivers must wear the company's special uniform and (1) **cap.** That way, passengers will know they are legitimate and can be trusted.

My uncle's job can be dangerous. One time a passenger pulled out a pistol, pointed it at my uncle, and told him to stop the (2) **cab** and get out. Of course, all my uncle could do was cooperate. Besides, he figured that the robber probably wouldn't get far driving a well-marked cab. A cop would nab him as soon as the crime was reported.

The robber had thought of that possibility also. In fact, to reduce the chances of being caught he also wanted my uncle's uniform and cap. That way he would look more like the official

#1

#2

driver and less suspicious. A few minutes later, the robber drove away in my uncle's cab and left my uncle standing at the curb in his underwear. It was an experience he never forgot!

Contrasting Sentences

❑ A robber stole my uncle's _____. (hat)

❑ A robber stole my uncle's _____. (taxi)

Additional Practice

I need a new *rope/robe.* (C1f-b), Those *pills/bills* are very large! (C1i-A/a), Pete caught a fantastic *pass/bass.* (C1i-B/b), That was not a good place to *park/bark.* (C1i-C/c), Look at that *pear/bear.* (C1i-d), Here's the *pump/bump.* (C1i-e), What a beautiful *peach/beach!* (C1i-f), These *peas/bees* all look alike. (C1i-g), He has the *pox/box.* (C1i-h), *Rapid/Rabid* dogs are dangerous. (C1m-A/a)

Other Words

[p] ca**p**, co**p**, ro**p**e, ri**p**, sna**p**, cu**p**

[b] cur**b**, na**b**, ro**b**e, ri**b**, gra**b**, cu**b**

Other Practice Activities

❑ Partner Cards—Listening.
❑ Partner Cards—Speaking.
❑ Story Reading.
❑ Story Dictation.
❑ Cloze Reading.
❑ Story Retelling from Skeleton.
❑ Free Story Retelling.
❑ Parallel Story.
❑ Mini-drama.

Unit C2i-A [p] pan—[f] fan

Story

Listen to the story as your teacher reads it, or on tape, until you understand the main ideas.

Recently Frances moved out of her parents' home and into an apartment of her own. She felt happy to be independent, but she was surprised at (1) how expensive everything was. The deposit and first month's rent used up nearly all her money. Unfortunately, she still had to furnish the apartment—especially the kitchen. It already had a refrigerator, but she needed some small appliances. She also needed (2) a good frying **pan.** So Frances went to a department store to buy one.

When she got there Frances noticed something else that she needed—(3) an electric **fan.** Summer was just starting, and her bedroom was already hot and stuffy.

Frances had a big decision to make. She wouldn't get her next paycheck for several more days, and she had only enough money for one of the things she needed. She had to decide whether to buy a pan, or a fan. Which one do you think she bought?

#1

#2

#3

Contrasting Sentences

Listening: Write the appropriate key word in each blank. Later, as you hear each sentence, mark the box, point to the picture, make a gesture, and / or say the rejoinder. Speaking: Choose and say each sentence so that your listener(s) can respond correctly.

❏ She needed a _____. (for cooking)

❏ She needed a _____. (to keep cool)

Explanations and diagrams for this unit's target sounds are on pages 335 and 336 in Section 10.

Additional Practice

I need some *pins/fins*. (C2i-b), The hyena was *lapping/laughing*.
(C2m-A/a), Where's the *copy/coffee* machine? (C2m-b), Your *cup/cuff*
is dirty! (C2f-A/a), Look at that *clip/cliff!* (C2f-b)

Other Words

*Many, if not all, of the words listed below are in the story. Find them
and circle or underline them each time they occur. Say each marked
word aloud—individually and then in its entire sentence. Look for
additional words in the story that contain the target sounds. Mark
and say them also.*

[p] **p**arents, **p**aycheck, **p**ry, **p**ail, **p**in, **p**ride

[f] **F**rances, **f**irst, **f**urnish, **f**rying, **f**ail, **f**ast

Other Practice Activities

❏ Partner Cards—Listening. *Practice until
you can point to the right card every time.*
❏ Partner Cards—Speaking. *Practice until
you can say the contrasting sentences so
accurately that your partner points to the
right card every time.*
❏ Story Reading. *Practice reading the story
aloud. Mark any difficult words. Then
record the story on tape.*
❏ Story Dictation. *Write the story as your
teacher reads it or as you listen to it on the
audiotape.*
❏ Cloze Reading. *Choose some key words in
the story and black them out. Then read the
entire story aloud. Do this several times.*

*Each time black out more words. Continue
until most of the story is blacked out and
you can tell it without looking at the page
very often.*
❏ Story Retelling from Skeleton. *Black out all
the remaining words except those you need
in order to remind you of the story line.
Then, using just this skeleton, tell the story
to your partner or class.*
❏ Free Story Retelling. *Retell the whole story
from memory, without looking at your book.*
❏ Parallel Story. *Create your own story similar to the one in this unit.*
❏ Mini-drama. *Make up a skit or do a role
play based on the story.*

Unit C2m-A [p] lapping—[f] laughing

Story

I love to go to the zoo and see the animals. My favorite ones are

from Africa. (1) The giraffes are so tall that they can eat leaves

out of the tops of trees, but they are still graceful. (2) The ele-

phants are big and powerful, yet their trunks are so sensitive

they can find and pick up a peanut lying on the ground between their front legs. There is one African animal, however, that doesn't impress me—(3) the hyena.

When I was a child, I saw hyenas in cartoons. They were always (4) **laughing** hysterically. The two words—*laughing* and *hyena*—became inseparable in my mind. So, the first time I saw a hyena, I expected to hear it laughing uncontrollably. Boy, was I disappointed! I watched and waited for a long time, but all it did was sit quietly in its cage. Once in a while it would walk over to its (5) water dish and **lap** up some water. That's all. It never laughed once. I walked away muttering, "It should be called a *lapping* hyena, not a *laughing* hyena."

Contrasting Sentences

❏ The hyena was _____. (Ha ha, hee hee!)

❏ The hyena was _____. (drinking water)

Additional Practice

She needed a *pan/fan*. (C2i-A/a), I need some *pins/fins*. (C2i-b), Where's the *copy/coffee* machine? (C2m-b), Your *cup/cuff* is dirty! (C2f-A/a), Look at that *clip/cliff!* (C2f-b)

Other Words

[p] inse**p**arable, disa**pp**ointed, shi**pp**ed, lea**p**ing, su**pp**er, pu**pp**y

[f] grace**f**ul, ele**ph**ant, power**f**ul, A**f**rican, sni**ff**ing, cou**gh**s

Other Practice Activities

❏ Partner Cards—Listening.
❏ Partner Cards—Speaking.
❏ Story Reading.
❏ Story Dictation.
❏ Cloze Reading.

❏ Story Retelling
   from Skeleton.
❏ Free Story Retelling.
❏ Parallel Story.
❏ Mini-drama.

Unit C2f-A [p] cup—[f] cuff

Story

My wife is very particular when it comes to keeping everything clean. I try to satisfy her, but I have trouble meeting her high standards. For example, even though I am dressed in freshly washed clothes, she feels she has to inspect me and look for dirty spots. My socks, pants, and shirt may be perfectly clean, but if I happen to have rubbed the (1) **cuff** of my clean shirt on a dusty table she will exclaim, "Your cuff is dirty!" Then I have to change my shirt.

She does the same thing at the dinner table. She has to inspect all the dishes and silverware before she will let me eat. My plate, knife, fork, and spoon may be spotless, but if there is even a tiny speck of something on my (2) **cup** she will gasp, "Your cup is dirty!" Immediately, she will leap up and wipe it clean. It's not easy living with a perfectionist like my wife.

Contrasting Sentences

❏ Your _____ is dirty! (You'd better change your shirt.)

❏ Your _____ is dirty! (Don't drink from it.)

Additional Practice

She needed a *pan/fan.* (C2i-A/a), I need some *pins/fins.* (C2i-b), The hyena was *lapping/laughing* (C2m-A/a), Where's the *copy/coffee* machine? (C2m-b), Look at that *clip/cliff!* (C2f-b)

Other Words

[p] gas**p**, wi**p**e, stri**p**e, ti**p**, gul**p**, lea**p**

[f] wi**f**e, kni**f**e, bee**f**, sni**ff**, pu**ff**, cou**gh**

Other Practice Activities

- ❏ Partner Cards—Listening.
- ❏ Partner Cards—Speaking.
- ❏ Story Reading.
- ❏ Story Dictation.
- ❏ Cloze Reading.
- ❏ Story Retelling from Skeleton.
- ❏ Free Story Retelling.
- ❏ Parallel Story.
- ❏ Mini-drama.

Unit C3i-A [v] vote—[b] boat

Story

Listen to the story as your teacher reads it, or on tape, until you understand the main ideas.

In big cities, most people live relatively private lives. Many don't even know their neighbors. In small towns, however, everybody knows everyone else. They also tend to keep track of their neighbors. If you want to know where someone is, all you have to do is ask.

When I go to visit my cousin Vera, who lives in a very small town, she is easy to find. She is almost always at the lake. There is not much else to do. Last Saturday, however, when I went to visit her I couldn't find her when I arrived. I thought that she would be out on the lake (1) **boating** because it was a nice day. But she wasn't. Then I thought she might have gone to the little corner store to buy something, but she wasn't there either.

Finally I asked my cousin's neighbor where she was, and he said, "Oh, she's in town (2) **voting**." What a surprise! I had forgotten it was election day.

Contrasting Sentences

Listening: Write the appropriate key word in each blank. Later, as you hear each sentence, mark the box, point to the picture, make a gesture, and/or say the rejoinder. Speaking: Choose and say each sentence so that your listener(s) can respond correctly.

❏ She's _____. (on the lake)

❏ She's _____. (in the election)

Explanations and diagrams for this unit's target sounds are on pages 335–37 in Section 10.

Additional Practice

That's a lot of *volts/bolts!* (C3i-b), She has a *veil/bale.* (C3i-c), I saw *calves/cabs.* (C3m-A/a), The car went over the *curve/curb.* (C3f-A/a)

Other Words

Many, if not all, of the words listed below are in the story. Find them and circle or underline them each time they occur. Say each marked word aloud—individually and then in its entire sentence. Look for additional words in the story that contain the target sounds. Mark and say them also.

[v] **v**isit, **V**era, **v**ery, **v**an, **v**est, **v**owel

[b] **b**ig, **b**ecause, **b**uy, **b**eer, **b**erry, **b**ow

Other Practice Activities

❑ Partner Cards—Listening. *Practice until you can point to the right card every time.*
❑ Partner Cards—Speaking. *Practice until you can say the contrasting sentences so accurately that your partner points to the right card every time.*
❑ Story Reading. *Practice reading the story aloud. Mark any difficult words. Then record the story on tape.*
❑ Story Dictation. *Write the story as your teacher reads it or as you listen to it on the audiotape.*
❑ Cloze Reading. *Choose some key words in the story and black them out. Then read the entire story aloud. Do this several times.*

Each time black out more words. Continue until most of the story is blacked out and you can tell it without looking at the page very often.
❑ Story Retelling from Skeleton. *Black out all the remaining words except those you need in order to remind you of the story line. Then, using just this skeleton, tell the story to your partner or class.*
❑ Free Story Retelling. *Retell the whole story from memory, without looking at your book.*
❑ Parallel Story. *Create your own story similar to the one in this unit.*
❑ Mini-drama. *Make up a skit or do a role play based on the story.*

Unit C3m-A [v] calves—[b] cabs

Story

When you live in the city, you don't often see animals, especially farm animals. But last time I went to the park I was pleasantly surprised. They had brought in lots of baby animals for a special children's petting zoo. In a canvas-covered area on one side of the park there were (1) **calves,** piglets, and colts. On the other side there were chicks, kittens, and puppies. I am an animal lover, so I spent quite a bit of time there. I felt so much like I was in the country that I marveled at seeing (2) **cabs** when I finally left the park and walked back out on the street.

Contrasting Sentences

❏ I saw _____ . (baby cows)

❏ I saw _____ . (taxis)

Additional Practice

She's *voting / boating.* (C3i-A/a), That's a lot of *volts / bolts!* (C3i-b), She has a *veil / bale.* (C3i-c), The car went over the *curve / curb.* (C3f-A/a)

Other Words

[v] li**v**es, can**v**as, co**v**ered, lo**v**er, mar**v**eled, thie**v**es

[b] ba**b**y, cur**b**s, cup**b**oard, sa**b**er, mar**b**led, dri**bb**le

Other Practice Activities

❏ Partner Cards—Listening.
❏ Partner Cards—Speaking.
❏ Story Reading.
❏ Story Dictation.
❏ Cloze Reading.

❏ Story Retelling from Skeleton.
❏ Free Story Retelling.
❏ Parallel Story.
❏ Mini-drama.

Unit C3f-A [v] curve—[b] curb

Story

Yesterday the police received a call notifying them that a man in a dark blue (1) pickup truck had been observed driving strangely. Sometimes the truck stayed on the road even though it would weave in and out of its lane. Four or five times, however, it went over the (2) **curb** and up onto the sidewalk. Finally, as it came to a place where the road turned around the edge of a hill, the truck went over the (3) **curve,** off the road, down a slope, and into a ditch. There, it got stuck and couldn't go any farther.

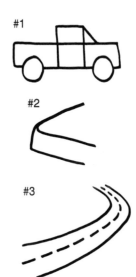

#1

#2

#3

When the police arrived on the scene, there were many witnesses to the event who told them what had happened. Fortunately, no one had been injured. The police arrested the driver, who was still sitting in the cab of the truck, and took him to the station. He was obviously very drunk. He should have known better than to drink and drive.

Contrasting Sentences

❑ The car went over the _____. (raised edge of the road)

❑ The car went over the _____. (turn in the road)

Additional Practice

She's *voting*/*boating*. (C3i-A/a), That's a lot of *volts*/*bolts!* (C3i-b), She has a *veil*/*bale*. (C3i-c), I saw *calves*/*cabs*. (C3m-A/a)

Other Words

[v] wea**v**e, o**f**, fi**v**e, dri**v**e, obser**v**e, ha**v**e

[b] ca**b**, ro**b**e, ru**b**, gra**b**, tri**b**e, swa**b**

Other Practice Activities

❑ Partner Cards—Listening.
❑ Partner Cards—Speaking.
❑ Story Reading.
❑ Story Dictation.
❑ Cloze Reading.
❑ Story Retelling from Skeleton.
❑ Free Story Retelling.
❑ Parallel Story.
❑ Mini-drama.

Unit C4i-A [w] worse—[v] verse

Story

Listen to the story as your teacher reads it, or on tape, until you understand the main ideas.

My neighbor Wendy is an accomplished writer. She likes anything that has to do with words, but she particularly likes poetry. She has written and published many poems of her own. Some of her verse has even been put to music.

Sometimes I see myself as a poet. I have written a few poems, and once I asked Wendy to evaluate them. She did, but she was not favorably impressed. She kindly told me I needed to revise them.

So, I spent many hours trying to improve my poetry. I struggled to use just the right words. It was not easy to create the right images, rhythm, and rhyme. Unfortunately, all my hard work didn't help very much. When Wendy read my revised poems, she told me that they were (1) **worse.** I almost gave up at that point, but I decided to stick with my vision. I vowed that someday my poetry would win Wendy's approval.

For several more weeks I worked on my poems. Then I showed them to Wendy again. This time the outcome was different. My extra work had not been in vain. Although I was still far from being a poetry virtuoso, Wendy was very happy with my improvements and exclaimed, "Now, that's (2) **verse!**"

Contrasting Sentences

Listening: Write the appropriate key word in each blank. Later, as you hear each sentence, mark the box, point to the picture, make a gesture, and/or say the rejoinder. Speaking: Choose and say each sentence so that your listener(s) can respond correctly.

❑ That's _____. (not as good)

❑ That's _____. (poetry)

Explanations and diagrams for this unit's target sounds are on pages 336 and 337 in Section 10.

Additional Practice

It's in the *west/vest*. (C4i-b), That's a strong *wine/vine*. (C4i-c), They were *rowing/roving* around in the dark. (C4m-A/a)

Other Words

Many, if not all, of the words listed below are in the story. Find them and circle or underline them each time they occur. Say each marked word aloud—individually and then in its entire sentence. Look for additional words in the story that contain the target sounds. Mark and say them also.

[w] **W**endy, **w**ords, **w**ith, **w**as, **w**ork, **w**in

[v] **v**ery, **v**owed, **v**ision, **v**ain, **v**irtuoso, **v**ital

Other Practice Activities

❏ Partner Cards—Listening. *Practice until you can point to the right card every time.*
❏ Partner Cards—Speaking. *Practice until you can say the contrasting sentences so accurately that your partner points to the right card every time.*
❏ Story Reading. *Practice reading the story aloud. Mark any difficult words. Then record the story on tape.*
❏ Story Dictation. *Write the story as your teacher reads it or as you listen to it on the audiotape.*
❏ Cloze Reading. *Choose some key words in the story and black them out. Then read the entire story aloud. Do this several times.*

Each time black out more words. Continue until most of the story is blacked out and you can tell it without looking at the page very often.
❏ Story Retelling from Skeleton. *Black out all the remaining words except those you need in order to remind you of the story line. Then, using just this skeleton, tell the story to your partner or class.*
❏ Free Story Retelling. *Retell the whole story from memory, without looking at your book.*
❏ Parallel Story. *Create your own story similar to the one in this unit.*
❏ Mini-drama. *Make up a skit or do a role play based on the story.*

Unit C4m-A [w] rowing—[v] roving

Story

When my friends get together for an activity at the lake, you can never tell what they will do next. They are always on the move.

For example, one night I was camping at the lake with a

bunch of my friends. We decided to go for a hike, but we couldn't find Owen and Kevin. When we saw that the rowboat was gone, we thought that they were probably (1) **rowing** around the lake in the dark. So we went on our hike without them.

#1

We had been walking for only about ten minutes when we ran into Owen and Kevin. They hadn't gone rowing after all. They had gone on a hike of their own and had gotten lost in the woods. They had been (2) **roving** around in the dark for over an hour trying to find the camp. They had walked for several miles and were very happy to see us.

#2

Contrasting Sentences

❏ They were _____ around. (in the boat)

❏ They were _____ around. (in the woods)

Additional Practice

That's *worse/verse*. (C4i-A/a), It's in the *west/vest*. (C4i-b), That's a strong *wine/vine* . (C4i-c)

Other Words

[w] O**w**en, al**w**ays, re**w**ard, a**w**aken, t**w**ist, s**w**ing

[v] acti**v**ity, ne**v**er, Ke**v**in, o**v**er, se**v**eral, e**v**aluate

Other Practice Activities

❏ Partner Cards—Listening.
❏ Partner Cards—Speaking.
❏ Story Reading.
❏ Story Dictation.
❏ Cloze Reading.

❏ Story Retelling
  from Skeleton.
❏ Free Story Retelling.
❏ Parallel Story.
❏ Mini-drama.

Unit C5i-A [f] fan—[v] van

Story

Listen to the story as your teacher reads it, or on tape, until you understand the main ideas.

Nancy always loves to go shopping with her friends, but last Friday she was even more excited than usual. She was planning to buy something for her favorite season—summer. The very first thing she found was a (1) **fan.** "I want to buy this fan so I can keep cool and sleep well during hot summer nights," she thought.

At that moment, she looked out the window and saw a nice (2) **van** go by. She thought out loud, "Wow! If I had that van, I wouldn't need the fan. I could drive to the beach or visit the mountains to keep cool. And all my friends could go with me in my van. We could even go to drive-in movies at night. It would be wonderful!"

Then her friend Valerie asked, "Do you have enough money to buy a van? They're very expensive, you know."

"No," said Nancy. "I guess I'll have to go home and ask my parents very nicely." They laughed, and then they went to buy the fan. They had just enough money left over to rent a video.

Contrasting Sentences

Listening: Write the appropriate key word in each blank. Later, as you hear each sentence, mark the box, point to the picture, make a gesture, and/or say the rejoinder. Speaking: Choose and say each sentence so that your listener(s) can respond correctly.

❑ I want to buy the _____. (to sleep well)

❑ I want to buy the _____. (to drive around)

Explanations and diagrams for this unit's target sounds are on pages 336–37 in Section 10.

Additional Practice

My grandfather *shuffles/shovels* slowly. (C5m-A/a), What a fantastic
safe/save! (C5f-A/a)

Other Words

*Many, if not all, of the words listed below are in the story. Find them
and circle or underline them each time they occur. Say each marked
word aloud—individually and then in its entire sentence. Look for
additional words in the story that contain the target sounds. Mark
and say them also.*

[f] **f**riends, **F**riday, **f**avorite, **f**irst, **f**ound, **f**ather

[v] **v**ery, **v**isit, **V**alerie, **v**ideo, **v**oice, **v**iew

Other Practice Activities

❑ Partner Cards—Listening. *Practice until you can point to the right card every time.*
❑ Partner Cards—Speaking. *Practice until you can say the contrasting sentences so accurately that your partner points to the right card every time.*
❑ Story Reading. *Practice reading the story aloud. Mark any difficult words. Then record the story on tape.*
❑ Story Dictation. *Write the story as your teacher reads it or as you listen to it on the audiotape.*
❑ Cloze Reading. *Choose some key words in the story and black them out. Then read the entire story aloud. Do this several times.*

Each time black out more words. Continue until most of the story is blacked out and you can tell it without looking at the page very often.
❑ Story Retelling from Skeleton. *Black out all the remaining words except those you need in order to remind you of the story line. Then, using just this skeleton, tell the story to your partner or class.*
❑ Free Story Retelling. *Retell the whole story from memory, without looking at your book.*
❑ Parallel Story. *Create your own story similar to the one in this unit.*
❑ Mini-drama. *Make up a skit or do a role play based on the story.*

Unit C5m-A [f] shuffle—[v] shovel

Story

My grandfather lives up in the mountains, and it's fun to visit
him—especially in winter. We often go sledding and have a
great time. Of course, he doesn't go sledding with us. He is 82
years old, and his bones are brittle, so he does safer things, like
hiking. He can't walk fast anymore. He barely (1) **shuffles**

#1

#2

along. However, he is still healthy and has a lot of energy and determination. The first thing he does on winter mornings is (2) **shovel** the snow. It often snows a lot during the night, and he has to clear a path from his front door to the road, or else he'll be trapped. He goes slowly, but he refuses any help. It takes him about an hour, and he does it after every snowstorm. I guess it's good for him. He is strong for his age, and he rarely gets sick in winter—not even a case of the sniffles. My grandfather is truly an amazing man. I admire him, but I'm glad I don't have to shovel snow so often.

Contrasting Sentences

❏ My grandfather _____ slowly. (slides his feet)

❏ My grandfather _____ slowly. (clears the snow)

Additional Practice

I want to buy the *fan/van*. (C5i-A/a), What a fantastic *safe/save!* (C5f-A/a)

Other Words

  [f] safer, often, refuses, sniffles, rifle, infest

  [v] lives, seven, however, every, review, invest

Other Practice Activities

❏ Partner Cards—Listening.
❏ Partner Cards—Speaking.
❏ Story Reading.
❏ Story Dictation.
❏ Cloze Reading.

❏ Story Retelling
  from Skeleton.
❏ Free Story Retelling.
❏ Parallel Story.
❏ Mini-drama.

Unit C5f-A [f] safe—[v] save

Story

Last week, Jeff and Dave went walking in the woods. There they found an old, abandoned house. Inside there was a rusty (1) **safe.** Jeff was excited and said, "Fantastic! There must be money or treasure in it! We'll split it half and half."

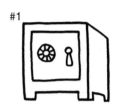

"Do you really believe there's something valuable in there?" asked Dave.

"Why not?" said Jeff. Slowly, he opened the door of the safe, but there was nothing inside—only a dry leaf and four or five stones.

"Oh well, that's life," said Dave.

After that, they went home and turned on the television. There was an exciting soccer match on. Dave said, "Let's watch. I love soccer." The score was tied, and time was running out. One of the forwards attempted a low shot at the goal. The ball would have gone in, but the goalie made an unbelievable stop. He dove and caught the ball before it reached the net. (2) "What a fantastic **save**!" Jeff shouted.

"What a relief!" said Dave. He had been cheering for the goalie's team.

Contrasting Sentences

❑ What a fantastic _____! (in the old house)

❑ What a fantastic _____! (by the goalie)

Additional Practice

I want to buy the *fan/van.* (C5i-A/a), My grandfather *shuffles/shovels* slowly. (C5m-A/a)

Other Words

[f] Je**ff**, hal**f**, lea**f**, li**f**e, enou**gh**, relie**f**

[v] Da**v**e, belie**v**e, fi**v**e, lo**v**e, ha**v**e, do**v**e

Other Practice Activities

- ❏ Partner Cards—Listening.
- ❏ Partner Cards—Speaking.
- ❏ Story Reading.
- ❏ Story Dictation.
- ❏ Cloze Reading.
- ❏ Story Retelling from Skeleton.
- ❏ Free Story Retelling.
- ❏ Parallel Story.
- ❏ Mini-drama.

Unit C6i-A [f] fought—[θ] thought

Story

Listen to the story as your teacher reads it, or on tape, until you understand the main ideas.

Mr. and Mrs. Adams don't always get along. Last week, for example, they had a disagreement about how they would spend their vacation. Mrs. Adams loves hiking, so she wanted to go to the mountains. Mr. Adams just wanted to relax, so he insisted on going to the beach. Soon, their talk turned into an argument. They said things they shouldn't have said. Then the argument became a full-scale fight, and they started shouting. (1) They **fought** this way for quite a while—at least twenty or thirty minutes.

After that, they went through a long, silent period. It lasted two or three hours. They wouldn't talk, but Mr. Adams kept thinking of how he was right and his wife was wrong. On the other hand, Mrs. Adams (2) **thought** of how right she was and how wrong Mr. Adams was. Finally, each cooled down and started thinking of the other person's point of view. When they thought about it carefully, they realized that there was no reason for them to fight so much. They thought of several possible solutions. Can you think of some too?

Contrasting Sentences

Listening: Write the appropriate key word in each blank. Later, as you hear each sentence, mark the box, point to the picture, make a gesture, and/or say the rejoinder. Speaking: Choose and say each sentence so that your listener(s) can respond correctly.

❏ They _____ about it. (and came up with solutions)

❏ They _____ about it. (and started to shout)

Explanations and diagrams for this unit's target sounds are on pages 336 and 337–38 in Section 10.

Additional Practice

Mr. Murphy was *roofless/ruthless.* (C6m-A/a), The *reef/wreath* was beautiful. (C6f-A/a)

Other Words

Many, if not all, of the words listed below are in the story. Find them and circle or underline them each time they occur. Say each marked word aloud—individually and then in its entire sentence. Look for additional words in the story that contain the target sounds. Mark and say them also.

[f] **for, full, finally, fight, first, free**

[θ] **think, things, thirty, three, threaten, thrill**

Other Practice Activities

❑ Partner Cards—Listening. *Practice until you can point to the right card every time.*
❑ Partner Cards—Speaking. *Practice until you can say the contrasting sentences so accurately that your partner points to the right card every time.*
❑ Story Reading. *Practice reading the story aloud. Mark any difficult words. Then record the story on tape.*
❑ Story Dictation. *Write the story as your teacher reads it or as you listen to it on the audiotape.*
❑ Cloze Reading. *Choose some key words in the story and black them out. Then read the entire story aloud. Do this several times.*

Each time black out more words. Continue until most of the story is blacked out and you can tell it without looking at the page very often.

❑ Story Retelling from Skeleton. *Black out all the remaining words except those you need in order to remind you of the story line. Then, using just this skeleton, tell the story to your partner or class.*
❑ Free Story Retelling. *Retell the whole story from memory, without looking at your book.*
❑ Parallel Story. *Create your own story similar to the one in this unit.*
❑ Mini-drama. *Make up a skit or do a role play based on the story.*

Unit C6m-A [f] roofless—[θ] ruthless

Story

Mr. Murphy was rich, but he was not happy. Although he owned a big, fancy house on top of the highest hill in town, people did not admire him. In fact, they hated him because he got all his money by taking advantage of people. When it came to business, he was (1) **ruthless.** He was cruel and without pity. If someone

owed him money, whether it was a thousand dollars or just ten, he would get it from them no matter how much it made them suffer.

Then one day the tables were turned. A storm with very strong winds passed through town. It blew down many trees. It even (2) blew the roof off of Mr. Murphy's big house on the hill and ruined it. All he could do was sit and look at his **roofless** house. Many people thought he got what he deserved. "Let him suffer now," they said.

Others disagreed. "He was powerful and ruthless before, but now he is roofless," they said. "Let's help him." What do you think they should have done?

Contrasting Sentences

❑ Mr. Murphy was _____. (without a roof)

❑ Mr. Murphy was _____. (without mercy)

Additional Practice

They *fought/thought* about it. (C6i-A/a), The *reef/wreath* was beautiful. (C6f-A/a)

Other Words

[f] Mur**ph**y, su**ff**er, lau**gh**ing, **f**rom, o**ff**, re**f**reshing

[θ] wi**th**out, **th**ousand, **th**ought, dea**th**ly, **th**ink, my**th**ical

Other Practice Activities

❑ Partner Cards—Listening.
❑ Partner Cards—Speaking.
❑ Story Reading.
❑ Story Dictation.
❑ Cloze Reading.

❑ Story Retelling from Skeleton.
❑ Free Story Retelling.
❑ Parallel Story.
❑ Mini-drama.

Unit C6f-A [f] reef—[θ] wreath

Story

Elizabeth was on her way to Hawaii, and she could hardly wait to get there. She wanted to see all the sights of "paradise." As her plane descended through the clouds, she held her breath. Then she saw the tops of lush green mountains beneath her. After that, she saw the deep blue-green ocean and white beaches surrounding the island. Farther out in the ocean, the waves were breaking on the coral (1) **reef.** It was beautiful! But even more beautiful was the (2) **wreath** of tropical flowers that was placed around her neck as she got off the plane. In Hawaiian, this wreath is called a lei. What a beautiful beginning to her vacation! She couldn't help but laugh out loud with joy. She knew that she was going to enjoy this tropical paradise.

Contrasting Sentences

❑ The _____ was beautiful. (around her neck)

❑ The _____ was beautiful. (in the ocean)

Additional Practice

They *fought/thought* about it. (C6i-A/a), Mr. Murphy was *roofless/ruthless.* (C6m-A/a)

Other Words

[f] o**ff**, lau**gh**, lea**f**, hal**f**, sta**ff**, rou**gh**

[θ] Elizabe**th**, brea**th**, benea**th**, wi**th**, warm**th**, ten**th**

Other Practice Activities

❑ Partner Cards—Listening.
❑ Partner Cards—Speaking.
❑ Story Reading.
❑ Story Dictation.
❑ Cloze Reading.

❑ Story Retelling
   from Skeleton.
❑ Free Story Retelling.
❑ Parallel Story.
❑ Mini-drama.

Unit C7i-A [θ] thigh—[ð] thy

Story

Listen to the story as your teacher reads it, or on tape, until you understand the main ideas.

Every year the fifth grade has a spelling bee. Last year, Sally wanted to be the champion. She studied the words on the spelling bee list every day after school. Some of the words were hard to spell, but after two weeks of practice there were just three that Sally still had trouble spelling—*thermometer, withhold,* and *complementary.* After a little more practice, she could spell even those three perfectly. Then she continued to practice until she could spell all the words automatically, without even thinking about them. She was certain that she was going to win the spelling bee.

Unfortunately, on the day of the spelling bee, Sally was eliminated in the third round. She was so overconfident that she didn't pay close attention and mixed up the spelling of the words (1) **thigh** and (2) **thy.** She was sad, but all she said was, "Wait until next year. The sixth grade has a spelling bee too."

Contrasting Sentences

Listening: Write the appropriate key word in each blank. Later, as you hear each sentence, mark the box, point to the picture, make a gesture, and/or say the rejoinder. Speaking: Choose and say each sentence so that your listener(s) can respond correctly.

❏ Sally didn't spell _____ correctly. (T-H-I-G-H)

❏ Sally didn't spell _____ correctly. (T-H-Y)

Explanations and diagrams for this unit's target sounds are on pages 337–39 in Section 10.

Additional Practice

She didn't want *ether/either.* (C7m-A/a), He needs *two teeth / to teethe* before he can eat corn. (C7f-A/a)

Other Words

Many, if not all, of the words listed below are in the story. Find them and circle or underline them each time they occur. Say each marked word aloud—individually and then in its entire sentence. Look for additional words in the story that contain the target sounds. Mark and say them also.

[θ] **th**ree, **th**ermometer, wi**thh**old, wi**th**out, **th**inking, **th**ird

[ð] **th**e, **th**ere, **th**at, **th**en, **th**ose, **th**is

Other Practice Activities

❏ Partner Cards—Listening. *Practice until you can point to the right card every time.*

❏ Partner Cards—Speaking. *Practice until you can say the contrasting sentences so accurately that your partner points to the right card every time.*

❏ Story Reading. *Practice reading the story aloud. Mark any difficult words. Then record the story on tape.*

❏ Story Dictation. *Write the story as your teacher reads it or as you listen to it on the audiotape.*

❏ Cloze Reading. *Choose some key words in the story and black them out. Then read the entire story aloud. Do this several times.*

Each time black out more words. Continue until most of the story is blacked out and you can tell it without looking at the page very often.

❏ Story Retelling from Skeleton. *Black out all the remaining words except those you need in order to remind you of the story line. Then, using just this skeleton, tell the story to your partner or class.*

❏ Free Story Retelling. *Retell the whole story from memory, without looking at your book.*

❏ Parallel Story. *Create your own story similar to the one in this unit.*

❏ Mini-drama. *Make up a skit or do a role play based on the story.*

Unit C7m-A [θ] ether—[ð] either

Story

Surgery is very painful, so when patients have an operation they are usually given anesthetic medication to help with the pain. When my friend Kathy went into the hospital for a major operation she needed general anesthesia, and the doctor gave her two choices. She could have an injection or (1) **ether.** Kathy said that she didn't want ether. Breathing through the mask over her mouth and nose was scary for her.

#1

Nevertheless, when the anesthesiologist came with the needle, Kathy decided she didn't want an injection either. She said that she didn't like (2) **either** choice. She then asked if there were any other options. There weren't, unless she wanted no anesthetic at all. That option didn't sound very attractive to Kathy, so she decided she would choose ether even though she didn't really want it.

#2

Thankfully, that was the last decision she had to make that day. The doctors took over from there, and when Kathy woke up she learned that her operation had been a success.

Contrasting Sentences

❏ She didn't want _____. (gas)

❏ She didn't want _____. (neither one)

Additional Practice

Sally didn't spell *thigh* / *thy* correctly. (C7i-A/a), He needs *two teeth* / *to teethe* before he can eat corn. (C7f-A/a)

Other Words

[θ] anes**th**etic, Ka**th**y, anes**th**esia, anes**th**esiologist, fai**th**ful, mou**th**y

[ð] brea**th**ing, never**th**eless, whe**th**er, wea**th**er, ba**th**ing, soo**th**ing

Other Practice Activities

❏ Partner Cards—Listening.
❏ Partner Cards—Speaking.
❏ Story Reading.
❏ Story Dictation.
❏ Cloze Reading.

❏ Story Retelling from Skeleton.
❏ Free Story Retelling.
❏ Parallel Story.
❏ Mini-drama.

Unit C7f-A [θ] teeth—[ð] teethe

Story

My young cousin, Tim, who is seven years old, is very unhappy. He loves eating fresh, sweet corn on the cob in the summer. Somehow it tastes better that way. In fact, Tim thinks it's the best tasting food on earth. But this summer, because he has lost his (1) two front **teeth,** he can't bite the corn off the cob. Instead, he has to cut it off with a knife and then eat it with a fork. That's no fun, and the corn just doesn't taste the same. In a month or so, his two permanent teeth will appear, but by then summer will be over and there will be no more fresh corn on the cob until next year.

Tim's younger brother can't eat corn on the cob either, but it's because he doesn't have any teeth at all yet. He's only two months old, and his gums are still as smooth as they can be. He needs to (2) **teethe** before he can eat corn or any food that needs to be chewed.

Contrasting Sentences

❑ He needs two _____ before he can eat corn. (He's seven years old.)

❑ He needs to _____ before he can eat corn. (He's a baby.)

Additional Practice

Sally didn't spell *thigh/thy* correctly. (C7i-A/a), She didn't want *ether/either.* (C7m-A/a)

Other Words

[θ] ear**th**, wi**th**, mon**th**, nor**th**, brea**th**, ba**th**

[ð] smoo**th**, brea**the**, ba**the**, bro**ther**, ei**ther**, **the**

Other Practice Activities

- ❏ Partner Cards—Listening.
- ❏ Partner Cards—Speaking.
- ❏ Story Reading.
- ❏ Story Dictation.
- ❏ Cloze Reading.
- ❏ Story Retelling from Skeleton.
- ❏ Free Story Retelling.
- ❏ Parallel Story.
- ❏ Mini-drama.

Unit C8i-A [θ] thought—[t] taught

Story

Listen to the story as your teacher reads it, or on tape, until you understand the main ideas.

Teresa is teaching at an elementary school. Today she (1) **taught** the children about Abraham Lincoln. She showed them pictures of the tall, thin president with his famous beard and stovepipe hat. She also read some stories about him. Some were inspiring, like how he grew up on the frontier and had to work and study for many years to achieve his goals. Others were sad, like how he was shot from behind as he sat in a theater. The stories really made the children think.

Later, at home, Teresa (2) **thought** about President Lincoln some more. She felt thankful that the United States had had such a strong president to lead the country through the difficult years of the Civil War. Without his leadership, things might have turned out very different. She also wondered how anyone could shoot such a good man. For her, it was a mystery as well as a tragedy.

Contrasting Sentences

Listening: Write the appropriate key word in each blank. Later, as you hear each sentence, mark the box, point to the picture, make a gesture, and/or say the rejoinder. Speaking: Choose and say each sentence so that your listener(s) can respond correctly.

❑ Teresa _____ about Abraham Lincoln. (in school)

❑ Teresa _____ about Abraham Lincoln. (at home)

Explanations and diagrams for this unit's target sounds are on pages 337–38 and 339 Section 10.

Additional Practice

Please don't touch my *thigh/tie.* (C8i-B/b), They had been *rethreaded/retreaded.* (C8m-A/a), It was just an old *myth/mitt.* (C8f-A/a)

Other Words

Many, if not all, of the words listed below are in the story. Find them and circle or underline them each time they occur. Say each marked word aloud—individually and then in its entire sentence. Look for additional words in the story that contain the target sounds. Mark and say them also.

[θ] **th**in, **th**ink, **th**ankful, **th**rough, **th**ings, **th**eater

[t] **T**eresa, **t**eaching, **t**oday, **t**all, **t**urned, **t**ragedy

Other Practice Activities

❑ Partner Cards—Listening. *Practice until you can point to the right card every time.*

❑ Partner Cards—Speaking. *Practice until you can say the contrasting sentences so accurately that your partner points to the right card every time.*

❑ Story Reading. *Practice reading the story aloud. Mark any difficult words. Then record the story on tape.*

❑ Story Dictation. *Write the story as your teacher reads it or as you listen to it on the audiotape.*

❑ Cloze Reading. *Choose some key words in the story and black them out. Then read the entire story aloud. Do this several times.*

Each time black out more words. Continue until most of the story is blacked out and you can tell it without looking at the page very often.

❑ Story Retelling from Skeleton. *Black out all the remaining words except those you need in order to remind you of the story line. Then, using just this skeleton, tell the story to your partner or class.*

❑ Free Story Retelling. *Retell the whole story from memory, without looking at your book.*

❑ Parallel Story. *Create your own story similar to the one in this unit.*

❑ Mini-drama. *Make up a skit or do a role play based on the story.*

Unit C8i-B [θ] thigh—[t] tie

Story

Tom loves expensive clothes and often wears a fancy suit and nice tie. His friends sometimes admire his clothing. Tom likes the attention, but he warns them, "Look all you want, but don't touch my clothes, especially my (1) **tie.** It's from Italy and very expensive."

#1

Today Tom was walking with a limp. His friends asked him, "What's wrong? Did you hurt your leg?" One of them joked, "Do you want me to rub it for you?"

Tom backed away quickly and pleaded, "No! Please don't

touch my (2) **thigh**!" Then, he explained, "Yesterday, when I was playing basketball, I hurt it. I must have pulled a muscle. Today it's even more painful."

#2

One of the friends then asked, "Well, then can we touch your tie?" Everyone except Tom laughed. He was in pain and didn't think anything was funny.

Contrasting Sentences

❑ Please don't touch my _____. (It's expensive.)

❑ Please don't touch my _____. (It hurts.)

Additional Practice

Teresa *thought / taught* about Abraham Lincoln. (C8i-A/a), They had been *rethreaded / retreaded*. (C8m-A/a), It was just an old *myth / mitt*. (C8f-A/a)

Other Words

[θ] **th**ink, **th**ank, **th**irsty, **th**ousand, **th**ick, **th**eme

[t] **t**o, **t**ouch, **t**oday, **t**ank, **t**eam, **t**ick

Other Practice Activities

❑ Partner Cards—Listening.
❑ Partner Cards—Speaking.
❑ Story Reading.
❑ Story Dictation.
❑ Cloze Reading.

❑ Story Retelling from Skeleton.
❑ Free Story Retelling.
❑ Parallel Story.
❑ Mini-drama.

Unit C8m-A [θ] rethreaded—[t] retreaded

Story

Terry works in a shop. She loves operating machines and making things, but she also loves nature and the outdoors. In fact, she is quite concerned about the environment. She dreams of a world without pollution and waste, so she is interested in reusing and recycling things instead of just throwing them away.

For example, when the tires on her car got old, she didn't buy brand new tires. Instead, she got (1) tires that had been **retreaded.** In other words they were used tires with new treads on them. She was proud that they ended up on her car instead of in some landfill.

Here's another example. The other day Terry was working on some metal equipment in her shop. A couple of parts would not hold together properly. The problem was that the threads in some holes were damaged and the bolts in them kept slipping out. Instead of just throwing the parts away and getting new ones, Terry got out some special tools and (2) **rethreaded** the holes. Then the bolts didn't slip anymore. Doing that took only a few minutes, and it made Terry feel happy. Instead of throwing something away unnecessarily, she had done one more small thing to help the environment.

Contrasting Sentences

❑ They had been _____. (the tires)

❑ They had been _____. (the holes)

Additional Practice

Teresa *thought / taught* about Abraham Lincoln. (C8i-A/a), Please don't touch my *thigh / tie.* (C8i-B/b), It was just an old *myth / mitt.* (C8f-A/a)

Other Words

[θ] wi**th**out, some**th**ing, **th**rowing, too**th**less, fai**th**ful

[t] opera**t**ing, ou**t**doors, ha**t**es, in**t**erested, ins**t**ead, me**t**al

Other Practice Activities

- ❏ Partner Cards—Listening.
- ❏ Partner Cards—Speaking.
- ❏ Story Reading.
- ❏ Story Dictation.
- ❏ Cloze Reading.

- ❏ Story Retelling from Skeleton.
- ❏ Free Story Retelling.
- ❏ Parallel Story.
- ❏ Mini-drama.

Unit C8f-A [θ] myth—[t] mitt

Story

My neighbor Keith is an enthusiastic fan of everything connected with baseball. He watches every baseball game that he can. He also has a huge collection of baseball cards and over a dozen baseballs autographed by major league stars. Some of them are very valuable.

Keith often goes to big baseball conventions and sales so that he can add to his collection. Once he paid three thousand dollars for a (1) **mitt** because he thought it had previously belonged to Hank Aaron. The seller told Keith an incredible story about how he got the mitt. He explained that he and Hank were fourth cousins and played baseball together when they were kids, and Keith believed him.

Unfortunately, the story turned out to be a (2) **myth.** Keith was angry to learn the truth—that he had spent three thousand dollars for an ordinary old baseball mitt that was really worth only about three dollars. It was an expensive lesson, but now Keith is much more careful about what he believes. He takes nothing on faith and double-checks everything before he pays a cent.

Contrasting Sentences

❏ It was just an old _____. (baseball glove)

❏ It was just an old _____. (made-up story)

Additional Practice

Teresa *thought/taught* about Abraham Lincoln. (C8i-A/a), Please don't touch my *thigh/tie*. (C8i-B/b), They had been *rethreaded/retreaded*. (C8m-A/a)

Other Words

[θ] Kei**th**, wi**th**, four**th**, tru**th**, wor**th**, fai**th**

[t] tha**t**, though**t**, i**t**, go**t**, for**t**, fa**t**e

Other Practice Activities

❏ Partner Cards—Listening.
❏ Partner Cards—Speaking.
❏ Story Reading.
❏ Story Dictation.
❏ Cloze Reading.

❏ Story Retelling from Skeleton.
❏ Free Story Retelling.
❏ Parallel Story.
❏ Mini-drama.

Unit C9i-A [θ] think—[s] sink

Story

Listen to the story as your teacher reads it, or on tape, until you understand the main ideas.

Paul and Matthew were walking along the lake when they found  something exciting. It was (1) an old canoe. They pushed it into the water, got into it, and started to paddle toward the middle of the lake. They thought it was fun, but after they had gone a short distance they noticed a lot of water leaking into the canoe. There were big cracks in the bottom. Paul screamed, "Oh no! I  can't swim! I don't want to (2) **sink.** I might die!"

Matthew laughed and said, "Relax. You don't need to worry about a thing. This lake is not deep at all. You can stand on the bottom." Then Paul was embarrassed. All he had to do was walk to the shore.

On the way back home, Matthew joked, "Aren't you going to  thank me for saving you?"

But Paul was still embarrassed. He just said, "I don't want to (3) **think** about it again."

Contrasting Sentences

Listening: Write the appropriate key word in each blank. Later, as you hear each sentence, mark the box, point to the picture, make a gesture, and/or say the rejoinder. Speaking: Choose and say each sentence so that your listener(s) can respond correctly.

❏ Paul didn't want to _____. (in the lake)

❏ Paul didn't want to _____. (about what happened)

Explanations and diagrams for this unit's target sounds are on pages 337–38 and 342 in Section 10.

Additional Practice

That's a good *thimble/symbol*. (C9i-b), One sister is very *mouthy/mousy*. (C9m-A/a), Ken tried not to lose *faith/face*. (C9f-

A/a), That's a big *mouth/mouse.* (C9f-b), Look at that beautiful *moth/moss.* (C9f-c)

Other Words

Many, if not all, of the words listed below are in the story. Find them and circle or underline them each time they occur. Say each marked word aloud—individually and then in its entire sentence. Look for additional words in the story that contain the target sounds. Mark and say them also.

[θ] **th**ought, **th**ing, **th**ank, **th**in, **th**ick, **th**umb

[s] **s**omething, **s**tarted, **s**wim, **s**aid, **s**till, **s**ick

Other Practice Activities

❑ Partner Cards—Listening. *Practice until you can point to the right card every time.*
❑ Partner Cards—Speaking. *Practice until you can say the contrasting sentences so accurately that your partner points to the right card every time.*
❑ Story Reading. *Practice reading the story aloud. Mark any difficult words. Then record the story on tape.*
❑ Story Dictation. *Write the story as your teacher reads it or as you listen to it on the audiotape.*
❑ Cloze Reading. *Choose some key words in the story and black them out. Then read the entire story aloud. Do this several times.*

Each time black out more words. Continue until most of the story is blacked out and you can tell it without looking at the page very often.
❑ Story Retelling from Skeleton. *Black out all the remaining words except those you need in order to remind you of the story line. Then, using just this skeleton, tell the story to your partner or class.*
❑ Free Story Retelling. *Retell the whole story from memory, without looking at your book.*
❑ Parallel Story. *Create your own story similar to the one in this unit.*
❑ Mini-drama. *Make up a skit or do a role play based on the story.*

Unit C9m-A [θ] mouthy—[s] mousy

Story

I have two friends who are sisters. They have the same father and the same mother, but they have very different personalities.

One of them is named Suzanne. She (1) never stops talking, and sometimes she's even rude. Lots of people say she is really **mouthy.** In fact, her mouthiness sometimes offends people and gets her in trouble.

#1

#2

On the other hand, Ruth Ann, her sister, (2) is too shy to say even one word. She is timid and **mousy.** In a crowd, she would rather remain faceless than stand out.

Sometimes I find it impossible to believe that Suzanne and Ruth Ann are even related even though I know they are sisters. It is something many people have trouble understanding.

Contrasting Sentences

❏ One sister is very _____. (talkative and rude)

❏ One sister is very _____. (quiet and shy)

Additional Practice

Paul didn't want to *think / sink*. (C9i-A/a), That's a good *thimble / symbol*. (C9i-b), Ken tried not to lose *faith / face*. (C9f-A/a), That's a big *mouth / mouse*. (C9f-b), Look at that beautiful *moth / moss*. (C9f-c)

Other Words

[θ] mou**th**iness, some**th**ing, un**th**inkable, un**th**ankful, re**th**ink, fai**th**less

[s] **s**i**s**ter**s**, per**s**onalitie**s**, facele**ss**, impo**ss**ible, un**s**inkable

Other Practice Activities

❏ Partner Cards—Listening.
❏ Partner Cards—Speaking.
❏ Story Reading.
❏ Story Dictation.
❏ Cloze Reading.

❏ Story Retelling
   from Skeleton.
❏ Free Story Retelling.
❏ Parallel Story.
❏ Mini-drama.

Unit C9f-A [θ] faith—[s] face

Story

Ken was not born in the United States, but he believed in the American dream. He had confidence that if he worked hard he would succeed. When he first came to the States, he had no money and no job. He didn't speak very much English either. He survived by doing work that no one else would do. It was hard, and sometimes he felt like giving up, but he tried not to (1) lose **faith.**

In the evenings, he took ESL classes to improve his English language skills. That wasn't easy either. Sometimes he thought his English was getting worse instead of better. The biggest problem was that he would not take risks when he spoke because he was worried about making mistakes. He didn't want to (2) lose **face.** He was afraid people would laugh at him.

Then one day Ken realized that making mistakes was essential to learning. Mistakes were part of the path to success. After that, he wasn't afraid to open his mouth and speak up. His English skills improved steadily, and soon he was able to get a better job. Now he owns his own business, which is worth half a million dollars, and he is making big plans for the future.

Contrasting Sentences

❏ Ken tried not to lose _____. (give up)

❏ Ken tried not to lose _____. (be embarrassed)

Additional Practice

Paul didn't want to *think / sink.* (C9i-A/a), That's a good *thimble / symbol.* (C9i-b), One sister is very *mouthy / mousy.* (C9m-A/a), That's a big *mouth / mouse.* (C9f-b), Look at that beautiful *moth / moss.* (C9f-c)

Other Words

[θ] pa**th**, mou**th**, wor**th**, ba**th**, ma**th**, four**th**

[s] State**s**, confiden**c**e, wor**s**e, risk**s**, mistake**s**, busine**ss**

Other Practice Activities

- ❏ Partner Cards—Listening.
- ❏ Partner Cards—Speaking.
- ❏ Story Reading.
- ❏ Story Dictation.
- ❏ Cloze Reading.
- ❏ Story Retelling from Skeleton.
- ❏ Free Story Retelling.
- ❏ Parallel Story.
- ❏ Mini-drama.

Unit C10i-A [ð] they—[d] day

Story

Listen to the story as your teacher reads it, or on tape, until you understand the main ideas.

Once I went on a camping trip with my friend Dave. He was an experienced outdoorsman, but I was not. I worried about a lot of things, but he reassured me that there was no reason to be concerned. For example, we were supposed to meet some friends at a lake in the mountains, and we got there before they did. I started to imagine all kinds of things that might have happened to them along the trail, but Dave said, "Don't worry. (1) **They** will come soon." And they did.

We camped overnight at the lake, and when the sun went down everything was very dark. I went to sleep, but I woke up in the night and stayed awake. The night seemed very long, and when I noticed Dave was awake, too, I commented on how long the night seemed. He said, "Don't worry. (2) **Day** will come soon." And it did. Soon the sun rose over the mountains in the east, and another enjoyable day in the mountains began.

Contrasting Sentences

Listening: Write the appropriate key word in each blank. Later, as you hear each sentence, mark the box, point to the picture, make a gesture, and / or say the rejoinder. Speaking: Choose and say each sentence so that your listener(s) can respond correctly.

❏ Don't worry, _____ will come soon. (our friends)

❏ Don't worry, _____ will come soon. (morning)

Explanations and diagrams for this unit's target sounds are on pages 338–40 in Section 10.

Additional Practice

It is forbidden to *those/doze* in class. (C10i-B/b), It was *Mother's/Mudder's* Day. (C10m-A/a), They really love their *father/fodder.* (C10m-B/b), They really *loathe/load* their old washer. (C10f-A/a), Rabbits *breathe/breed* quickly. (C10f-b)

Other Words

Many, if not all, of the words listed below are in the story. Find them and circle or underline them each time they occur. Say each marked word aloud—individually and then in its entire sentence. Look for additional words in the story that contain the target sounds. Mark and say them also.

[ð] **th**at, **th**ere, **th**e, **th**em, **th**en, **th**ose

[d] **D**ave, **d**id, **d**on't, **d**ark, **d**en, **d**are

Other Practice Activities

❏ Partner Cards—Listening. *Practice until you can point to the right card every time.*
❏ Partner Cards—Speaking. *Practice until you can say the contrasting sentences so accurately that your partner points to the right card every time.*
❏ Story Reading. *Practice reading the story aloud. Mark any difficult words. Then record the story on tape.*
❏ Story Dictation. *Write the story as your teacher reads it or as you listen to it on the audiotape.*
❏ Cloze Reading. *Choose some key words in the story and black them out. Then read the entire story aloud. Do this several times.*

Each time black out more words. Continue until most of the story is blacked out and you can tell it without looking at the page very often.
❏ Story Retelling from Skeleton. *Black out all the remaining words except those you need in order to remind you of the story line. Then, using just this skeleton, tell the story to your partner or class.*
❏ Free Story Retelling. *Retell the whole story from memory, without looking at your book.*
❏ Parallel Story. *Create your own story similar to the one in this unit.*
❏ Mini-drama. *Make up a skit or do a role play based on the story.*

Unit C10i-B [ð] those—[d] doze

Story

Juan is from Mexico, but he is studying in an intensive English program in the United States. He goes to class several hours every day and loves it. Juan has a small problem, though. He stays up late every night watching TV. Then, when he goes to school the next day he (1) dozes in class. The teachers are nice, but they don't want their students to sleep when they should be

#1

learning. Therefore, they have a rule about sleeping in class. The rule states that it is forbidden to **doze** while class is in session.

Juan's class has another rule. All the students really want to practice English as much as possible, and they want to make friends with their classmates from other countries, so they have agreed to speak only English when class is in session. Therefore, the second rule states that it is forbidden to **those** in class to speak their native languages (2). Everybody must communicate in English. The students like this rule even though it's sometimes hard for them to obey it.

Contrasting Sentences

❏ It is forbidden to _____ in class. (Students must stay awake.)

❏ It is forbidden to _____ in class. (to speak their native languages)

Additional Practice

Don't worry, *they/day* will come soon. (C10i-A/a), It was *Mother's/Mudder's* Day. (C10m-A/a), They really love their *father/fodder*. (C10m-B/b), They really *loathe/load* their old washer. (C10f-A/a), Rabbits *breathe/breed* quickly. (C10f-b)

Other Words

[ð] **th**e, **th**ough, **th**en, **th**eir, **th**ey, **th**erefore

[d] **d**ay, **d**on't, **d**en, **d**are, **d**iscipline, **d**og

Other Practice Activities

❏ Partner Cards—Listening.
❏ Partner Cards—Speaking.
❏ Story Reading.
❏ Story Dictation.
❏ Cloze Reading.
❏ Story Retelling from Skeleton.
❏ Free Story Retelling.
❏ Parallel Story.
❏ Mini-drama.

Unit C10m-A [ð] mother—[d] mudder

Story

The Kentucky Derby may be the most famous of all horse races. It has been run for over 120 years, and every spring well over a hundred thousand fans go to Churchill Downs to watch it. Saturday, May 7, 1994, was an unforgettable day in Derby history. It had been raining hard, and for the first time in 46 years the track was muddy. The sloppy, rain-soaked track made it difficult for many of the horses to run. Holy Bull, the horse favored to win, didn't even come close to first place. Instead, another horse, Go for Gin, was the surprise winner. Go for Gin was a (1) mudder, a horse that ran well in the mud. The next day, the headline on the sports page in the newspaper read, "It was **Mudder's** Day at Churchill Downs."

As I read the newspaper story about Go for Gin's victory in the Kentucky Derby, I noticed something else. Sunday, May 8, 1994, was **Mother's** Day, and there were all kinds of advertisements for (2) gifts for mothers. As I looked at them, I realized that I didn't have a gift for my mother. I hadn't even bought her a card. I dropped the newspaper and hurried to get something for her before it was too late.

Contrasting Sentences

❏ It was _____ Day. (And Go for Gin won.)

❏ It was _____ Day. (And I had forgotten to get a gift.)

Additional Practice

Don't worry, *they/day* will come soon. (C10i-A/a), It is forbidden to *those/doze* in class. (C10i-B/b), They really love their *father/fodder*. (C10m-B/b), They really *loathe/load* their old washer. (C10f-A/a), Rabbits *breathe/breed* quickly. (C10f-b)

Other Words

[ð] ano**th**er, toge**th**er, o**th**er, ei**th**er, brea**th**ing, la**th**er

[d] hun**d**red, Satur**d**ay, mu**dd**y, di**d**n't, hea**d**line, ri**d**ing

Other Practice Activities

❏ Partner Cards—Listening.
❏ Partner Cards—Speaking.
❏ Story Reading.
❏ Story Dictation.
❏ Cloze Reading.

❏ Story Retelling
　from Skeleton.
❏ Free Story Retelling.
❏ Parallel Story.
❏ Mini-drama.

Unit C10m-B [ð] father—[d] fodder

Story

My neighbor Roy raises horses. He has four, and he takes very good care of them. He keeps their stalls clean and brushes them regularly. He also makes certain they have plenty of clean water to drink and fresh (1) **fodder** to eat. He has his own special fodder mixture that is both healthy and tasty for his horses. They love their fodder. They eat it with enthusiasm.

Of course, Roy doesn't do all this work alone. He has two teenage children, and they help him. Caring for the horses teaches Roy's kids to work together and help each other. In addition, it also teaches them another virtue—responsibility. The horses need to be cared for every day, no matter what, and if Roy and his children don't do it no one does. But the horses aren't all work. Roy's whole family goes horseback riding in the mountains nearly every week. It's great fun, and the kids really like that. They also really love their (2) **father.** He teaches them good things, and they have fun in the process.

Contrasting Sentences

❏ They really love their _____. (They're horses.)

❏ They really love their _____. (They're children.)

Additional Practice

Don't worry, *they/day* will come soon. (C10i-A/a), It is forbidden to *those/doze* in class. (C10i-B/b), It was *Mother's/Mudder's* Day. (C10m-A/a), They really *loathe/load* their old washer. (C10f-A/a), Rabbits *breathe/breed* quickly. (C10f-b)

Other Words

[ð] toge**th**er, o**th**er, ano**th**er, ei**th**er, brea**th**ing, wor**th**y

[d] a**dd**ition, ri**d**ing, u**dd**er, la**dd**er, bree**d**ing, wor**d**y

Other Practice Activities

❏ Partner Cards—Listening.
❏ Partner Cards—Speaking.
❏ Story Reading.
❏ Story Dictation.
❏ Cloze Reading.

❏ Story Retelling
   from Skeleton.
❏ Free Story Retelling.
❏ Parallel Story.
❏ Mini-drama.

Unit C10f-A [ð] loathe—[d] load

Story

The members of the Kent family are all very busy. Sandra, the mother, writes computer programs; Samuel, the father, teaches; and the kids all go to school. Because they have little time during the week to clean their home, the Kents spend most of the day Saturday doing laundry, washing dishes, vacuuming the floors, and cleaning their rooms. They barely have time to bathe. Sometimes they feel as if they don't even have time to breathe.

One thing that all the kids hate to do is the wash. The Kent's (1) washing machine is very old. The door is hard to open, the controls don't always work, and sometimes it won't even

#1

turn on. Then, when it is running, the washer rattles and makes other scary noises. The kids really (2) **loathe** their old washer and refuse to go near it.

Sandra and Samuel are usually left with all the laundry to do at the end of the day. Then, because there is so much laundry, they (3) **load** the washer as full as it will go. The clothes never get really clean, and the children complain. But when Samuel tells them to do their own laundry, they stop complaining and hurry away.

Contrasting Sentences

❏ They really _____ their old washer. (hate)

❏ They really _____ their old washer. (put in a lot of clothes)

Additional Practice

Don't worry, *they/day* will come soon. (C10i-A/a), It is forbidden to *those/doze* in class. (C10i-B/b), It was *Mother's/Mudder's* Day. (C10m-A/a), They really love their *father/fodder*. (C10m-B/b), Rabbits *breathe/breed* quickly. (C10f-b)

Other Words

[ð] ba**th**e, brea**th**e, soo**th**e, clo**th**e, **th**ere, fa**th**er

[d] an**d**, spen**d**, ol**d**, har**d**, ki**d**, en**d**

Other Practice Activities

❏ Partner Cards—Listening.
❏ Partner Cards—Speaking.
❏ Story Reading.
❏ Story Dictation.
❏ Cloze Reading.
❏ Story Retelling from Skeleton.
❏ Free Story Retelling.
❏ Parallel Story.
❏ Mini-drama.

Unit C11i-A [ð] then—[z] Zen

Story

Listen to the story as your teacher reads it, or on tape, until you understand the main ideas.

My uncle has had a lot of interesting hobbies. The first one that I became aware of was stamp collecting. He had stamps from all over the world. They were all interesting, but he was especially proud of the many beautiful Japanese stamps in his collection.

My uncle didn't stick with that hobby, however. He switched to collecting coins. That hobby was good in the winter because he could do it indoors when it was cold outside. But when spring and warm weather arrived, he wanted to be outdoors.

Then (1) gardening became his new hobby. He enjoyed working with plants, but by the end of the summer he got involved in a type of gardening that uses mostly rocks and gravel. They are arranged and raked into artistic patterns. He first learned about this kind of gardening when he saw a picture of a (2) **Zen** garden on one of his Japanese stamps. Then he checked out a book from the library on Zen gardening and read all about it. Zen gardening became his new hobby, and he really enjoyed it—at least for a few months—but it didn't last either. Now he's raising tropical fish.

Contrasting Sentences

Listening: Write the appropriate key word in each blank. Later, as you hear each sentence, mark the box, point to the picture, make a gesture, and/or say the rejoinder. Speaking: Choose and say each sentence so that your listener(s) can respond correctly.

❏ _____ gardening became his hobby. (flowers and plants)

❏ _____ gardening became his hobby. (rocks and gravel)

Explanations and diagrams for this unit's target sounds are on pages 338–39 and 343 in Section 10.

Additional Practice

Show me the *thee/Z*. (C11i-b), He was *teething/teasing*. (C11m-A/a), That's a *clothing/closing* store. (C11m-B/b), Jim gave his *tithe/ties*. (C11f-A/a)

Other Words

Many, if not all, of the words listed below are in the story. Find them and circle or underline them each time they occur. Say each marked word aloud—individually and then in its entire sentence. Look for additional words in the story that contain the target sounds. Mark and say them also.

[ð] **the, that, they, this, there, thee**

[z] **zero, zip, zinc, zany, zealous, zebra**

Other Practice Activities

❏ Partner Cards—Listening. *Practice until you can point to the right card every time.*
❏ Partner Cards—Speaking. *Practice until you can say the contrasting sentences so accurately that your partner points to the right card every time.*
❏ Story Reading. *Practice reading the story aloud. Mark any difficult words. Then record the story on tape.*
❏ Story Dictation. *Write the story as your teacher reads it or as you listen to it on the audiotape.*
❏ Cloze Reading. *Choose some key words in the story and black them out. Then read the entire story aloud. Do this several times.*

Each time black out more words. Continue until most of the story is blacked out and you can tell it without looking at the page very often.
❏ Story Retelling from Skeleton. *Black out all the remaining words except those you need in order to remind you of the story line. Then, using just this skeleton, tell the story to your partner or class.*
❏ Free Story Retelling. *Retell the whole story from memory, without looking at your book.*
❏ Parallel Story. *Create your own story similar to the one in this unit.*
❏ Mini-drama. *Make up a skit or do a role play based on the story.*

Unit C11m-A [ð] teething—[z] teasing

Story

Watching and caring for children is a difficult job. I usually avoid it when I can, but yesterday I couldn't. My sister asked me to watch her two little boys while she went to the doctor. One is five years old, and the other is just a baby.

#1

#2

They really kept me busy. The older one is very mischievous and jealous of the baby. For that reason, he loves to (1) tease his little brother whenever he gets a chance. On top of that, the baby had a (2) new tooth coming in, so he was in pain. He cried and fussed quite a bit.

I tried to get some other things done when I was watching my nephews, but I just couldn't. The baby kept crying. I never knew why. Sometimes it was because he was **teething** and in pain. Other times it was because his older brother was **teasing** him.

After an hour of this, my nerves started to go. I was really glad when my sister returned.

Contrasting Sentences

❏ He was _____. (painful gums)

❏ He was _____. (tormenting his brother.)

Additional Practice

Then/Zen gardening became his hobby. (C11i-A/a), Show me the *thee/Z*. (C11i-b), That's a *clothing/closing* store. (C11m-B/b), Jim gave his *tithe/ties*. (C11f-A/a)

Other Words

[ð] o**th**er, bro**th**er, ei**th**er, clo**th**ing, brea**th**ing, **th**is

[z] bu**s**y, rea**s**on, ri**s**ing, i**s**, wa**s**, becau**s**e

Other Practice Activities

❏ Partner Cards—Listening.
❏ Partner Cards—Speaking.
❏ Story Reading.
❏ Story Dictation.
❏ Cloze Reading.

❏ Story Retelling from Skeleton.
❏ Free Story Retelling.
❏ Parallel Story.
❏ Mini-drama.

Unit C11m-B [ð] clothing—[z] closing

Story

It is tough to keep a business going these days. In my town, a lot of stores just come and go. Yesterday, I was out walking with my friend Susan, and she saw a lot of people going into a store. "What's going on there?" she asked.

I answered, "Oh, that store is (1) **closing.** They're having a final, close-out sale."

Susan was surprised. "Are they going out of business already? It seems like they just opened." Then she suggested, "Let's go in and see if we can find any bargains."

Well, we went into the closing store, but I didn't find anything I liked, and Susan didn't either. So we kept walking. Soon we passed (2) another interesting store. Susan said, "That store looks new. I wonder what they sell there."

"Oh, that's a **clothing** store," I said. "It just opened last week. They carry the latest casual clothes for both men and women."

Since both of us are interested in fashion, we decided to check out the new clothing store. Did we buy anything? Of course not. We didn't even have any money with us.

Contrasting Sentences

❑ That's a _____ store. (It's going out of business.)

❑ That's a _____ store. (It carries casual clothes.)

Additional Practice

Then/Zen gardening became his hobby. (C11i-A/a), Show me the *thee/Z.* (C11i-b), He was *teething/teasing.* (C11m-A/a), Jim gave his *tithe/ties.* (C11f-A/a)

Other Words

[ð] ano**th**er, ei**th**er, **th**ese, **th**ere, **th**at, **th**ey're

[z] bu**s**ine**ss**, Su**s**an, the**s**e, clo**s**e-out, surpri**s**ed, ri**s**er

Other Practice Activities

- ❏ Partner Cards—Listening.
- ❏ Partner Cards—Speaking.
- ❏ Story Reading.
- ❏ Story Dictation.
- ❏ Cloze Reading.

- ❏ Story Retelling from Skeleton.
- ❏ Free Story Retelling.
- ❏ Parallel Story.
- ❏ Mini-drama.

Unit C11f-A [ð] tithe—[z] ties

Story

Many organizations exist to help the poor. Often these organizations have no money of their own. Rather, they collect funds and goods and then redistribute them to the needy.

Jim likes to help people. In (1) the church that he belongs to, people pay tithes to help the poor. Jim's tithe is money that he contributes to the church. The church then uses this money for various causes. Jim gives his **tithe** every month.

#1

Of course, people can make donations of other kinds. In fact, churches and other organizations often organize drives to encourage and collect donations of clothing or household goods. These donations are also used to help people in need. When there is a drive, Jim often contributes his old clothes. Last month he donated two pairs of pants that no longer fit him. He also gave (2) several **ties.** He had just bought some new ones, so it wasn't hard for him to give away the old ties. In fact, it made him feel good.

#2

Contrasting Sentences

❑ Jim gave his _____. (neckties)

❑ Jim gave his _____. (money)

Additional Practice

Then/Zen gardening became his hobby. (C11i-A/a), Show me the *thee/Z*. (C11i-b), He was *teething/teasing*. (C11m-A/a), That's a *clothing/closing* store. (C11m-B/b)

Other Words

[ð] ba**the**, clo**the**, ra**the**r, o**the**r, clo**the**ing, **the**

[z] belong**s**, Jim'**s**, cause**s**, organi**z**e, drive**s**, clothe**s**

Other Practice Activities

❑ Partner Cards—Listening.
❑ Partner Cards—Speaking.
❑ Story Reading.
❑ Story Dictation.
❑ Cloze Reading.
❑ Story Retelling from Skeleton.
❑ Free Story Retelling.
❑ Parallel Story.
❑ Mini-drama.

Unit C12f-A [t] cart—[d] card

Story

Listen to the story as your teacher reads it, or on tape, until you understand the main ideas.

Today is my mother's birthday, and my father and I decided to cook a special dinner for her tonight. This afternoon we went to a grocery store. We needed to buy cake mix, potatoes, chicken, some vegetables, frosting, candles, and ice cream. I hurried around the store looking for these things. Dad followed behind me. Soon I had so many things in my arms that I couldn't hold them all. "Dad, help me!" I called. My father smiled and said, "We need a (1) **cart** so we can carry more." Soon the cart was full of food, and we had everything we needed.

#1

"OK, let's go home and start cooking," said my father. When we were just about to leave the store, I remembered something important. "Dad, we need a (2) **card**!" I ran to the card section and picked out the prettiest one. At home, we both signed the card and then started to cook.

#2

Mom will be home from work soon. I'm sure she will love both the card and the food.

Contrasting Sentences

Listening: Write the appropriate key word in each blank. Later, as you hear each sentence, mark the box, point to the picture, make a gesture, and/or say the rejoinder. Speaking: Choose and say each sentence so that your listener(s) can respond correctly.

❑ We need a _____. (so we can carry more)

❑ We need a _____. (to sign and give to Mom)

Explanations and diagrams for this unit's target sounds are on pages 339–40 in Section 10.

Additional Practice

Have you seen this *coat/code* before? (C12f-B/b), He gave me his *seat/seed*. (C12f-c)

Other Words

Many, if not all, of the words listed below are in the story. Find them and circle or underline them each time they occur. Say each marked word aloud—individually and then in its entire sentence. Look for additional words in the story that contain the target sounds. Mark and say them also.

[t] tonigh**t**, wen**t**, star**t**, jus**t**, abou**t**, picke**d**

[d] decide**d**, aroun**d**, followe**d**, behin**d**, hol**d**, foo**d**

Other Practice Activities

❑ Partner Cards—Listening. *Practice until you can point to the right card every time.*

❑ Partner Cards—Speaking. *Practice until you can say the contrasting sentences so accurately that your partner points to the right card every time.*

❑ Story Reading. *Practice reading the story aloud. Mark any difficult words. Then record the story on tape.*

❑ Story Dictation. *Write the story as your teacher reads it or as you listen to it on the audiotape.*

❑ Cloze Reading. *Choose some key words in the story and black them out. Then read the entire story aloud. Do this several times.*

Each time black out more words. Continue until most of the story is blacked out and you can tell it without looking at the page very often.

❑ Story Retelling from Skeleton. *Black out all the remaining words except those you need in order to remind you of the story line. Then, using just this skeleton, tell the story to your partner or class.*

❑ Free Story Retelling. *Retell the whole story from memory, without looking at your book.*

❑ Parallel Story. *Create your own story similar to the one in this unit.*

❑ Mini-drama. *Make up a skit or do a role play based on the story.*

Unit C12f-B [t] coat—[d] code

Story

I work in a clothing store that is very organized. Each item is tagged with a (1) **code** that can be scanned at the register. That way, we know what items have been sold, and we can order replacements. Also, this code makes it easy for customers to return items.

One day a customer brought in a (2) **coat** that I didn't think I had seen before. She wanted to return it, but I told her that she couldn't. It had not come from our store. Then the customer showed me the tag that was still attached to the coat and asked me if I'd seen the code before. It was definitely one of our tags. When I scanned the code, I found out that the customer was right and I was wrong. It was an embarrassing situation for me.

Contrasting Sentences

❏ Have you seen this _____ before? (symbol on the tag)

❏ Have you seen this _____ before? (clothing)

Additional Practice

We need a *cart / card*. (C12f-A/a), He gave me his *seat / seed*. (C12f-c)

Other Words

[t] tha**t**, wha**t**, brough**t**, i**t**, no**t**, righ**t**

[d] tagge**d**, scanne**d**, ha**d**, wante**d**, tol**d**, I'**d**

Other Practice Activities

❏ Partner Cards—Listening.
❏ Partner Cards—Speaking.
❏ Story Reading.
❏ Story Dictation.
❏ Cloze Reading.

❏ Story Retelling
   from Skeleton.
❏ Free Story Retelling.
❏ Parallel Story.
❏ Mini-drama.

Unit C13i-A [n] nap—[l] lap

Story

Listen to the story as your teacher reads it, or on tape, until you understand the main ideas.

My cat, whose name is Nikki, thinks that she is the queen of the world. In reality, she does lead a very luxurious life with everything she needs provided for her. When she is hungry, she calls me and I feed her. She never works, she goes out every night, and most of the day she just lies around. During the day she (1) **naps** whenever and wherever she wants. Often she takes her naps on the sofa, but sometimes she chooses a sunny spot by the window.

Nikki's favorite napping spot of all is on my (2) **lap.** If she sees me sitting down, she will climb up on my lap and have a nice nap. It doesn't matter what I'm doing as long as I'm sitting down. In fact, if you come to my home and sit down somewhere, she will probably crawl into your lap too. Then she will fall asleep. Nikki definitely likes laps, and she also likes naps. Whenever she can combine these two pleasures, she does.

Contrasting Sentences

Listening: Write the appropriate key word in each blank. Later, as you hear each sentence, mark the box, point to the picture, make a gesture, and/or say the rejoinder. Speaking: Choose and say each sentence so that your listener(s) can respond correctly.

❑ Nikki likes _____. (She sleeps frequently.)

❑ Nikki likes _____. (If you sit down, she'll crawl into yours.)

Explanations and diagrams for this unit's target sounds are on pages 340–41 in Section 10.

Additional Practice

Please don't *nick/lick* it. (C13i-b), Don't choose a *snob/slob* for a roommate. (C13m-A/a), He's a *tenor/teller*. (C13m-b), The dog wants its *bone/bowl*. (C13f-A/a), Where's the *spoon/spool?* (C13f-b)

Other Words

Many, if not all, of the words listed below are in the story. Find them and circle or underline them each time they occur. Say each marked word aloud—individually and then in its entire sentence. Look for additional words in the story that contain the target sounds. Mark and say them also.

[n] **n**ame, **N**ikki, **n**eeds, **n**ever, **n**ice, **kn**ife

[l] **l**uxurious, **l**ife, **l**eads, **l**ies, **l**ong, **l**ikes

Other Practice Activities

❑ Partner Cards—Listening. *Practice until you can point to the right card every time.*
❑ Partner Cards—Speaking. *Practice until you can say the contrasting sentences so accurately that your partner points to the right card every time.*
❑ Story Reading. *Practice reading the story aloud. Mark any difficult words. Then record the story on tape.*
❑ Story Dictation. *Write the story as your teacher reads it or as you listen to it on the audiotape.*
❑ Cloze Reading. *Choose some key words in the story and black them out. Then read the entire story aloud. Do this several times.*

Each time black out more words. Continue until most of the story is blacked out and you can tell it without looking at the page very often.
❑ Story Retelling from Skeleton. *Black out all the remaining words except those you need in order to remind you of the story line. Then, using just this skeleton, tell the story to your partner or class.*
❑ Free Story Retelling. *Retell the whole story from memory, without looking at your book.*
❑ Parallel Story. *Create your own story similar to the one in this unit.*
❑ Mini-drama. *Make up a skit or do a role play based on the story.*

Unit C13m-A [n] snob—[l] slob

Story

When you look for a roommate, you should make your decision carefully. There are several personal characteristics you should consider.

First of all, you don't want a roommate who is too messy. If your roommate is a (1) **slob,** you will always be cleaning, or else you will have to live in a constant mess. On the other hand, you don't want a roommate who is too neat because you might feel messy in comparison.

#1

#2

Secondly, you probably want a roommate who is friendly and easy to talk to. You won't enjoy rooming with someone who is always acting superior. In other words, don't choose a (2) **snob** for a roommate.

These are just two of the many things to consider when making your decision. You definitely have to be extra careful when choosing a roommate.

Contrasting Sentences

❑ Don't choose a _____ for a roommate. (a person who acts superior)

❑ Don't choose a _____ for a roommate. (a messy person)

Additional Practice

Nikki likes *naps/laps*. (C13i-A/a), Please don't *nick/lick* it. (C13i-b), He's a *tenor/teller*. (C13m-b), The dog wants its *bone/bowl*. (C13f-A/a), Where's the *spoon/spool?* (C13f-b)

Other Words

[n] perso**n**al, co**n**sider, wa**n**t, clea**n**ing, e**n**joy, defi**n**itely

[l] carefu**ll**y, a**l**ways, c**l**eaning, e**l**se, second**l**y, friend**l**y

Other Practice Activities

❑ Partner Cards—Listening.
❑ Partner Cards—Speaking.
❑ Story Reading.
❑ Story Dictation.
❑ Cloze Reading.

❑ Story Retelling from Skeleton.
❑ Free Story Retelling.
❑ Parallel Story.
❑ Mini-drama.

Unit C13f-A [n] bone—[l] bowl

Story

Ann claims that she can understand what her dog, Ember, is saying when he barks. Last week when I visited her she interpreted everything that her dog "said." First of all Ember barked in a particular tone. Ann said that meant he wanted his (1) **bone.** So she gave him a rawhide "bone." He chewed on it for a while; then he barked again. It sounded the same to me, but Ann said that bark meant that Ember wanted his ball. When she gave it to him, however, he didn't seem at all interested. A little while after that, he barked excitedly. According to Ann, that meant he wanted to go outside. So she let him out. He went, but not for long. When Ember came back in, he barked with a rough voice. Ann said that meant he was thirsty and wanted his (2) **bowl.** He did drink the water she gave him, but I'm still not convinced that Ann was really understanding his barking. What do you think? Can people really understand their pets?

#1

#2

Contrasting Sentences

❏ The dog wants its _____. (to chew on)

❏ The dog wants its _____. (to drink from)

Additional Practice

Nikki likes *naps/laps.* (C13i-A/a), Please don't *nick/lick* it. (C13i-b), Don't choose a *snob/slob* for a roommate. (C13m-A/a), He's a *tenor/teller.* (C13m-b), Where's the *spoon/spool?* (C13f-b)

Other Words

[n] A**nn**, ca**n**, whe**n**, i**n**, chi**n**, mai**n**

[l] a**ll**, ba**ll**, whi**l**e, sti**ll**, mea**l**, mai**l**

Other Practice Activities

❏ Partner Cards—Listening.

❏ Partner Cards—Speaking.

❏ Story Reading.

❏ Story Dictation.

❏ Cloze Reading.

❏ Story Retelling from Skeleton.

❏ Free Story Retelling.

❏ Parallel Story.

❏ Mini-drama.

Unit C14i-A [l] long—[r] wrong

Story

Listen to the story as your teacher reads it, or on tape, until you understand the main ideas.

Rebecca knew she should study for her history examination, but she didn't. She doesn't like history, and she didn't even want to think about the exam, so she went to a party instead. She planned to study the next day, but she slept in because she was tired. She woke up around eleven, just in time to rush to her class and take the exam.

The examination consisted of one essay question. When she looked at the question, Rebecca realized that she didn't know anything about it. Her mind formed a desperate plan. She thought that if she wrote a lot, she might get a good grade anyway. She wrote an answer that was not even related to the question, but it was (1) five pages **long.**

Unfortunately, Rebecca's plan did not work. When she got her test back she saw that her answer was marked completely (2) **wrong.** Her grade was a big red F. She was shocked. In fact, she felt like she'd been struck by lightning. Luckily, it was only the midterm exam. She decided that she had better go to the library and start studying for the final right away.

Contrasting Sentences

Listening: Write the appropriate key word in each blank. Later, as you hear each sentence, mark the box, point to the picture, make a gesture, and/or say the rejoinder. Speaking: Choose and say each sentence so that your listener(s) can respond correctly.

❏ Rebecca's answer was _____. (She wrote five pages.)

❏ Rebecca's answer was _____. (She got a bad grade.)

Explanations and diagrams for this unit's target sounds are on pages 341–42 in Section 10.

Additional Practice

They found a *lake/rake*. (C14i-B/b), I need a big *lock/rock*. (C14i-C/c), There are *lamps/ramps* in the tomb. (C14i-D/d), The substitute *collected/corrected* the essays. (C14m-A/a), The account was lost in the *file/fire*. (C14f-A/a)

Other Words

Many, if not all, of the words listed below are in the story. Find them and circle or underline them each time they occur. Say each marked word aloud—individually and then in its entire sentence. Look for additional words in the story that contain the target sounds. Mark and say them also.

[l] **l**ike, **l**ooked, **l**ot, **l**ightning, **l**uckily, **l**ibrary

[r] **r**ush, **r**ealized, **wr**ote, **r**elated, **r**ed, **r**ight

Other Practice Activities

❑ Partner Cards—Listening. *Practice until you can point to the right card every time.*
❑ Partner Cards—Speaking. *Practice until you can say the contrasting sentences so accurately that your partner points to the right card every time.*
❑ Story Reading. *Practice reading the story aloud. Mark any difficult words. Then record the story on tape.*
❑ Story Dictation. *Write the story as your teacher reads it or as you listen to it on the audiotape.*
❑ Cloze Reading. *Choose some key words in the story and black them out. Then read the entire story aloud. Do this several times.*

Each time black out more words. Continue until most of the story is blacked out and you can tell it without looking at the page very often.
❑ Story Retelling from Skeleton. *Black out all the remaining words except those you need in order to remind you of the story line. Then, using just this skeleton, tell the story to your partner or class.*
❑ Free Story Retelling. *Retell the whole story from memory, without looking at your book.*
❑ Parallel Story. *Create your own story similar to the one in this unit.*
❑ Mini-drama. *Make up a skit or do a role play based on the story.*

Unit C14i-B [l] lake—[r] rake

Story

Larry and Ron were walking in the woods. It was fall, and red and yellow leaves covered the ground. As they walked, the boys found an old ranch house by a (1) **lake.** It seemed abandoned. It was all broken down, and there were no signs of life anywhere—

#1

except for a rat that quickly ran away. They decided to stop there and have a rest. The weather was cool, and the sun's rays were weak.

"Let's make a campfire," said Larry.

"Yeah, that's a great idea," answered Ron. "I'll clear a spot, and you get some wood."

Larry started hunting for dead branches. Soon he smiled and said, "Look what I found. It's an old (2) **rake.**" The rake was rusty, and the handle was broken, but Ron was happy to see it. Using the rake, he was able to clear a place for the fire quickly. Then Larry and Ron both used the rake to gather piles of leaves to rest on. They were comfortable, and they enjoyed the view of the lake. It was a leisurely way to spend an afternoon.

#2

Contrasting Sentences

❏ They found a _____. (and decided to rest by it)

❏ They found a _____. (and used it to gather leaves)

Additional Practice

Rebecca's answer was *long / wrong*. (C14i-A/a), I need a big *lock / rock*. (C14i-C/c), There are *lamps / ramps* in the tomb. (C14i-D/d), The substitute *collected / corrected* the essays. (C14m-A/a), The account was lost in the *file / fire*. (C14f-A/a)

Other Words

[l] **L**arry, **l**eaves, **l**ife, **l**et's, **l**ook, **l**eisurely

[r] **r**ed, **r**anch, **r**at, **r**ays, **r**usty, **r**est

Other Practice Activities

❏ Partner Cards—Listening.
❏ Partner Cards—Speaking.
❏ Story Reading.
❏ Story Dictation.
❏ Cloze Reading.

❏ Story Retelling
　from Skeleton.
❏ Free Story Retelling.
❏ Parallel Story.
❏ Mini-drama.

Unit C14i-C [l] lock—[r] rock

Story

My little sister Rachel got a big doll for her birthday present. She named the doll Rosy. Rachel loved her doll very much, but when we went on a trip she had to leave Rosy behind. No matter how much we reassured Rachel that her doll would be safe, she was very worried that something would happen to Rosy.

She decided to put Rosy in her closet. "I need a big (1) **lock** to keep Rosy safe," said Rachel. I let her use a lock I had bought a long time ago, and then I hid the key.

When we returned from our trip, the first thing Rachel wanted to do was get Rosy out of the closet. But I couldn't find the key. She got angry and said, "Rosy wants to come out right now. I'm going to get a big (2) **rock** and break the lock." She ran out of the house to get a rock.

Luckily, by the time she came back, I had found the key and opened the closet. She was happy to have Rosy back, and I was relieved to get my lock back safely.

Contrasting Sentences

❏ I need a big _____. (to keep Rosy safe)

❏ I need a big _____. (to break the lock)

Additional Practice

Rebecca's answer was *long/wrong*. (C14i-A/a), They found a *lake/rake*. (C14i-B/b), There are *lamps/ramps* in the tomb. (C14i-D/d), The substitute *collected/corrected* the essays. (C14m-A/a), The account was lost in the *file/fire*. (C14f-A/a)

Other Words

[l] little, loved, leave, let, long, luckily

[r] Rachel, Rosy, ran, reassured, returned, right

Other Practice Activities

- ❏ Partner Cards—Listening.
- ❏ Partner Cards—Speaking.
- ❏ Story Reading.
- ❏ Story Dictation.
- ❏ Cloze Reading.

- ❏ Story Retelling from Skeleton.
- ❏ Free Story Retelling.
- ❏ Parallel Story.
- ❏ Mini-drama.

Unit C14i-D [l] lamps—[r] ramps

Story

Have you ever been to the Ming Tombs near Beijing? Visiting them is a memorable and remarkable experience. These thirteen tombs were the burial places for the Ming emperors. The Sacred Way leading to the tombs is guarded by huge stone statues— lions, elephants, camels, etc. Each tomb consists of a tall pagoda and an underground palace, where the emperor's body was placed.

Today, some of the tombs are open to visitors, and you can actually go down into one of the underground palaces. Unfortunately, the tombs were raided and robbed centuries ago. Any remaining objects are now in museums, so there aren't any treasures or bodies to see in the underground palace. Still it is impressive.

To get to the underground palace, you walk down long stairways and big (1) **ramps.** They lead you to large halls and smaller chambers. Because you are so far underground, it is cool and dark. (2) **Lamps** light the way. In one room you can see three imperial thrones. In another you will find three coffins. They once held the bodies of some of the most powerful rulers on earth. It certainly makes you reflect on life and death.

Contrasting Sentences

❏ There are _____ in the tomb. (to go down)

❏ There are _____ in the tomb. (to light the way)

Additional Practice

Rebecca's answer was *long/wrong*. (C14i-A/a), They found a *lake/rake*. (C14i-B/b), I need a big *lock/rock*. (C14i-C/c), The substitute *collected/corrected* the essays. (C14m-A/a), The account was lost in the *file/fire*. (C14f-A/a)

Other Words

[l] **l**eading, **l**ions, **l**ong, **l**ead, **l**arge, **l**ife

[r] **r**emarkable, **r**aided, **r**obbed, **r**oom, **r**ulers, **r**eflect

Other Practice Activities

❏ Partner Cards—Listening.
❏ Partner Cards—Speaking.
❏ Story Reading.
❏ Story Dictation.
❏ Cloze Reading.

❏ Story Retelling from Skeleton.
❏ Free Story Retelling.
❏ Parallel Story.
❏ Mini-drama.

Unit C14m-A [l] collect—[r] correct

Story

Ms. Jones is a teacher, but yesterday she was so sick she couldn't teach her classes. Mr. Harrison, a substitute teacher, came and taught her classes for the day. Ms. Jones had already written out a lesson plan, but he didn't follow it. He had his own plans.

When Mr. Harrison got to class, the students were excited because they didn't like Ms. Jones. They were happy to see she wouldn't be there that day. This happiness didn't last long, though, because Mr. Harrison made the students write essays the whole hour. They couldn't believe it. It was very boring. The whole time, Mr. Harrison sat there filing his fingernails. When the hour was finished he (1) **collected** the papers from the students.

During the next class hour, while the students in that class were writing their essays, he read and (2) **corrected** the essays from the previous hour. At the end of the day, Mr. Harrison delivered the essays to Ms. Jones's mailbox in the school office so that she could record the scores in her roll book the next day.

Today, when Ms. Jones returned, she was surprised to see that the students were very happy to see her.

Contrasting Sentences

❏ The substitute _____ the essays. (gathered them)

❏ The substitute _____ the essays. (marked them)

Additional Practice

Rebecca's answer was *long/wrong*. (C14i-A/a), They found a *lake/rake*. (C14i-B/b), I need a big *lock/rock*. (C14i-C/c), There are *lamps/ramps* in the tomb. (C14i-D/d), The account was lost in the *file/fire*. (C14f-A/a)

Also, for [l] and [r] following consonants: George puts in *glass/grass* for a living. (CC1-A/a), Look at the *clown/crown*. (CC1-B/b), Grace went to *glamour/grammar* school (CC1-C/c)

Other Words

[l] already, follow, believe, filing, deliver, mailbox

[r] yesterday, boring, during, record, returned, very

Other Practice Activities

❏ Partner Cards—Listening.
❏ Partner Cards—Speaking.
❏ Story Reading.
❏ Story Dictation.
❏ Cloze Reading.
❏ Story Retelling from Skeleton.
❏ Free Story Retelling.
❏ Parallel Story.
❏ Mini-drama.

Unit C14f-A [l] file—[r] fire

Story

Jill works in the head office of a large company. Her job is to (1) **file** papers related to clients' accounts. All day long she puts papers in files. There are hundreds of accounts and hundreds of papers in each account, so she must be very careful to put each paper in the proper place. If a paper is put in the wrong file it may be lost forever.

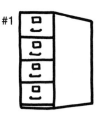

Last week there was a problem with the electrical wiring, and a (2) **fire** started in the wall of the office. The fire department came quickly and put it out, but the fire still damaged several file cabinets. Some papers in them were burned in the fire. Others were damaged by the water used in putting the fire out. The papers that were not damaged were put in a new file cabinet. In the process, however, many of them got mixed up and put in wrong places.

Today, when Jill was looking for a client's account, she couldn't find it. She couldn't figure out if it had been lost in the fire last week, or if it was still there but just lost in the file. It was a frustrating experience for her.

Contrasting Sentences

❑ The account was lost in the_____ . (burned up)

❑ The account was lost in the_____ . (misplaced in the cabinet)

Additional Practice

Rebecca's answer was *long/wrong*. (C14i-A/a), They found a *lake/rake*. (C14i-B/b), I need a big *lock/rock*. (C14i-C/c), There are *lamps/ramps* in the tomb. (C14i-D/d), The substitute *collected/corrected* the essays. (C14m-A/a)

Other Words

[l] **all, careful, electrical, wall, still, several**

[r] he**r**, pape**r**, wate**r**, we**r**e, figu**r**e, o**r**

Other Practice Activities

- ❏ Partner Cards—Listening.
- ❏ Partner Cards—Speaking.
- ❏ Story Reading.
- ❏ Story Dictation.
- ❏ Cloze Reading.
- ❏ Story Retelling from Skeleton.
- ❏ Free Story Retelling.
- ❏ Parallel Story.
- ❏ Mini-drama.

Unit C15i-A [s] sip—[z] zip

Story

Listen to the story as your teacher reads it, or on tape, until you understand the main ideas.

Last summer, I went backpacking with some friends. We saw many animals in the mountains. It was better than a zoo. I took lots of pictures, and with my zoom lens I could take close-ups from far away.

Since we were far from civilization, we carried our drinking water in canteens. As we zigzagged up steep trails, I got thirsty, and my friends gave me conflicting advice. Some told me to drink plenty of water whenver I felt like it. Others advised me to (1) drink only a little at a time. "Just **sip** it slowly and make it last longer," they said.

When we found a spring of fresh, cold water, we decided to camp there. Unfortunately, when I set up my tent I found that (2) the zipper was broken. It would either jam or else not stay closed. Once again, my friends gave me conflicting advice. Some said, "To make the zipper work, **zip** it fast and don't stop." Others insisted that I should just zip it slowly and carefully. I tried both methods and neither worked.

In that alpine zone there were lots of mosquitoes, and I worried that they would get into my tent and I would get zero rest that night. Then I came up with a solution. It was a little zany, but it worked. What do you think I did?

Contrasting Sentences

Listening: Write the appropriate key word in each blank. Later, as you hear each sentence, mark the box, point to the picture, make a gesture, and/or say the rejoinder. Speaking: Choose and say each sentence so that your listener(s) can respond correctly.

❏ _____ it slowly. (Make it last longer.)

❏ _____ it slowly. (Maybe it will stay closed.)

Explanations and diagrams for this unit's target sounds are on pages 342–43 in Section 10.

Additional Practice

David pretended it was a *racer / razor*. (C15m-A/a), The *prices / prizes* are great! (C15m-B/b), That's a *fussy / fuzzy* dog! (C15m-c), She looked at my *ice / eyes*. (C15f-A/a)

Other Words

Many, if not all, of the words listed below are in the story. Find them and circle or underline them each time they occur. Say each marked word aloud—individually and then in its entire sentence. Look for additional words in the story that contain the target sounds. Mark and say them also.

[s] **s**ummer, **s**ome, **s**aw, civili**z**ation, **s**aid, **s**olution

[z] **z**oo, **z**oom, **z**ig**z**agged, **z**ipper, **z**one, **z**ero

Other Practice Activities

❏ Partner Cards—Listening. *Practice until you can point to the right card every time.*

❏ Partner Cards—Speaking. *Practice until you can say the contrasting sentences so accurately that your partner points to the right card every time.*

❏ Story Reading. *Practice reading the story aloud. Mark any difficult words. Then record the story on tape.*

❏ Story Dictation. *Write the story as your teacher reads it or as you listen to it on the audiotape.*

❏ Cloze Reading. *Choose some key words in the story and black them out. Then read the entire story aloud. Do this several times.*

Each time black out more words. Continue until most of the story is blacked out and you can tell it without looking at the page very often.

❏ Story Retelling from Skeleton. *Black out all the remaining words except those you need in order to remind you of the story line. Then, using just this skeleton, tell the story to your partner or class.*

❏ Free Story Retelling. *Retell the whole story from memory, without looking at your book.*

❏ Parallel Story. *Create your own story similar to the one in this unit.*

❏ Mini-drama. *Make up a skit or do a role play based on the story.*

Unit C15m-A [s] racer—[z] razor

Story

My little nephew David loves electrical things. Anything that has batteries or plugs into the wall interests him. His father has an electric (1) **razor** that makes a buzzing sound when you turn it on. David loves it and always wants to play with it after his dad is finished shaving. But since the razor is not a toy, David's father does not let him play with it.

One day, while David's father was at work, I heard a mysterious buzzing sound coming from the bathroom. I looked in and saw David moving a small car up and down his face and making the buzzing noise. He was pretending the car was a razor.

I realized that he needed something fun to do, so I took him in the other room. We built a track on the floor. Then we raced his car around it. David now made different noises. He went, "Zoom! Zoom!" In his mind the car was now a speeding (2) **racer**!

Contrasting Sentences

❑ David pretended it was a _____ . (shaver—Buzz, buzz)

❑ David pretended it was a _____ . (fast car—Zoom, zoom)

Additional Practice

Sip / Zip it slowly. (C15i-A/a), The *prices / prizes* are great! (C15m-B/b), That's a *fussy / fuzzy* dog! (C15m-c), She looked at my *ice / eyes*. (C15f-A/a)

Other Words

[s] interes**t**s, my**s**terious, ra**c**ed, la**c**y, mu**s**cle, ra**c**ing

[z] bu**zz**ing, reali**z**ed, di**zz**y, pri**z**es, la**z**y, rai**s**ing

Other Practice Activities

❏ Partner Cards—Listening.
❏ Partner Cards—Speaking.
❏ Story Reading.
❏ Story Dictation.
❏ Cloze Reading.

❏ Story Retelling
   from Skeleton.
❏ Free Story Retelling.
❏ Parallel Story.
❏ Mini-drama.

Unit C15m-B [s] prices—[z] prizes

Story

Have you ever been to Las Vegas? It's one of the most fantastic places in the world. There are big hotels and casinos all along the Strip. One looks like a giant Egyptian pyramid. Another famous one makes you feel like you're in ancient Rome. In the evening, most of the big hotels also have shows with live entertainment by top stars. Everywhere you look, people are putting money into slot machines and playing other games of chance. The casinos are big moneymakers, and they are never closed.

To attract customers, a lot of the hotels and casinos also offer good food at great (1) **prices.** Many of them offer buffets for just a few dollars.

#1

Nowadays Las Vegas isn't just for adults. There are attractions for younger people also. In fact, the larger casinos have special arcades with lots of fun games for children and teenagers. When you play these games, you can win fun (2) **prizes.** Of course, since it's illegal for kids to gamble, the prizes aren't money. Instead, winners get stuffed animals, funny hats, and things like that.

#2

Contrasting Sentences

❏ The _____ are great! (for the food)

❏ The _____ are great! (in the arcades)

Additional Practice

Sip / Zip it. (C15i-A/a), David pretended it was a *racer / razor*. (C15m-A/a), That's a *fussy / fuzzy* dog! (C15m-c), She looked at my *ice / eyes.* (C15f-A/a)

Other Words

[s] most, fantastic, places, casino, also, customer

[z] closed, stars, lazy, teaser, rising, mazes

Other Practice Activities

❏ Partner Cards—Listening.
❏ Partner Cards—Speaking.
❏ Story Reading.
❏ Story Dictation.
❏ Cloze Reading.

❏ Story Retelling
   from Skeleton.
❏ Free Story Retelling.
❏ Parallel Story.
❏ Mini-drama.

Unit C15f-A [s] ice—[z] eyes

Story

I used to have a cute little dog. His name was Buzz, and I loved him very much. But one day he got loose, ran out on the street, and was hit by a car. It's always hard when someone or something you love dies. When Buzz died, I felt a great loss and emptiness. I stayed in my room and cried all day.

My sister was worried about me and came into my room. She looked at my (1) **eyes.** "Please stop crying," she said. "You've been crying since this morning, and your eyes are all red." Then she offered, "Let me get you something to eat." A few minutes later she brought my favorite snack, iced tea and a sandwich.

As I was sipping the iced tea, I saw something black in the (2) **ice.** "What's this?" I asked.

My sister took a look and said, "Oops. It's a bug." Feeling disgusted, I started to cry again.

Contrasting Sentences

❏ She looked at my _____. (They were red.)

❏ She looked at my _____. (There was a bug in it.)

Additional Practice

Sip / Zip it slowly. (C15i-A/a), David pretended it was a *racer / razor*. (C15m-A/a), The *prices / prizes* are great! (C15m-B/b), That's a *fussy / fuzzy* dog! (C15m-c)

Other Words

    [s] loose, it'**s**, lo**ss**, emptine**ss**, **s**ince, thi**s**

    [z] hi**s**, wa**s**, alway**s**, die**s**, plea**s**e, a**s**

Other Practice Activities

❏ Partner Cards—Listening.
❏ Partner Cards—Speaking.
❏ Story Reading.
❏ Story Dictation.
❏ Cloze Reading.

❏ Story Retelling
   from Skeleton.
❏ Free Story Retelling.
❏ Parallel Story.
❏ Mini-drama.

Unit C16i-A [s] sip—[ʃ] ship

Story

Listen to the story as your teacher reads it, or on tape, until you understand the main ideas.

My sister Shirley works for a company with branches all over the country. In the last few years she has been transferred several times. Every time Shirley moves she has lots of boxes to (1) **ship.** Since she doesn't have a car, she sends most of her boxes by way of a parcel delivery service. It's expensive, but her company pays for it. Besides, it's convenient and fast. Unfortunately, Shirley herself is quite slow. It always takes her longer than she plans to pack her stuff.

Last month I went to help Shirley take her boxes to the parcel delivery service's office. She had asked me to come at five thirty sharp because the office closed at six o'clock. But when I got to Shirley's apartment, I was shocked. The boxes she needed to ship were not even packed and sealed. In fact, several of her things were still lying around the room or sitting on shelves. But, instead of hurrying to finish her packing, Shirley was sitting on her bed (2) **sipping** a drink. She complained that she was tired, but I told her that if she didn't hurry we wouldn't be able to ship her stuff.

Contrasting Sentences

Listening: Write the appropriate key word in each blank. Later, as you hear each sentence, mark the box, point to the picture, make a gesture, and/or say the rejoinder. Speaking: Choose and say each sentence so that your listener(s) can respond correctly.

❑ Can you_____ it quickly? (the drink)

❑ Can you_____ it quickly? (the stuff)

Explanations and diagrams for this unit's target sounds are on pages 342 and 343–44 in Section 10.

Additional Practice

Look at that *sack / shack*. (C16i-b), This *seat / sheet* is dirty. (C16i-c), There are many *classes / clashes* at that school. (C16m-A/a), He has it on a *lease / leash*. (C16f-A/a)

Other Words

Many, if not all, of the words listed below are in the story. Find them and circle or underline them each time they occur. Say each marked word aloud—individually and then in its entire sentence. Look for additional words in the story that contain the target sounds. Mark and say them also.

[s] **s**ister, **s**everal, **s**ends, **s**ervice, **s**low, **s**tuff, **s**ix

[ʃ] **Sh**irley, **sh**e, **sh**arp, **sh**elves, **sh**ock, **sh**eet

Other Practice Activities

❑ Partner Cards—Listening. *Practice until you can point to the right card every time.*
❑ Partner Cards—Speaking. *Practice until you can say the contrasting sentences so accurately that your partner points to the right card every time.*
❑ Story Reading. *Practice reading the story aloud. Mark any difficult words. Then record the story on tape.*
❑ Story Dictation. *Write the story as your teacher reads it or as you listen to it on the audiotape.*
❑ Cloze Reading. *Choose some key words in the story and black them out. Then read the entire story aloud. Do this several times.*

Each time black out more words. Continue until most of the story is blacked out and you can tell it without looking at the page very often.
❑ Story Retelling from Skeleton. *Black out all the remaining words except those you need in order to remind you of the story line. Then, using just this skeleton, tell the story to your partner or class.*
❑ Free Story Retelling. *Retell the whole story from memory, without looking at your book.*
❑ Parallel Story. *Create your own story similar to the one in this unit.*
❑ Mini-drama. *Make up a skit or do a role play based on the story.*

Unit C16m-A [s] classes—[ʃ] clashes

Story

My mother is a substitute teacher at a large high school. There are many (1) **classes** at the school, so my mother teaches a different class almost every day. Some days she teaches chemistry; another day it's girls' basketball or maybe social studies. Some

[#1] Chemistry
Russian
Social Studies
Auto Shop

days she even has to cover classes in Russian or auto shop. She enjoys her work, but sometimes she wishes there wasn't quite so much variety.

With so many classes and students, it's hard to get to know all the students. One of her big challenges is classroom management. But there are even bigger problems outside of the classroom. There are quite a few gangs and groups of students that don't get along. Students from different groups often trade insults, begin shouting at each other, start pushing, and end up fighting right in the hall. Because there are so many (2) **clashes** among the students, the school has hired security officers to patrol the halls.

Sometimes it worries me that my mother works there. What if there were a fight when the security officers weren't around? My mother might get caught in the middle and be hurt.

Contrasting Sentences

❏ There are many _____ at that school. (courses)

❏ There are many _____ at that school. (fights)

Additional Practice

Can you *sip/ship* it quickly? (C16i-A/a), Look at that *sack/shack*. (C16i-b), This *seat/sheet* is dirty. (C16i-c), He has it on a *lease/leash*. (C16f-A/a)

Other Words

[s] substitute, chemistry, basketball, classroom, officers

[ʃ] Russian, social, wishes, pushing, fashion, shout

Other Practice Activities

- ❏ Partner Cards—Listening.
- ❏ Partner Cards—Speaking.
- ❏ Story Reading.
- ❏ Story Dictation.
- ❏ Cloze Reading.
- ❏ Story Retelling from Skeleton.
- ❏ Free Story Retelling.
- ❏ Parallel Story.
- ❏ Mini-drama.

Unit C16f-A [s] lease—[ʃ] leash

Story

My neighbor Mr. Parish likes to show off. He drives a very expensive car, and he lives in the biggest house in town. He's always talking about his trips to Paris and a book he's going to publish about his world travels. He thinks everyone admires him. Some people do. They think he's rich, but he really isn't. Those people would be astonished to learn that Mr. Parish is all show and no substance. The reality is that he's deeply in debt. He's quite foolish with his money, and he owns almost nothing. He has his car on a (1) **lease,** and he rents his house. Even the fancy clothes he wears are often borrowed.

About the only valuable thing Mr. Parish really owns is his dog. It's a special, rare breed, and he's very proud of it. Maybe that's why he takes his dog for a walk on its fancy **leash** (2) twice a day. It's one more way for him to show off and make people think he is rich.

Contrasting Sentences

❏ He has it on a _____. (the car)

❏ He has it on a _____. (the dog)

Additional Practice

Can you *sip/ship* it quickly? (C16i-A/a), Look at that *sack/shack*. (C16i-b), This *seat/sheet* is dirty. (C16i-c), There are many *classes/clashes* at that school. (C16m-A/a)

Other Words

[s] like**s**, hou**s**e, trip**s**, think**s**, sub**s**tan**c**e, rent**s**

[ʃ] Pari**sh**, publi**sh**, fooli**sh**, astoni**sh**, wa**sh**, refre**sh**

Other Practice Activities

❏ Partner Cards—Listening.
❏ Partner Cards—Speaking.
❏ Story Reading.
❏ Story Dictation.
❏ Cloze Reading.

❏ Story Retelling
   from Skeleton.
❏ Free Story Retelling.
❏ Parallel Story.
❏ Mini-drama.

Unit C17m-A [ʃ] dilution—[ʒ] delusion

Story

Listen to the story as your teacher reads it, or on tape, until you understand the main ideas.

Many people are very health conscious. They exercise faithfully, get plenty of rest, and eat only nutritious foods. Some even take special dietary supplements. Natural supplements are growing in popularity. They usually contain herbs, acids, and minerals— unusual things like licorice root, benzoic acid, and chromium. Some of the herbs are native to America; others come from Asia or even Polynesia.

Because of their exotic ingredients, these supplements are expensive. Many people, however, are willing to pay any price for good health. Besides, a small bottle of the supplement solution lasts a long time because users take just a few drops per day mixed in a glass of water. It's only a weak (1) **dilution.**

#1

Other people argue that these supplements are really poison. Taken in strong doses, they can actually harm the user's health or even cause death. These people say that users' claims of better health are a (2) **delusion.** They insist that any benefits are purely psychological.

#2

Obviously, there is a lot of confusion and contention on this topic.

Contrasting Sentences

Listening: Write the appropriate key word in each blank. Later, as you hear each sentence, mark the box, point to the picture, make a gesture, and/or say the rejoinder. Speaking: Choose and say each sentence so that your listener(s) can respond correctly.

❏ It's only a _____. (thin liquid)

❏ It's only a _____. (false belief)

Explanations and diagrams for this unit's target sounds are on pages 343–44 in Section 10.

Additional Practice

That's a good *mesher/measure.* (C17m-b)

For [ʃ]: Can you *sip/ship* it quickly? (C16i-A/a), Look at that *sack/shack.* (C16i-b), This *seat/sheet* is dirty. (C16i-c), There are many *classes/clashes* at that school. (C16m-A/a), He has it on a *lease/leash.* (C16f-A/a)

Other Words

Many, if not all, of the words listed below are in the story. Find them and circle or underline them each time they occur. Say each marked word aloud—individually and then in its entire sentence. Look for additional words in the story that contain the target sounds. Mark and say them also.

[ʃ] con**s**cious, nutri**ti**ous, spe**ci**al, licori**c**e, solu**ti**on, conten**ti**on

[ʒ] u**s**ually, unu**s**ual, A**s**ia, Polyne**s**ia, confu**s**ion, trea**s**ure

Other Practice Activities

❏ Partner Cards—Listening. *Practice until you can point to the right card every time.*

❏ Partner Cards—Speaking. *Practice until you can say the contrasting sentences so accurately that your partner points to the right card every time.*

❏ Story Reading. *Practice reading the story aloud. Mark any difficult words. Then record the story on tape.*

❏ Story Dictation. *Write the story as your teacher reads it or as you listen to it on the audiotape.*

❏ Cloze Reading. *Choose some key words in the story and black them out. Then read the entire story aloud. Do this several times.*

Each time black out more words. Continue until most of the story is blacked out and you can tell it without looking at the page very often.

❏ Story Retelling from Skeleton. *Black out all the remaining words except those you need in order to remind you of the story line. Then, using just this skeleton, tell the story to your partner or class.*

❏ Free Story Retelling. *Retell the whole story from memory, without looking at your book.*

❏ Parallel Story. *Create your own story similar to the one in this unit.*

❏ Mini-drama. *Make up a skit or do a role play based on the story.*

Unit C18i-A [ʃ] shin—[tʃ] chin

Story

Listen to the story as your teacher reads it, or on tape, until you understand the main ideas.

Sherman loves to ride his bike, but for two weeks he has not been able to. Here's why. A couple of weeks ago, while riding his bike, he started showing off for his friends. At that moment, he hit a rock in the road. He lost control of his bike, fell on a sharp rock, and cut his (1) **chin.** It was a bad cut, and he needed five stitches. This accident shook him up a little, but he didn't shed any tears. In fact, he was ready to get back on his bike immediately. The doctor, however, told Sherman to take it easy and not ride his bike for two weeks while the cut healed.

But Sherman chose not to listen to the doctor. He didn't want to change. The next day, he ran outside and jumped on his bike. In his hurry, he didn't see the lawn chair someone had left in the driveway. His leg slammed into the chair, and he fell again. This time his (2) **shin** was hurt. Sherman slowly limped back to his house, put his bike away, and stayed off it for two weeks just as the doctor ordered.

Contrasting Sentences

Listening: Write the appropriate key word in each blank. Later, as you hear each sentence, mark the box, point to the picture, make a gesture, and/or say the rejoinder. Speaking: Choose and say each sentence so that your listener(s) can respond correctly.

❏ He hurt his _____ when he fell. (bottom of his face)

❏ He hurt his _____ when he fell. (front of his leg)

Explanations and diagrams for this unit's target sounds are on pages 343–44 and 345 in Section 10.

Additional Practice

Sherry *shows/chose* her software at conventions. (C18i-B/b), Richard *washes/watches* cars. (C18m-A/a), The captain made sure the chests were *lashed/latched*. (C18f-A/a)

Other Words

Many, if not all, of the words listed below are in the story. Find them and circle or underline them each time they occur. Say each marked word aloud—individually and then in its entire sentence. Look for additional words in the story that contain the target sounds. Mark and say them also.

[ʃ] **Sh**erman, **sh**owing, **sh**arp, **sh**ook, **sh**ed, **sh**ame

[tʃ] **ch**ose, **ch**air, **ch**ange, **ch**allenge, **ch**icken, stit**ch**es

Other Practice Activities

❏ Partner Cards—Listening. *Practice until you can point to the right card every time.*
❏ Partner Cards—Speaking. *Practice until you can say the contrasting sentences so accurately that your partner points to the right card every time.*
❏ Story Reading. *Practice reading the story aloud. Mark any difficult words. Then record the story on tape.*
❏ Story Dictation. *Write the story as your teacher reads it or as you listen to it on the audiotape.*
❏ Cloze Reading. *Choose some key words in the story and black them out. Then read the entire story aloud. Do this several times.*

Each time black out more words. Continue until most of the story is blacked out and you can tell it without looking at the page very often.
❏ Story Retelling from Skeleton. *Black out all the remaining words except those you need in order to remind you of the story line. Then, using just this skeleton, tell the story to your partner or class.*
❏ Free Story Retelling. *Retell the whole story from memory, without looking at your book.*
❏ Parallel Story. *Create your own story similar to the one in this unit.*
❏ Mini-drama. *Make up a skit or do a role play based on the story.*

Unit C18i-B [ʃ] shows—[tʃ] chose

Story

Sherry is a computer whiz. She writes her own programs, and she also buys a lot of computer software. Software is not cheap, and Sherry is very choosy. To make sure she is getting what she wants, Sherry prefers to see software in operation before she buys it. You can't do that in most computer stores or by mail. For that reason, she went to several computer conventions last year and shopped for software there. She was glad that she did. At the conventions, she checked a lot of software that she had read about. Many of the programs did not perform as well as she expected they would. After seeing everything firsthand, she (1) **chose** only the best software.

At the conventions, Sherry realized two things. First, there is a real need for quality software. Second, she can write computer programs as well as other people can. Therefore, Sherry has started her own business. She now writes software and sells it. She even goes to computer conventions and (2) **shows** her products. She likes to demonstrate them to people because she enjoys the challenge of explaining and selling her creations. Chatting with customers also gives her ideas for making changes in her software or creating new products.

Contrasting Sentences

❑ Sherry _____ her software at conventions. (selected)

❑ Sherry _____ her software at conventions. (demonstrates)

Additional Practice

He hurt his *shin/chin* when he fell. (C18i-A/a), Richard *washes/watches* cars. (C18m-A/a), The captain made sure the chests were *lashed/latched*. (C18f-A/a)

Other Words

[ʃ] **Sh**erry, **sh**e, **s**ure, **sh**opped, **sh**are, crea**ti**ons

[tʃ] **ch**eap, **ch**oosy, **ch**ecked, **ch**allenge, **ch**atting, **ch**anges

Other Practice Activities

❑ Partner Cards—Listening.
❑ Partner Cards—Speaking.
❑ Story Reading.
❑ Story Dictation.
❑ Cloze Reading.

❑ Story Retelling
   from Skeleton.
❑ Free Story Retelling.
❑ Parallel Story.
❑ Mini-drama.

Unit C18m-A [ʃ] washes— [tʃ] watches

Story

Richard loves all kinds of cars, but his big dream is to become a race car driver. He spends every weekend at the racetrack catching as many races as he can. Sometimes it's hard to see the cars from the stand, so he always brings his binoculars. Through them he (1) **watches** all the action and sees everything clearly. He cheers for his favorite cars and drivers and wishes he were down there on the track himself.

Because it costs money to watch the races, Richard works after school to earn cash to pay for his admission to the track. He used to wash dishes in a restaurant, but recently he switched jobs. Now he makes his money a different way. He works for a used car dealer and (2) **washes** cars. Strange as it may seem, he loves to wash cars because he thinks it's fun work. He enjoys squirting water from the hose, and he likes to see the cars shine when he's done. One day he would like to combine his two loves and have his own race car washing business. I think he is car crazy. Don't you?

Contrasting Sentences

❑ Richard _____ cars. (with binoculars)

❑ Richard _____ cars. (with a hose)

Additional Practice

He hurt his *shin/chin* when he fell. (C18i-A/a), Sherry *shows/chose* her software at conventions. (C18i-B/b), The captain made sure the chests were *lashed/latched*. (C18f-A/a)

Other Words

[ʃ] ac**ti**on, admi**ss**ion, wi**sh**es, di**sh**es, ca**sh**ier, swi**sh**ing

[tʃ] Ri**ch**ard, ca**tch**ing, swi**tch**ed, ca**tch**er, ma**tch**es, mar**ch**ing

Other Practice Activities

❑ Partner Cards—Listening.
❑ Partner Cards—Speaking.
❑ Story Reading.
❑ Story Dictation.
❑ Cloze Reading.

❑ Story Retelling
   from Skeleton.
❑ Free Story Retelling.
❑ Parallel Story.
❑ Mini-drama.

Unit C18f-A [ʃ] lash—[tʃ] latch

Story

Many years ago, a shipful of English pirates attacked a Spanish ship, captured the rich passengers, and took three large chests full of gold and jewels. They put those treasure chests on the deck of their ship, but the pirate captain was afraid that some of his men might take treasure from the chests when no one was looking. So he made certain that the chests were (1) **latched** securely. Then he locked them with three large padlocks. He put the only keys in a pouch he wore around his neck.

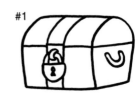

#1

The captain thought his treasure was safe until he noticed a big storm approaching. The waves were getting bigger. The captain was afraid the chests might wash overboard in the storm, but there was no time to carry them down into the ship. "Fetch some ropes," he ordered. With them, his men (2) **lashed** the heavy chests to the deck. Then they went below while the

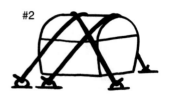

#2

storm passed. In the morning, they were astonished. The chests were gone. In their places were three silvery fish. "Search the ship!" ordered the captain, but the chests were nowhere to be found. It was a great mystery. What do you think happened?

Contrasting Sentences

❏ The captain made sure the chests were _____ . (closed)

❏ The captain made sure the chests were _____ . (to the deck)

Additional Practice

He hurt his *shin/chin* when he fell. (C18i-A/a), Sherry *shows/chose* her software at conventions. (C18i-B/b), Richard *washes/watches* cars. (C18m-A/a)

Other Words

[ʃ] Engli**sh**, Spani**sh**, wa**sh**, astoni**sh**, fi**sh**, fre**sh**

[tʃ] ri**ch**, pou**ch**, approa**ch**ing, fe**tch**, capture, sear**ch**

Other Practice Activities

❏ Partner Cards—Listening.
❏ Partner Cards—Speaking.
❏ Story Reading.
❏ Story Dictation.
❏ Cloze Reading.

❏ Story Retelling from Skeleton.
❏ Free Story Retelling.
❏ Parallel Story.
❏ Mini-drama.

Unit C19i-A [tʃ] choking—[dʒ] joking

Story

Listen to the story as your teacher reads it, or on tape, until you understand the main ideas.

My friend John likes to fool people. When I introduced my sister to him, he pretended he didn't understand English well. So she talked to him very slowly and clearly. I couldn't help bursting into laughter. "He's just (1) **joking**," I chuckled. "He speaks perfect English."

My sister was embarrassed and angry. "What a jerk!" she said.

"Sorry," John apologized, smiling. "To make up for the joke, I'll buy you a cup of coffee." We all went to a coffee shop and had coffee and chocolate chip cookies.

While we were chatting, John started to cough, and his face turned red. "Oh, no! He's (2) **choking**!" I shouted. I jumped up and patted his back.

"I won't fall for that, you jolly jester," said my sister. "You can't fool me twice in one day."

"He's serious," I insisted. "Pass me the water." After drinking some water, John swallowed what was stuck in his throat.

"You'd better stop fooling people. You won't be taken seriously," chastened my sister.

John the joker may have finally learned his lesson. Maybe he will change and stop joking so much.

Contrasting Sentences

Listening: Write the appropriate key word in each blank. Later, as you hear each sentence, mark the box, point to the picture, make a gesture, and/or say the rejoinder. Speaking: Choose and say each sentence so that your listener(s) can respond correctly.

❏ He's _____. (He needs some water.)

❏ He's _____. (He really speaks English.)

Explanations and diagrams for this unit's target sounds are on pages 345–46 in Section 10.

Additional Practice

She's *cheering/jeering.* (C19i-b), The *etching/edging* looked great. (C19m-A/a), Everyone needs to make and bring a *batch/badge.* (C19f-A/a)

Other Words

Many, if not all, of the words listed below are in the story. Find them and circle or underline them each time they occur. Say each marked word aloud—individually and then in its entire sentence. Look for additional words in the story that contain the target sounds. Mark and say them also.

[tʃ] **ch**uckled, **ch**ocolate, **ch**ip, **ch**atting, **ch**astened, **ch**ange

[dʒ] **J**ohn, **j**ust, **j**erk, **j**umped, **j**olly, **j**ester

Other Practice Activities

❏ Partner Cards—Listening. *Practice until you can point to the right card every time.*
❏ Partner Cards—Speaking. *Practice until you can say the contrasting sentences so accurately that your partner points to the right card every time.*
❏ Story Reading. *Practice reading the story aloud. Mark any difficult words. Then record the story on tape.*
❏ Story Dictation. *Write the story as your teacher reads it or as you listen to it on the audiotape.*
❏ Cloze Reading. *Choose some key words in the story and black them out. Then read the entire story aloud. Do this several times.*

Each time black out more words. Continue until most of the story is blacked out and you can tell it without looking at the page very often.
❏ Story Retelling from Skeleton. *Black out all the remaining words except those you need in order to remind you of the story line. Then, using just this skeleton, tell the story to your partner or class.*
❏ Free Story Retelling. *Retell the whole story from memory, without looking at your book.*
❏ Parallel Story. *Create your own story similar to the one in this unit.*
❏ Mini-drama. *Make up a skit or do a role play based on the story.*

Unit C19m-A [tʃ] etching—[dʒ] edging

Story

Mike does the maintenance work around the Ridge Realty office building, and he certainly earns his wages. He can fix just about anything. In addition, he's a fantastic gardener and artist. For example, when we wanted to put the name of our company on the door of our building, he volunteered to (1) etch the name into the glass. I don't have any idea how he did it. I imagine he used acid or something. I wish I had watched him. Someday maybe I can get him to teach me. However Mike did it, the **etching** looks great. Now, anyone searching for our office will be impressed when they see the name on the door.

The great-looking door encouraged Mike to make other improvements outside the entrance to our building. He made the flower bed larger, and he neatly (2) edged the lawn along the sidewalk. The flowers added color, and the **edging** looked great. It was the finishing touch. Mike's good work really adds to our company's image.

Contrasting Sentences

❏ The _____ looked great. (the name on the glass)

❏ The _____ looked great. (the border of the lawn)

Additional Practice

He's *choking / joking.* (C19i-A/a), She's *cheering / jeering.* (C19i-b), Everyone needs to make and bring a *batch / badge.* (C19f-A/a)

Other Words

[tʃ] wat**ch**ed, sear**ch**ing, tea**ch**er, ar**ch**ing, ri**ch**es, mar**ch**ed

[dʒ] Ri**dg**e, wa**g**es, ima**g**ine, encoura**g**ed, lar**g**er, coura**g**eous

Other Practice Activities

- ❏ Partner Cards—Listening.
- ❏ Partner Cards—Speaking.
- ❏ Story Reading.
- ❏ Story Dictation.
- ❏ Cloze Reading.
- ❏ Story Retelling from Skeleton.
- ❏ Free Story Retelling.
- ❏ Parallel Story.
- ❏ Mini-drama.

Unit C19f-A [tʃ] batch—[dʒ] badge

Story

My school is large, so it's hard to get to know everyone. At the start of the school year, our grade has a special way of helping people get to know each other. We have a big after-school party, and everyone in the grade is invited. There are only two requirements for admission.

First, everyone must make and wear a name (1) **badge.** Besides the person's name, the badge should show or tell something special about him or her. For example, if someone is interested in drama, the badge could have a picture of a stage on it. These badges really encourage conversation. It doesn't take much courage to talk to someone about the picture on his or her badge.

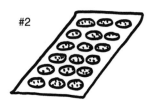

The other requirement is that everyone must make and bring (2) a **batch** of their favorite cookies. Each time you talk to a new person, you give that person one of your cookies. The refreshments are very rich, but we don't mind. It's fun to watch everyone walking around, talking, making new friends, and eating cookies.

Contrasting Sentences

- ❏ Everyone needs to make and bring a _____. (that tells something about them)

- ❏ Everyone needs to make and bring a _____. (of cookies)

Additional Practice

He's *choking / joking*. (C19i-A/a), She's *cheering / jeering*. (C19i-b),
The *etching / edging* looked great. (C19m-A/a)

Other Words

[tʃ] ea**ch**, ri**ch**, wat**ch**, sear**ch**, bran**ch**, cat**ch**

[dʒ] lar**ge**, sta**ge**, encoura**ge**, coura**ge**, a**ge**, bri**dge**

Other Practice Activities

❏ Partner Cards—Listening.
❏ Partner Cards—Speaking.
❏ Story Reading.
❏ Story Dictation.
❏ Cloze Reading.

❏ Story Retelling
   from Skeleton.
❏ Free Story Retelling.
❏ Parallel Story.
❏ Mini-drama.

Unit C20i-A [dʒ] jail—[y] Yale

Story

Listen to the story as your teacher reads it, or on tape, until you understand the main ideas.

From the day he started kindergarten, Jeff was always a good student. He worked hard, did his homework, and learned a lot. As a result, he got high scores on his tests and excellent grades. When he finished high school, he was at the head of his class. It was no surprise that he got a great scholarship and went to (1) **Yale.** He hasn't graduated yet, but he will soon.

Jesse was Jeff's twin brother. On the outside, Jesse looked a lot like Jeff, but inside he was totally different. Maybe he was jealous of his brother. Maybe he was just rebellious. Instead of studying, he joked around in school. He did poorly and got bad grades. Every year he got worse. When he was just thirteen, he ended up in juvenile court. In high school, he failed many classes. He chose friends who were a bad influence on him, and they started him on a life of crime. He dropped out of high school and started using illegal drugs. Eventually, he became a junkie. Later, he was arrested for armed robbery. When the jury convicted him, the judge sent him to (2) **jail.** He's still there.

Contrasting Sentences

Listening: Write the appropriate key word in each blank. Later, as you hear each sentence, mark the box, point to the picture, make a gesture, and/or say the rejoinder. Speaking: Choose and say each sentence so that your listener(s) can respond correctly.

❏ He went to _____. (university)

❏ He went to _____. (prison)

Explanations and diagrams for this unit's target sounds are on pages 345–46 in Section 10.

Additional Practice

Please pass the *jam/yam.* (C20i-B/b), *I like Jell-O/yellow.* (C20i-c)

Other Words

Many, if not all, of the words listed below are in the story. Find them and circle or underline them each time they occur. Say each marked word aloud—individually and then in its entire sentence. Look for additional words in the story that contain the target sounds. Mark and say them also.

[dʒ] **j**ealous, **j**oked, **j**uvenile, **j**unkie, **j**ury, **j**udge

[y] **Y**ale, **y**ear, **y**et, **y**awn, **y**ou, **y**es

Other Practice Activities

❏ Partner Cards—Listening. *Practice until you can point to the right card every time.*
❏ Partner Cards—Speaking. *Practice until you can say the contrasting sentences so accurately that your partner points to the right card every time.*
❏ Story Reading. *Practice reading the story aloud. Mark any difficult words. Then record the story on tape.*
❏ Story Dictation. *Write the story as your teacher reads it or as you listen to it on the audiotape.*
❏ Cloze Reading. *Choose some key words in the story and black them out. Then read the entire story aloud. Do this several times.*

Each time black out more words. Continue until most of the story is blacked out and you can tell it without looking at the page very often.
❏ Story Retelling from Skeleton. *Black out all the remaining words except those you need in order to remind you of the story line. Then, using just this skeleton, tell the story to your partner or class.*
❏ Free Story Retelling. *Retell the whole story from memory, without looking at your book.*
❏ Parallel Story. *Create your own story similar to the one in this unit.*
❏ Mini-drama. *Make up a skit or do a role play based on the story.*

Unit C20i-B [dʒ] jam—[y] yam

Story

Thanksgiving is a popular holiday in the United States and Canada. It is a day to give thanks for blessings received during the year. That tradition began with the Pilgrims in New England in 1621.

Today, Americans celebrate Thanksgiving by eating a big meal with their family or friends. Usually people eat roast turkey with stuffing, mashed potatoes, rolls, and (1) **yams** (sweet potatoes). To make the food taste extra good there are cranberry sauce to go with the turkey, gravy for the mashed potatoes, and (2) **jam** for the rolls.

Everyone sits around the table loaded with food and asks others to pass the things they cannot reach themselves. At a Thanksgiving dinner table you will hear a lot of sentences beginning with "Please pass the…" You will also hear a lot of jokes and stories. Thanksgiving is a joyful time.

Even though there is a lot of food on the table at the start of the meal, everyone eats a lot. By the end there may be just one roll, one yam, or one serving of stuffing left. When they can eat no more, people spend the rest of the day sleeping, talking, or watching football on television.

Contrasting Sentences

❑ Please pass the _____. (the last sweet potato)

❑ Please pass the _____. (to put on a roll)

Additional Practice

He went to *jail/Yale.* (C20i-A/a), I like *Jell-O/yellow.* (C20i-c)

Other Words

[dʒ] **j**okes, **j**oyful, **j**ust, **j**ealous, **j**elly, **j**oin

[y] **y**ear, **U**nited, **u**sually, **y**ou, **y**awn, **y**et

Other Practice Activities

❑ Partner Cards—Listening.
❑ Partner Cards—Speaking.
❑ Story Reading.
❑ Story Dictation.
❑ Cloze Reading.

❑ Story Retelling from Skeleton.
❑ Free Story Retelling.
❑ Parallel Story.
❑ Mini-drama.

Unit C21i-A [yiy] yeast—[iy] east

Story

Listen to the story as your teacher reads it, or on tape, until you understand the main ideas.

Yesterday my friends and I were at my home. We were playing a fun game, but we started feeling hungry and finally decided to yield to our hunger. We went to the kitchen to see what we could find. Unfortunately, the refrigerator and cupboards were almost empty. There was nothing that was ready to eat. We did find some yeast, spices, flour, and a few cans of fruit, but that was about it.

When she saw those things, Eva suggested that we make pita bread. Some of the others didn't know what pita bread was, so Eva explained that it was pocket bread, a bread often made in (1) the Middle **East.** Her family made it several times a year, so she knew the recipe. Everyone said, "Yes, that sounds good. Let's try it."

The pita bread was quick and easy to make. All we needed was flour, salt, water and (2) **yeast.** It was delicious.

Contrasting Sentences

Listening: Write the appropriate key word in each blank. Later, as you hear each sentence, mark the box, point to the picture, make a gesture, and/or say the rejoinder. Speaking: Choose and say each sentence so that your listener(s) can respond correctly.

❑ Let's make bread from the _____. (Middle East)

❑ Let's make bread from the _____. (in the package)

Explanations and diagrams for this unit's target sounds are on pages 331 and 346 in Section 10.

Additional Practice

This *year/ear* seems longer than normal (C21i-b)

Other Words

Many, if not all, of the words listed below are in the story. Find them and circle or underline them each time they occur. Say each marked word aloud—individually and then in its entire sentence. Look for additional words in the story that contain the target sounds. Mark and say them also.

[yiy] **yie**ld, **ye**ar, **ye**

[iy] **ea**t, **E**va, **ea**r

Other Practice Activities

❏ Partner Cards—Listening. *Practice until you can point to the right card every time.*

❏ Partner Cards—Speaking. *Practice until you can say the contrasting sentences so accurately that your partner points to the right card every time.*

❏ Story Reading. *Practice reading the story aloud. Mark any difficult words. Then record the story on tape.*

❏ Story Dictation. *Write the story as your teacher reads it or as you listen to it on the audiotape.*

❏ Cloze Reading. *Choose some key words in the story and black them out. Then read the entire story aloud. Do this several times.*

Each time black out more words. Continue until most of the story is blacked out and you can tell it without looking at the page very often.

❏ Story Retelling from Skeleton. *Black out all the remaining words except those you need in order to remind you of the story line. Then, using just this skeleton, tell the story to your partner or class.*

❏ Free Story Retelling. *Retell the whole story from memory, without looking at your book.*

❏ Parallel Story. *Create your own story similar to the one in this unit.*

❏ Mini-drama. *Make up a skit or do a role play based on the story.*

Unit C22i-A [k] coat—[g] goat

Story

Listen to the story as your teacher reads it, or on tape, until you understand the main ideas.

My uncle and cousins live in the country. They have a large garden and quite a few farm animals. They have a few sheep, a cow, and some goats. They keep the animals in a small barn. There's not a lot of room, but every spring they get a few more animals. This year my uncle got a new (1) **goat** and two new sheep.

#1

There is no heating in the barn, and it gets cold in the winter. The animals' body heat keeps it a little warmer inside than it is outside but not much. Sometimes my cousins have to break the ice in the water troughs so the animals can drink. No matter how cold it gets, my uncle and cousins have to get up early every morning to take care of the animals. I asked my uncle if he ever wanted to stay in bed on the mornings when it was cold. He said that since he got his new (2) **coat** for Christmas he never got cold anymore. He was glad for that, but it was still hard to get up early and go out to the barn in the dark.

#2

Contrasting Sentences

Listening: Write the appropriate key word in each blank. Later, as you hear each sentence, mark the box, point to the picture, make a gesture, and/or say the rejoinder. Speaking: Choose and say each sentence so that your listener(s) can respond correctly.

❑ My uncle has a new _____. (He has to feed it every day.)

❑ My uncle has a new _____. (It keeps him warm.)

Explanations and diagrams for this unit's target sounds are on pages 346–48 in Section 10.

Additional Practice

They looked at the *coast/ghost.* (C22i-b), She's very *picky/piggy.* (C22m-A/a), We needed a *tack/tag* for each picture. (C22f-A/a), Don't do that. You're going to break my *back/bag.* (C22f-B/b), This *dock/dog* is old. (C22f-c), Look at that *buck/bug!* (C22f-d), That's my *pick/pig.* (C22f-e)

Other Words

Many, if not all, of the words listed below are in the story. Find them and circle or underline them each time they occur. Say each marked word aloud—individually and then in its entire sentence. Look for additional words in the story that contain the target sounds. Mark and say them also.

[k] **c**ousins, **c**ountry, **qu**ite, **k**eep, **c**ow, **c**old

[g] **g**arden, **g**et, **g**ot, **g**lad, **g**o, **g**ame

Other Practice Activities

❑ Partner Cards—Listening. *Practice until you can point to the right card every time.*

❑ Partner Cards—Speaking. *Practice until you can say the contrasting sentences so accurately that your partner points to the right card every time.*

❑ Story Reading. *Practice reading the story aloud. Mark any difficult words. Then record the story on tape.*

❑ Story Dictation. *Write the story as your teacher reads it or as you listen to it on the audiotape.*

❑ Cloze Reading. *Choose some key words in the story and black them out. Then read the entire story aloud. Do this several times.*

Each time black out more words. Continue until most of the story is blacked out and you can tell it without looking at the page very often.

❑ Story Retelling from Skeleton. *Black out all the remaining words except those you need in order to remind you of the story line. Then, using just this skeleton, tell the story to your partner or class.*

❑ Free Story Retelling. *Retell the whole story from memory, without looking at your book.*

❑ Parallel Story. *Create your own story similar to the one in this unit.*

❑ Mini-drama. *Make up a skit or do a role play based on the story.*

Unit C22m-A [k] picky—[g] piggy

Story

Megan has been looking for a roommate, but she's been having a hard time finding a good one. According to Megan, her new roommate has to be quiet, neat, nonsmoking, and responsible. Her friends say she's very (1) **picky.** They think she'll never find such perfection in a roommate, especially considering the type of person Megan is.

#1

What kind of person is Megan? "Well," says one of her friends, "She's OK, but she has one big, ugly problem. She's very (2) **piggy.** In other words, she's messy and leaves her things all over the place. Picking them up never occurs to her. That makes it difficult for anyone to live with Megan. But an even bigger problem is that when Megan sees someone eating something, she wants to eat it, too. Not just a bite. She actually wants the whole thing." Do you know anyone who would like to live with her?

Contrasting Sentences

❑ She's very _____. (She wants perfection.)

❑ She's very _____. (She leaves things messy.)

Additional Practice

My uncle has a new *coat/goat.* (C22i-A/a), They looked at the *coast/ghost.* (C22i-b), We needed a *tack/tag* for each picture. (C22f-A/a), Don't do that. You're going to break my *back/bag.* (C22f-B/b), This *dock/dog* is old. (C22f-c), Look at that *buck/bug!* (C22f-d), That's my *pick/pig.* (C22f-e)

Other Words

[k] looking, according, smoking, perfection, actually, difficult

[g] Megan, ugly, bigger, degree, regain, plugging

Other Practice Activities

❑ Partner Cards—Listening.
❑ Partner Cards—Speaking.
❑ Story Reading.
❑ Story Dictation.
❑ Cloze Reading.

❑ Story Retelling from Skeleton.
❑ Free Story Retelling.
❑ Parallel Story.
❑ Mini-drama.

Unit C22f-A [k] tack—[g] tag

Story

My friend Greg is a fantastic artist. He draws a lot of beautiful pictures with pencil and charcoal. He also sells a lot of them. Last week he had a one-man show at a gallery in town, and I helped him get everything ready. He had a big stack of pictures to display, so it was a lot of work.

First we decided where to hang each picture on the wall. Then we needed to put a tack in the wall in just the right place. We needed a (1) **tack** for each picture. After that, we hung each picture on its tack.

Then we went around the room and labeled each of Greg's drawings. To do that, we needed a (2) **tag** for each picture. Each tag showed the picture's title and price.

It was such a big show that it took us four hours to hang and tag all the pictures. To show his appreciation, Greg gave me one of his smaller pictures. It was a sketch of a mountain scene with a dog running through a field and a hawk circling in the sky. I love it.

Contrasting Sentences

❏ We needed a _____ for each picture. (to hang it)

❏ We needed a _____ for each picture. (to label it)

Additional Practice

My uncle has a new *coat/goat.* (C22i-A/a), They looked at the *coast/ghost.* (C22i-b), She's very *picky/piggy.* (C22m-A/a), Don't do that. You're going to break my *back/bag.* (C22f-B/b), This *dock/dog* is old. (C22f-c), Look at that *buck/bug!* (C22f-d), That's my *pick/pig.* (C22f-e)

Other Words

[k] fantasti**c**, wee**k**, sta**ck**, wor**k**, too**k**, haw**k**

[g] Gre**g**, bi**g**, do**g**, pe**g**, ri**g**, bu**g**

Other Practice Activities

❏ Partner Cards—Listening.
❏ Partner Cards—Speaking.
❏ Story Reading.
❏ Story Dictation.
❏ Cloze Reading.

❏ Story Retelling
  from Skeleton.
❏ Free Story Retelling.
❏ Parallel Story.
❏ Mini-drama.

Unit C22f-B [k] back—[g] bag

Story

Last summer I took my two little kids to Disneyland. We had a great time even though we spent a lot of our time standing in big lines. At first, the kids had trouble standing still. They couldn't run around or they would lose their places in line, so they climbed all over me. After a while they got tired. Then they wanted me to carry them. They didn't understand that I was tired too. Sometimes I thought they were going to break my (1) **back.**

Around noon, they got very hungry, but we were standing in line so we couldn't go eat. Luckily, I had some snacks in my (2) bag. When I told my kids that there was food in the bag, they grabbed it and started fighting over it. My daughter jerked on one of the straps, and my son pulled on the other one. Neither would let go as they cried and yanked on the straps. "Don't do that," I barked. "You're going to break my **bag.**" Quickly, I opened the bag and gave each child a snack. Then they were happy again—at least for a little while. They hugged my leg and waited patiently.

Contrasting Sentences

❏ Don't do that. You're going to break my _____. (spine)

❏ Don't do that. You're going to break my _____. (purse)

Additional Practice

My uncle has a new *coat*/*goat*. (C22i-A/a), They looked at the *coast*/*ghost*. (C22i-b), She's very *picky*/*piggy*. (C22m-A/a), We needed a *tack*/*tag* for each picture. (C22f-A/a), This *dock*/*dog* is old. (C22f-c), Look at that *buck*/*bug!* (C22f-d), That's my *pick*/*pig*. (C22f-e)

Other Words

[k] too**k**, brea**k**, lu**ck**, sna**ck**, yan**k**, jer**k**

[g] bi**g**, hu**g**, le**g**, ra**g**, lu**g**, fro**g**

Other Practice Activities

❏ Partner Cards—Listening.
❏ Partner Cards—Speaking.
❏ Story Reading.
❏ Story Dictation.
❏ Cloze Reading.

❏ Story Retelling from Skeleton.
❏ Free Story Retelling.
❏ Parallel Story.
❏ Mini-drama.

Section 4

Consonant Clusters (CC)

Unit CC1-A [C + l] glass—[C + r] grass

Story

Listen to the story as your teacher reads it, or on tape, until you understand the main ideas.

Everybody does something different for a living. Glen is glad for any job that allows him to work outside. He likes the freedom and the sunshine outdoors. He especially likes to work on new houses.

When a new home is built, Glen's favorite job is installing (1) **glass** in the windows. He likes windows because they let light into the house and make the inside bright and cheery.

Then he works on the landscaping. He puts in all of the plants—bushes, flowers, trees, and (2) **grass.**

After a new house is finished, Glen tries to drive by it as often as he can in the following months. He enjoys watching people turn the house into a home, and he likes watching the new plants grow. Glen is grateful for the variety in his work and the sense of accomplishment it gives him.

Contrasting Sentences

Listening: Write the appropriate key word in each blank. Later, as you hear each sentence, mark the box, point to the picture, make a gesture, and/or say the rejoinder. Speaking: Choose and say each sentence so that your listener(s) can respond correctly.

❏ Glen puts in _____ for a living. (windows)

❏ Glen puts in _____ for a living. (lawn)

Explanations and diagrams for this unit's target sounds are on pages 341, 342, and 348–49 in Section 10.

Additional Practice

Look at the *clown/crown.* (CC1-B/b), Grace went to *glamour/grammar* school. (CC1-C/c)

Other Words

Many, if not all, of the words listed below are in the story. Find them and circle or underline them each time they occur. Say each marked word aloud—individually and then in its entire sentence. Look for additional words in the story that contain the target sounds. Mark and say them also.

[C + l] **gl**ad, **fl**owers, **pl**ants accom**pl**ishment, **gl**ow, **pl**ay

[C + r] **fr**eedom, **br**ight, **tr**ees, **tr**ies, **dr**ive, **gr**ow

Other Practice Activities

❏ Partner Cards—Listening. *Practice until you can point to the right card every time.*

❏ Partner Cards—Speaking. *Practice until you can say the contrasting sentences so accurately that your partner points to the right card every time.*

❏ Story Reading. *Practice reading the story aloud. Mark any difficult words. Then record the story on tape.*

❏ Story Dictation. *Write the story as your teacher reads it or as you listen to it on the audiotape.*

❏ Cloze Reading. *Choose some key words in the story and black them out. Then read the entire story aloud. Do this several times.*

Each time black out more words. Continue until most of the story is blacked out and you can tell it without looking at the page very often.

❏ Story Retelling from Skeleton. *Black out all the remaining words except those you need in order to remind you of the story line. Then, using just this skeleton, tell the story to your partner or class.*

❏ Free Story Retelling. *Retell the whole story from memory, without looking at your book.*

❏ Parallel Story. *Create your own story similar to the one in this unit.*

❏ Mini-drama. *Make up a skit or do a role play based on the story.*

Unit CC1-B [C + l] clown—[C + r] crown

Story

I went to the city with my friend Chris the other day. We went to the circus together. It wasn't a great circus, but we had a good time anyway. The circus had food, rides, shows, and a lot of fun things. Once, we saw a crowd laughing, and we went to see what was making them laugh. It was a (1) **clown** performing tricks. He was very funny, and we laughed hard.

After that, we went into a large trailer that was advertised as the "French Royal Collection." Inside, it was like a small museum. "Look at this!" said Chris. According to a sign, it was a (2) **crown** that had belonged to one of the French kings. It was very beautiful although I'm not convinced it was authentic.

At the end of the day, we were both happy we had gone to the circus. We had seen funny things, and we had seen beautiful things.

Contrasting Sentences

❑ Look at the _____. (He's funny.)

❑ Look at the _____. (It's beautiful.)

Additional Practice

Glen puts in *glass/grass* for a living. (CC1-A/a), Grace went to *glamour/grammar* school. (CC1-C/c)

Other Words

[C + l] **gl**ad, **bl**ow, **gl**ass, **gl**ow, **bl**eed

[C + r] **fr**iend, **Chr**is, **gr**eat, **cr**owd, **tr**ailer, **Fr**ench

Other Practice Activities

❑ Partner Cards—Listening.
❑ Partner Cards—Speaking.
❑ Story Reading.
❑ Story Dictation.
❑ Cloze Reading.

❑ Story Retelling from Skeleton.
❑ Free Story Retelling.
❑ Parallel Story.
❑ Mini-drama.

Unit CC1-C [l] [C + l] glamour—
[C + r] grammar

Story

Some people are naturally elegant and beautiful. Despite her name, Grace was not one of those people. Still, she desperately wanted to be graceful and glamorous. She dreamed of dressing up in expensive clothes, going to plays and the opera, eating in fancy restaurants, and impressing people. The main problem was not lack of money; Grace's family was rich. The problem was that Grace was a klutz, a clumsy person. No matter what she wore, she couldn't look glamorous because of the way she walked and acted. So, she went to a (1) special school where she could learn to act graceful and charming.

#1

Grace learned a lot in **glamour** school, but it wasn't enough. Even though she knew how to look and act glamorous, she didn't know how to speak properly. The minute she opened her mouth to talk, it was obvious that she was not as cultured as she looked. For example, the subjects and verbs in her sentences frequently didn't agree. She would say, "We is happy" instead of "We are happy." So she went to a (2) **grammar** school where she could learn to speak properly. Once Grace's grammar improved, her dream of being glamorous came true.

#2

Contrasting Sentences

❏ Grace went to a _____ school. (and learned to act glamorous)

❏ Grace went to a _____ school. (and learned to speak properly)

Additional Practice

Glen puts in *glass/grass* for a living. (CC1-A/a), Look at the *clown/crown*. (CC1-B/b)

Other Words

[C + l] **gl**amorous, **cl**othes, **pl**ays, pro**bl**em, **kl**utz, **cl**umsy

[C + r] **gr**aceful, **dr**essing, imp**r**ess, p**r**oblem, p**r**operly, **fr**equently

Other Practice Activities

❏ Partner Cards—Listening.
❏ Partner Cards—Speaking.
❏ Story Reading.
❏ Story Dictation.
❏ Cloze Reading.

❏ Story Retelling
   from Skeleton.
❏ Free Story Retelling.
❏ Parallel Story.
❏ Mini-drama.

Unit CC2-A [sp] spouse—[εsp] espouse

Story

Listen to the story as your teacher reads it, or on tape, until you understand the main ideas.

Mr. Smart offers family financial success seminars. In other words, he teaches workshops on how to manage family finances. Many married couples who have trouble saving money attend his courses. Mr. Smart helps them become smart (1) **spouses.** He presents lots of ideas that apply to different family situations.

Actually, most of the ideas he presents aren't his own. Smart (2) **espouses** the theories of Dr. Getrich, an economist who believes all people like saving money. He believes this in spite of the fact that most people spend a lot more than they save.

Smart's especial talent is to apply Getrich's theories in a practical manner. In his seminars, he speaks about Getrich's ideas, but he presents them in specific, realistic situations. That makes the ideas easy to understand and useful for everyone. After attending Smart's seminars, most wives and husbands not only want to save money but also know how to do so.

Contrasting Sentences

Listening: Write the appropriate key word in each blank. Later, as you hear each sentence, mark the box, point to the picture, make a gesture, and/or say the rejoinder. Speaking: Choose and say each sentence so that your listener(s) can respond correctly.

❏ Smart _____ all like saving money. (husbands and wives)

❏ Smart _____ all like saving money. (He supports the theory.)

Explanations and diagrams for this unit's target sounds are on page 349 in Section 10.

Additional Practice

Your big *spills / S-pills* scare me. (CC2-b), The property belongs to the *state / estate*. (CC3-A/a), The candidate is losing *steam / esteem*. (CC3-B/b), He looked for a good *landscape / land escape*. (CC4-A/a), *Too strange / To estrange* for words. (CC5-A/a)

Other Words

Many, if not all, of the words listed below are in the story. Find them and circle or underline them each time they occur. Say each marked word aloud—individually and then in its entire sentence. Look for additional words in the story that contain the target sounds. Mark and say them also.

[sp] **sp**ite, **sp**end, **sp**ecial, **sp**eaks, **sp**ecific, **sp**ring

[ɛsp] e**sp**ecial, e**sp**resso, e**sp**ionage, e**sp**ousal, E**sp**eranto

Other Practice Activities

❏ Partner Cards—Listening. *Practice until you can point to the right card every time.*
❏ Partner Cards—Speaking. *Practice until you can say the contrasting sentences so accurately that your partner points to the right card every time.*
❏ Story Reading. *Practice reading the story aloud. Mark any difficult words. Then record the story on tape.*
❏ Story Dictation. *Write the story as your teacher reads it or as you listen to it on the audiotape.*
❏ Cloze Reading. *Choose some key words in the story and black them out. Then read the entire story aloud. Do this several times.*

Each time black out more words. Continue until most of the story is blacked out and you can tell it without looking at the page very often.
❏ Story Retelling from Skeleton. *Black out all the remaining words except those you need in order to remind you of the story line. Then, using just this skeleton, tell the story to your partner or class.*
❏ Free Story Retelling. *Retell the whole story from memory, without looking at your book.*
❏ Parallel Story. *Create your own story similar to the one in this unit.*
❏ Mini-drama. *Make up a skit or do a role play based on the story.*

Unit CC3-A [st] state—[ɛst] estate

Story

Listen to the story as your teacher reads it, or on tape, until you understand the main ideas.

Last summer I went to stay with my cousins for a few days. One day, we went for a long walk. We walked by a big house on a large lot completely surrounded by a fence. I stopped and looked at the property. I wanted to know who it belonged to. As we stood there, my cousin Mary told me that it belonged to the (1) **estate** of Mr. Stone, a strange old gentleman who had lived there all by himself. Mr. Stone had been quite eccentric, and there were many scary stories about him. But, Mr. Stone had died recently, and no one lived in the house anymore. The ownership of the property was being decided in court.

Mary's sister Stephanie interrupted and said that that was no longer true. Mr. Stone did not leave a will, and he had no living relatives to inherit his estate. So, the court had decided that the property belonged to the (2) **state.** I wonder what the government will do with Mr. Stone's estate. It would make a good park or museum.

Contrasting Sentences

Listening: Write the appropriate key word in each blank. Later, as you hear each sentence, mark the box, point to the picture, make a gesture, and/or say the rejoinder. Speaking: Choose and say each sentence so that your listener(s) can respond correctly.

❏ The property belongs to the _____. (Mr. Stone's possessions)

❏ The property belongs to the _____. (government)

Explanations and diagrams for this unit's target sounds are on page 349 in Section 10.

Additional Practice

The candidate is losing *steam / esteem*. (CC3-B/b), Smart *spouses / espouses* all like saving money. (CC2-A/a), Your big *spills / S-pills* scare me. (CC2-b), He looked for a good *landscape / land escape*. (CC4-A/a), *Too strange / To estrange* for words. (CC5-A/a)

Other Words

Many, if not all, of the words listed below are in the story. Find them and circle or underline them each time they occur. Say each marked word aloud—individually and then in its entire sentence. Look for additional words in the story that contain the target sounds. Mark and say them also.

[st] **st**ay, **st**opped, **st**ood, **St**one, **st**range, **st**ories

[εst] **est**imate, **est**eem, **est**ablish, **est**range, **est**imable, **Est**onia

Other Practice Activities

❏ Partner Cards—Listening. *Practice until you can point to the right card every time.*

❏ Partner Cards—Speaking. *Practice until you can say the contrasting sentences so accurately that your partner points to the right card every time.*

❏ Story Reading. *Practice reading the story aloud. Mark any difficult words. Then record the story on tape.*

❏ Story Dictation. *Write the story as your teacher reads it or as you listen to it on the audiotape.*

❏ Cloze Reading. *Choose some key words in the story and black them out. Then read the entire story aloud. Do this several times.*

Each time black out more words. Continue until most of the story is blacked out and you can tell it without looking at the page very often.

❏ Story Retelling from Skeleton. *Black out all the remaining words except those you need in order to remind you of the story line. Then, using just this skeleton, tell the story to your partner or class.*

❏ Free Story Retelling. *Retell the whole story from memory, without looking at your book.*

❏ Parallel Story. *Create your own story similar to the one in this unit.*

❏ Mini-drama. *Make up a skit or do a role play based on the story.*

Unit CC3-B [st] steam—[εst] esteem

Story

Stella Stewart wants to be elected governor of her state. The estimable candidate Stewart has worked hard for almost a year to make sure that people know who she is. In fact, she has spent so much time meeting people every day and night that she is

#1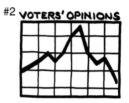

exhausted. She's really losing (1) **steam.** She doesn't know if she can continue until the election.

What's worse, her opponent has been attacking Stewart's reputation by telling lies about her personal life and finances. The stories are not true, but many people still believe them. They stain her character and hurt her chances of winning the election. Earlier estimates gave her a good chance of winning, but the stories have estranged the voters. A recent poll indicated that (2) Stewart's popularity rating is falling. She is losing voters' **esteem** and support. For now, she is still trying to win, but she is also thinking seriously about dropping out of politics.

#2 VOTERS' OPINIONS

Contrasting Sentences

❏ The candidate is losing _____. (getting tired)

❏ The candidate is losing _____. (confidence)

Additional Practice

The property belongs to the *state/estate.* (CC3-A/a), Smart *spouses/espouses* all like saving money. (CC2-A/a), Your big *spills/S-pills* scare me. (CC2-b), He looked for a good *landscape / land escape.* (CC4-A/a), *Too strange / To estrange* for words. (CC5-A/a)

Other Words

[st] **St**ella, **St**ewart, **st**ate, **st**ories, **st**ain, **st**ill

[ɛst] **est**imable, **est**imates, **est**eem, **est**ablish, **est**range, **est**ate

Other Practice Activities

❏ Partner Cards—Listening.
❏ Partner Cards—Speaking.
❏ Story Reading.
❏ Story Dictation.
❏ Cloze Reading.

❏ Story Retelling from Skeleton.
❏ Free Story Retelling.
❏ Parallel Story.
❏ Mini-drama.

Unit CC4-A [sk] scape—[ɛsk] escape

Story

Listen to the story as your teacher reads it, or on tape, until you understand the main ideas.

Harold was in prison for many years, but he just started painting pictures last year. He began painting because, after years of good behavior, he was finally allowed to go outside the prison walls to paint. All the prison guards admired the (1) **landscapes** he painted. They had beautiful skies and trees. Harold was quite a skillful painter.

What the guards didn't know was that Harold was actually looking for a way to (2) **escape** from the prison. Such an escapade would not be easy. On one side of the prison there was a river. On the other side was a large swamp. Harold knew the river was too swift and cold for him to swim across, and the swamp scared him also. So he was looking for a way to escape where there was dry land. Every time he painted a landscape around the prison, he scanned the ground looking for a way to escape over solid land. Finally, after months of looking and thinking, he figured out a path to freedom. The next day, Harold scaled the prison wall and escaped. He hasn't been seen since, but the landscapes he painted are still around.

Contrasting Sentences

Listening: Write the appropriate key word in each blank. Later, as you hear each sentence, mark the box, point to the picture, make a gesture, and/or say the rejoinder. Speaking: Choose and say each sentence so that your listener(s) can respond correctly.

❏ He looked for a good land_____. (scenery to paint)

❏ He looked for a good land _____. (route over dry land)

Explanations and diagrams for this unit's target sounds are on page 349 in Section 10.

Additional Practice

Smart *spouses/espouses* all like saving money. (CC2-A/a), Your big *spills/S-pills* scare me. (CC2-b), The property belongs to the *state/estate*. (CC3-A/a), The candidate is losing *steam/esteem*. (CC3-B/b), *Too strange / To estrange* for words. (CC5-A/a)

Other Words

Many, if not all, of the words listed below are in the story. Find them and circle or underline them each time they occur. Say each marked word aloud—individually and then in its entire sentence. Look for additional words in the story that contain the target sounds. Mark and say them also.

[sk] **sk**ies, **sk**illful, **sc**ared, **sc**anned, **sc**aled, **sk**im

[ɛsk] **esc**apade, **esc**alate, **esc**ort, **Esk**imo, **esc**row, **esc**alator

Other Practice Activities

❏ Partner Cards—Listening. *Practice until you can point to the right card every time.*

❏ Partner Cards—Speaking. *Practice until you can say the contrasting sentences so accurately that your partner points to the right card every time.*

❏ Story Reading. *Practice reading the story aloud. Mark any difficult words. Then record the story on tape.*

❏ Story Dictation. *Write the story as your teacher reads it or as you listen to it on the audiotape.*

❏ Cloze Reading. *Choose some key words in the story and black them out. Then read the entire story aloud. Do this several times.*

Each time black out more words. Continue until most of the story is blacked out and you can tell it without looking at the page very often.

❏ Story Retelling from Skeleton. *Black out all the remaining words except those you need in order to remind you of the story line. Then, using just this skeleton, tell the story to your partner or class.*

❏ Free Story Retelling. *Retell the whole story from memory, without looking at your book.*

❏ Parallel Story. *Create your own story similar to the one in this unit.*

❏ Mini-drama. *Make up a skit or do a role play based on the story.*

Unit CC5-A [str] strange—[ɛstr] estrange

Story

Listen to the story as your teacher reads it, or on tape, until you understand the main ideas.

I have a strange co-worker named Kenneth. He has many peculiar habits, and working with him is stressful and quite a strain. For example, when Kenneth works, he sings to himself. Then, right in the middle of a song, he starts screaming loudly and laughs like a madman. After that he goes back to work as if nothing had happened. This behavior really startles people around him, and it's only one of his peculiar habits. All in all, Kenneth is so unusual that it is difficult to find the vocabulary to describe him. He is (1) **too strange** for words.

Speaking of words, Kenneth uses lots of unusual ones. They are not just above people's heads; they're in the stratosphere. For example, he always calls his desk his escritoire. One warm afternoon last summer, he said that he'd like to estivate. Nobody knew what he meant until we looked up *estivate* in the dictionary. Kenneth thinks the big words he uses impress people, but they just alienate everyone. No one likes being around him. Our supervisor has told us that it is wrong for us (2) **to estrange** Kenneth for his words and behavior, but we can't help it.

Contrasting Sentences

Listening: Write the appropriate key word in each blank. Later, as you hear each sentence, mark the box, point to the picture, make a gesture, and/or say the rejoinder. Speaking: Choose and say each sentence so that your listener(s) can respond correctly.

❏ Too _____ for words. (is the only way to describe him)

❏ To _____ for words. (is wrong)

Explanations and diagrams for this unit's target sounds are on page 349 in Section 10.

Additional Practice

Smart *spouses/espouses* all like saving money. (CC2-A/a), The property belongs to the *state/estate*. (CC3-A/a), The candidate is losing *steam/esteem*. (CC3-B/b), He looked for a good *landscape / land escape*. (CC4-A/a)

Other Words

Many, if not all, of the words listed below are in the story. Find them and circle or underline them each time they occur. Say each marked word aloud—individually and then in its entire sentence. Look for additional words in the story that contain the target sounds. Mark and say them also.

[str] **str**essful, **str**ain, **str**atosphere, **str**ategy, **str**eam, **str**ict

[ɛstr] **estr**ogen, **escr**ow, **est**ablish, **est**eem, **Esth**er, **esq**uire

Other Practice Activities

❑ Partner Cards—Listening. *Practice until you can point to the right card every time.*

❑ Partner Cards—Speaking. *Practice until you can say the contrasting sentences so accurately that your partner points to the right card every time.*

❑ Story Reading. *Practice reading the story aloud. Mark any difficult words. Then record the story on tape.*

❑ Story Dictation. *Write the story as your teacher reads it or as you listen to it on the audiotape.*

❑ Cloze Reading. *Choose some key words in the story and black them out. Then read the entire story aloud. Do this several times.*

Each time black out more words. Continue until most of the story is blacked out and you can tell it without looking at the page very often.

❑ Story Retelling from Skeleton. *Black out all the remaining words except those you need in order to remind you of the story line. Then, using just this skeleton, tell the story to your partner or class.*

❑ Free Story Retelling. *Retell the whole story from memory, without looking at your book.*

❑ Parallel Story. *Create your own story similar to the one in this unit.*

❑ Mini-drama. *Make up a skit or do a role play based on the story.*

Unit CC6-A [ŋ] thing—[ŋk] think

Story

Listen to the story as your teacher reads it, or on tape, until you understand the main ideas.

Tom and Cathy have been dating for six months. Tom really likes Cathy, but recently she has been acting a little cold to him. He came to me for advice.

"Well," I suggested, "you could serenade her. Do you play the guitar or sing?" Unfortunately, Tom was a terrible singer.

"In that case, maybe you could take her boating on the lake in the park some evening. It's fun and romantic." But Tom, who can't swim, was afraid that the boat might sink.

All I could say was, "Well, go home and have a good (1) **think** about it."

The next day Tom said he had thought all night about what to do, and he finally got a good idea. He was thinking of buying a present for Cathy. We went to the shopping mall and looked around separately. After about twenty minutes, he came to me with a big smile and said he had found a good **thing.** It was (2) a cute pink T-shirt that said "LOVE" on the front. He bought it and gave it to Cathy that day. She loved the T-shirt, but they still broke up a week later.

Contrasting Sentences

Listening: Write the appropriate key word in each blank. Later, as you hear each sentence, mark the box, point to the picture, make a gesture, and/or say the rejoinder. Speaking: Choose and say each sentence so that your listener(s) can respond correctly.

❑ He had a good _____. (And he finally came up with an idea.)

❑ He had a good _____. (It was a cute T-shirt.)

Explanations and diagrams for this unit's target sounds are on pages 349–50 in Section 10.

Additional Practice

Captain Blackwing *sings / sinks.* (CC6-B/b)

Other Words

Many, if not all, of the words listed below are in the story. Find them and circle or underline them each time they occur. Say each marked word aloud—individually and then in its entire sentence. Look for additional words in the story that contain the target sounds. Mark and say them also.

[ŋ] dati**ng**, acti**ng**, si**ng**, eveni**ng**, thinki**ng**, buyi**ng**

[ŋk] si**nk**, pi**nk**, ri**nk**, wi**nk**, shri**nk**, zi**nc**

Other Practice Activities

❏ Partner Cards—Listening. *Practice until you can point to the right card every time.*

❏ Partner Cards—Speaking. *Practice until you can say the contrasting sentences so accurately that your partner points to the right card every time.*

❏ Story Reading. *Practice reading the story aloud. Mark any difficult words. Then record the story on tape.*

❏ Story Dictation. *Write the story as your teacher reads it or as you listen to it on the audiotape.*

❏ Cloze Reading. *Choose some key words in the story and black them out. Then read the entire story aloud. Do this several times.*

Each time black out more words. Continue until most of the story is blacked out and you can tell it without looking at the page very often.

❏ Story Retelling from Skeleton. *Black out all the remaining words except those you need in order to remind you of the story line. Then, using just this skeleton, tell the story to your partner or class.*

❏ Free Story Retelling. *Retell the whole story from memory, without looking at your book.*

❏ Parallel Story. *Create your own story similar to the one in this unit.*

❏ Mini-drama. *Make up a skit or do a role play based on the story.*

Unit CC6-B [ŋ] sings—[ŋk] sinks

Story

Last year I spent two months at the beach. I did a lot of fun things, but one of them was a little scary. One very foggy night when I was walking along the shore I thought I could hear singing. It was coming from somewhere out in the water. I told my friend, "I think I hear someone out there singing." In response, with a wink of his eye, he told me a strange tale.

More than two hundred years ago, on a night when a great, thick fog covered the coast, a pirate ship was coming in to shore. The ship hit some rocks and began to sink in the water. The crew abandoned ship, but instead of joining them, the captain, whose name was Blackwing, climbed up on the bow of the ship and began to (1) **sing.** He sang until the ship sank under the waves and he was drowned.

That was a long time ago, but even now, if you listen carefully on foggy nights, you can still hear the captain as he sings. Some people claim that on nights when the fog is not too thick they have even seen Captain Blackwing's ghost. They say that he (2) **sinks** into the ocean as he sings.

Contrasting Sentences

❏ Captain Blackwing _____. (songs)

❏ Captain Blackwing _____. (into the ocean)

Additional Practice

He had a good *thing / think.* (CC6-A/a)

Other Words

[ŋ] thi**ng**s, walki**ng**, si**ng**i**ng**, joini**ng**, sa**ng**, lo**ng**

[ŋk] thi**nk**, wi**nk**, sa**nk**, tha**nk**, pi**nk**, shri**nk**

Other Practice Activities

❏ Partner Cards—Listening.
❏ Partner Cards—Speaking.
❏ Story Reading.
❏ Story Dictation.
❏ Cloze Reading.

❏ Story Retelling from Skeleton.
❏ Free Story Retelling.
❏ Parallel Story.
❏ Mini-drama.

Unit CC7-A [rt] fort—[rs] force

Story

Listen to the story as your teacher reads it, or on tape, until you understand the main ideas.

Arthur and Linda Schwartz are both retired, but they don't stay at home much. They have plenty of money and like to travel, but they don't go to resorts. Rather, they like to go to historic sites. In the last two years, they have toured the royal courts of Europe and visited famous Mediterranean seaports.

This year Art and Linda have been focusing on ancient ruins—especially military fortresses. They think it is incredible how armies in the past built large (1) **forts** without using large machines. Of course, they sometimes used oxen, horses, or other animals, but most ancient military commanders and builders relied almost totally on human labor. It took (2) many thousands of people to build a fort—especially if it had thick stone walls. And those walls could not be short either. They had to be tall enough to keep out an attacking army. To construct such places, builders needed a large **force.** But it was worth it. Once the forts were built, a small force could defend them against a much larger army. Also, well-built forts would last for centuries. In fact, as Art and Linda know, many ancient forts are still standing today.

#1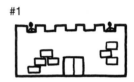

#2

Contrasting Sentences

Listening: Write the appropriate key word in each blank. Later, as you hear each sentence, mark the box, point to the picture, make a gesture, and/or say the rejoinder. Speaking: Choose and say each sentence so that your listener(s) can respond correctly.

❏ They needed a large _____. (fortified place)

❏ They needed a large _____. (group of people)

Explanations and diagrams for this unit's target sounds are on pages 350–51 in Section 10.

Additional Practice

You *fail / failed* every test. (CC8-A/a), I *fail / failed them*. (CC9-A/a), Don't forget your *car / card*. (CC9-B/b)

Other Words

Many, if not all, of the words listed below are in the story. Find them and circle or underline them each time they occur. Say each marked word aloud—individually and then in its entire sentence. Look for additional words in the story that contain the target sounds. Mark and say them also.

[rt] Schwa**rt**z, reso**rt**s, cou**rt**s, seapo**rt**s, sho**rt**, impo**rt**

[rs] cou**rs**e, ho**rs**es, enfo**rc**e, resou**rc**e, sou**rc**e, remo**rs**e

Other Practice Activities

❏ Partner Cards—Listening. *Practice until you can point to the right card every time.*

❏ Partner Cards—Speaking. *Practice until you can say the contrasting sentences so accurately that your partner points to the right card every time.*

❏ Story Reading. *Practice reading the story aloud. Mark any difficult words. Then record the story on tape.*

❏ Story Dictation. *Write the story as your teacher reads it or as you listen to it on the audiotape.*

❏ Cloze Reading. *Choose some key words in the story and black them out. Then read the entire story aloud. Do this several times.*

Each time black out more words. Continue until most of the story is blacked out and you can tell it without looking at the page very often.

❏ Story Retelling from Skeleton. *Black out all the remaining words except those you need in order to remind you of the story line. Then, using just this skeleton, tell the story to your partner or class.*

❏ Free Story Retelling. *Retell the whole story from memory, without looking at your book.*

❏ Parallel Story. *Create your own story similar to the one in this unit.*

❏ Mini-drama. *Make up a skit or do a role play based on the story.*

Unit CC8-A [C] pass—[C + t] passed

Story

Listen to the story as your teacher reads it, or on tape, until you understand the main ideas.

Laura works very hard in school. She has never missed a homework assignment or slept in class. Because of this, she normally passes every test easily. She also gets high grades. Her cumulative grade point average is 3.8 on a scale of 4. That's why she was shocked when she failed her final exam in math.

Laura's teacher told her, "Your score was a shock for me also. (1) During the school year, you **passed** every test you took, except the final. On that exam you missed more than half of the answers. What happened? Didn't you study? Did you have to guess a lot?"

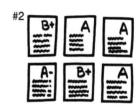

Laura didn't know. To the best of her memory, she had worked out all the answers. She hadn't guessed on any of them.

So the teacher looked at Laura's exam again. It turned out that the teacher had made a mistake scoring the test. She apologized and said, (2) "You **pass** every test you take. I should have known something was wrong." Laura was happy to learn that she hadn't failed after all.

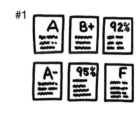

Contrasting Sentences

Listening: Write the appropriate key word in each blank. Later, as you hear each sentence, mark the box, point to the picture, make a gesture, and / or say the rejoinder. Speaking: Choose and say each sentence so that your listener(s) can respond correctly.

❏ You _____ every test. (except the final)

❏ You _____ every test. (all the time)

Explanations and diagrams for this unit's target sounds are on pages 350–51 in Section 10.

Additional Practice

I *fail* / *failed* them. (CC9-A/a), Don't forget your *car* / *card*. (CC9-B/b)

Other Words

Many, if not all, of the words listed below are in the story. Find them and circle or underline them each time they occur. Say each marked word aloud—individually and then in its entire sentence. Look for additional words in the story that contain the target sounds. Mark and say them also.

[C + t] mi**ss**ed, sle**p**t, poi**n**t, sho**ck**ed, did**n't**, be**st**

[C] gue**ss**, pa**ss**, sho**ck**, loo**k**, kee**p**, wor**k**

Other Practice Activities

❑ Partner Cards—Listening. *Practice until you can point to the right card every time.*
❑ Partner Cards—Speaking. *Practice until you can say the contrasting sentences so accurately that your partner points to the right card every time.*
❑ Story Reading. *Practice reading the story aloud. Mark any difficult words. Then record the story on tape.*
❑ Story Dictation. *Write the story as your teacher reads it or as you listen to it on the audiotape.*
❑ Cloze Reading. *Choose some key words in the story and black them out. Then read the entire story aloud. Do this several times.*

Each time black out more words. Continue until most of the story is blacked out and you can tell it without looking at the page very often.
❑ Story Retelling from Skeleton. *Black out all the remaining words except those you need in order to remind you of the story line. Then, using just this skeleton, tell the story to your partner or class.*
❑ Free Story Retelling. *Retell the whole story from memory, without looking at your book.*
❑ Parallel Story. *Create your own story similar to the one in this unit.*
❑ Mini-drama. *Make up a skit or do a role play based on the story.*

Unit CC9-A [C] fail—[C + d] failed

Story

Listen to the story as your teacher reads it, or on tape, until you understand the main ideas.

I have always been a terrible (1) test taker. Typically, I **fail** nearly every test that I take. (2) I fail them because I get nervous and my mind goes blank. That unnerves me even more, and I panic. I turn into a mindless fool and can't answer any of the questions.

At least I'm better now than I used to be. Last year, (3) I **failed** every test that I took the first term. That really disturbed me. The next term, I studied twice as hard, but when I took my exams I still failed them. Then I was really perturbed. I knew the material. I deserved to pass. The only reason that I failed the exams was because I was so nervous.

Those failures bugged me so much that I realized I needed special help. So I finally took a special course on test taking skills. It helped a little, but it solved my problem only partially. Now, I do much better on some tests, but I still fail those that are timed. The time pressure makes me nervous. I forget what I have studied, and I don't get the scores I deserve. I'll probably never do well on timed tests.

Contrasting Sentences

Listening: Write the appropriate key word in each blank. Later, as you hear each sentence, mark the box, point to the picture, make a gesture, and/or say the rejoinder. Speaking: Choose and say each sentence so that your listener(s) can respond correctly.

❏ I _____ them. (last year)

❏ I _____ them. (every time)

Explanations and diagrams for this unit's target sounds are on pages 350–51 in Section 10.

Additional Practice

Don't forget your *car/card.* (CC9-B/b), You *pass/passed* every test. (CC8-A/a)

Other Words

Many, if not all, of the words listed below are in the story. Find them and circle or underline them each time they occur. Say each marked word aloud—individually and then in its entire sentence. Look for additional words in the story that contain the target sounds. Mark and say them also.

[C] unne**rve**, tu**rn**, answe**r**, dese**rve**, distu**rb**, bu**g**

[C + d] distu**rbed,** pertu**rbed,** dese**rved,** bu**gged,** reali**zed,** so**lved**

Other Practice Activities

❑ Partner Cards—Listening. *Practice until you can point to the right card every time.*

❑ Partner Cards—Speaking. *Practice until you can say the contrasting sentences so accurately that your partner points to the right card every time.*

❑ Story Reading. *Practice reading the story aloud. Mark any difficult words. Then record the story on tape.*

❑ Story Dictation. *Write the story as your teacher reads it or as you listen to it on the audiotape.*

❑ Cloze Reading. *Choose some key words in the story and black them out. Then read the entire story aloud. Do this several times.*

Each time black out more words. Continue until most of the story is blacked out and you can tell it without looking at the page very often.

❑ Story Retelling from Skeleton. *Black out all the remaining words except those you need in order to remind you of the story line. Then, using just this skeleton, tell the story to your partner or class.*

❑ Free Story Retelling. *Retell the whole story from memory, without looking at your book.*

❑ Parallel Story. *Create your own story similar to the one in this unit.*

❑ Mini-drama. *Make up a skit or do a role play based on the story.*

Unit CC9-B [C] car—[C + d] card

Story

I believe I am losing my memory. I seem to always be forgetting things.

The other evening, for example, I went out to eat. My favorite restaurant is not far from my apartment, but I decided to drive because I was tired. After enjoying a delicious meal, I paid for it with my credit card and began to leave. Just as I was going out the door, the cashier called to me and said, "Don't forget your (1) **card.**" I had left it on the counter when I paid. I'm lucky that she was honest. I apologized for my mistake and told her thanks.

Then I started to walk home. It was farther than I remembered. I was just about to take a taxi when I realized that I had driven my own (2) car to the restaurant. It was back in the restaurant parking lot. "Now you forgot your **car,**" I said to myself.

I'm going to have to start writing everything down. Or maybe I'll get one of those little pocket voice recorders. Then I can tell myself, "Don't forget your card" and "Don't forget your car." But I probably won't remember to listen to the messages I record.

Contrasting Sentences

❏ Don't forget your _____. (automobile)

❏ Don't forget your _____. (credit card)

Additional Practice

I *fail/failed* them. (CC9-A/a), You *pass/passed* every test. (CC8-A/a)

Other Words

[C] believe, see**m**, drive, bega**n**, te**ll**, remember

[C + d] ti**red**, ca**lled**, apologi**zed**, to**ld**, remembe**red**, reali**zed**

Other Practice Activities

❏ Partner Cards—Listening.
❏ Partner Cards—Speaking.
❏ Story Reading.
❏ Story Dictation.
❏ Cloze Reading.

❏ Story Retelling from Skeleton.
❏ Free Story Retelling.
❏ Parallel Story.
❏ Mini-drama.

Unit CC10-A [C] beast—[C + s] beasts

Story

Listen to the story as your teacher reads it, or on tape, until you understand the main ideas.

Do you know the story "Beauty and the Beast"? Have you seen the movie? I like it very much. It's one of the cutest movies I've ever seen. I like the (1) **beast** best. He looks scary at first, but he turns out to be a nice guy.

When I told my brother how much I liked the beast in the movie, he laughed and said, "That's a movie for little kids." So I asked him which movie he liked.

He didn't remember its title, but he told me the story. "An evil mad scientist creates monsters to conquer the world, but the beasts he makes are not obedient. They kill the mad scientist and start to kill good scientists, too. Finally, the monsters attack a whole town. They eat lots of people and wreck everything. In the end, two news reporters trap the beasts."

It sounded like an awful movie to me, so I asked my brother what he liked about it. He answered, "I liked the (2) **beasts.** They were gross and cool." I guess different people have different tastes.

Contrasting Sentences

Listening: Write the appropriate key word in each blank. Later, as you hear each sentence, mark the box, point to the picture, make a gesture, and/or say the rejoinder. Speaking: Choose and say each sentence so that your listener(s) can respond correctly.

❑ I like the _____. (He is nice.)

❑ I like the _____. (They are cool.)

Explanations and diagrams for this unit's target sounds are on pages 350–51 in Section 10.

Additional Practice

The *dog / dogs* saw the mail carrier. (CC11-A/a)

Other Words

Many, if not all, of the words listed below are in the story. Find them and circle or underline them each time they occur. Say each marked word aloud—individually and then in its entire sentence. Look for additional words in the story that contain the target sounds. Mark and say them also.

[C] li**k**e, sta**r**t, atta**ck**, eat, wre**ck**, tra**p**

[C + s] loo**ks**, i**ts**, crea**tes**, ma**kes**, scienti**sts**, tas**tes**

Other Practice Activities

❑ Partner Cards—Listening. *Practice until you can point to the right card every time.*

❑ Partner Cards—Speaking. *Practice until you can say the contrasting sentences so accurately that your partner points to the right card every time.*

❑ Story Reading. *Practice reading the story aloud. Mark any difficult words. Then record the story on tape.*

❑ Story Dictation. *Write the story as your teacher reads it or as you listen to it on the audiotape.*

❑ Cloze Reading. *Choose some key words in the story and black them out. Then read the entire story aloud. Do this several times.*

Each time black out more words. Continue until most of the story is blacked out and you can tell it without looking at the page very often.

❑ Story Retelling from Skeleton. *Black out all the remaining words except those you need in order to remind you of the story line. Then, using just this skeleton, tell the story to your partner or class.*

❑ Free Story Retelling. *Retell the whole story from memory, without looking at your book.*

❑ Parallel Story. *Create your own story similar to the one in this unit.*

❑ Mini-drama. *Make up a skit or do a role play based on the story.*

Unit CC11-A [C] dog—[C + z] dogs

Story

Listen to the story as your teacher reads it, or on tape, until you understand the main ideas.

(1) The mail carrier who delivers mail to my house is getting very upset because whenever he comes down the street in my neighborhood the dogs see him, run out barking, and follow him around. He is nervous around these dogs because of what happened last month. One (2) **dog** saw him, growled, and followed him down the street. When the mail carrier tried to shoo him away, that dog bit him.

Now another neighbor's dog has begun to follow the mail carrier, too, so the poor guy has two dogs to worry about. There's also a third dog that is starting to join in this sport. Yesterday all three (3) **dogs** saw the mail carrier and followed him as he delivered letters.

The mail carrier is so nervous because of what happened before that if there's a dog on our porch when he comes he just skips our house. He takes out a pencil, writes "Dog on porch" on our letters, and puts them back in his bag. He doesn't bring them until the next day. With all the dogs watching for him, I hope he continues to deliver mail to my street.

Contrasting Sentences

Listening: Write the appropriate key word in each blank. Later, as you hear each sentence, mark the box, point to the picture, make a gesture, and/or say the rejoinder. Speaking: Choose and say each sentence so that your listener(s) can respond correctly.

❏ The _____ saw the mail carrier. (And it followed him.)

❏ The _____ saw the mail carrier. (And they followed him.)

Explanations and diagrams for this unit's target sounds are on pages 350–51 in Section 10.

Additional Practice

I liked the *beast / beasts.* (CC10-A/a)

Other Words

Many, if not all, of the words listed below are in the story. Find them and circle or underline them each time they occur. Say each marked word aloud—individually and then in its entire sentence. Look for additional words in the story that contain the target sounds. Mark and say them also.

[C] carrie**r**, begu**n**, neighborhoo**d**, ru**n**, joi**n**, penci**l**

[C + z] delive**rs**, lette**rs**, co**mes**, neighbo**r's**, the**re's**, bri**ngs**

Other Practice Activities

❏ Partner Cards—Listening. *Practice until you can point to the right card every time.*
❏ Partner Cards—Speaking. *Practice until you can say the contrasting sentences so accurately that your partner points to the right card every time.*
❏ Story Reading. *Practice reading the story aloud. Mark any difficult words. Then record the story on tape.*
❏ Story Dictation. *Write the story as your teacher reads it or as you listen to it on the audiotape.*
❏ Cloze Reading. *Choose some key words in the story and black them out. Then read the entire story aloud. Do this several times.*

Each time black out more words. Continue until most of the story is blacked out and you can tell it without looking at the page very often.
❏ Story Retelling from Skeleton. *Black out all the remaining words except those you need in order to remind you of the story line. Then, using just this skeleton, tell the story to your partner or class.*
❏ Free Story Retelling. *Retell the whole story from memory, without looking at your book.*
❏ Parallel Story. *Create your own story similar to the one in this unit.*
❏ Mini-drama. *Make up a skit or do a role play based on the story.*

Unit CC12-A [d] code—[ld] cold

Story

Listen to the story as your teacher reads it, or on tape, until you understand the main ideas.

Joan is in the military, and she has an unusual assignment. She works at a station north of the Arctic Circle. It's (1) **cold** there, extremely cold, but she stays inside her quarters most of the time. When she goes out, it's for only a few minutes, and then she goes back inside quickly. After all, there's no place to go. Everything is covered with ice and snow. There are not even any roads there. The only way for her to get in and out is by helicopter. Once a month, a helicopter flies in to unload supplies and load up things to be taken out.

At the station, Joan helps maintain machines that transmit military messages from one part of the world to another. If you think that she knows a lot of military secrets because of her work, you will be disappointed. Once, when I was bold enough to ask her about that, she told me that she really doesn't know any. Sometimes, when she's checking a machine, she sees a message on the screen, but it's in (2) **code.** She can't even read it.

#1

#2

```
XVDGDWE
GDXTAAN
FVVQSVX
KTMOEPS
XWEGRSP
```

Contrasting Sentences

Listening: Write the appropriate key word in each blank. Later, as you hear each sentence, mark the box, point to the picture, make a gesture, and / or say the rejoinder. Speaking: Choose and say each sentence so that your listener(s) can respond correctly.

❏ It's _____. (Let's go inside.)

❏ It's _____. (I can't read it.)

Explanations and diagrams for this unit's target sounds are on pages 351–52 in Section 10.

Additional Practice

Teri *sewed/sold* the dress. (CC12-B/b)

Other Words

Many, if not all, of the words listed below are in the story. Find them and circle or underline them each time they occur. Say each marked word aloud—individually and then in its entire sentence. Look for additional words in the story that contain the target sounds. Mark and say them also.

[d] **r**o**ad**, unl**oad**, l**oad**, corr**ode**, expl**ode**, t**oad**

[ld] b**old**, t**old**, h**old**, r**olled**, f**old**, sc**old**

Other Practice Activities

❑ Partner Cards—Listening. *Practice until you can point to the right card every time.*
❑ Partner Cards—Speaking. *Practice until you can say the contrasting sentences so accurately that your partner points to the right card every time.*
❑ Story Reading. *Practice reading the story aloud. Mark any difficult words. Then record the story on tape.*
❑ Story Dictation. *Write the story as your teacher reads it or as you listen to it on the audiotape.*
❑ Cloze Reading. *Choose some key words in the story and black them out. Then read the entire story aloud. Do this several times.*

Each time black out more words. Continue until most of the story is blacked out and you can tell it without looking at the page very often.
❑ Story Retelling from Skeleton. *Black out all the remaining words except those you need in order to remind you of the story line. Then, using just this skeleton, tell the story to your partner or class.*
❑ Free Story Retelling. *Retell the whole story from memory, without looking at your book.*
❑ Parallel Story. *Create your own story similar to the one in this unit.*
❑ Mini-drama. *Make up a skit or do a role play based on the story.*

Unit CC12-B [d] sewed—[ld] sold

Story

Teri is a super seamstress. She can sew clothes of all kinds, and she doesn't need a pattern to follow. If you show her a picture of what you want, she can create it. Of course, such talent and skill are rare and in demand, so Teri can charge a lot.

Once a woman asked Teri to make her a special dress. She already owed Teri some money from a previous job and said that

she would pay for both dresses when Teri finished this one. Teri (1) **sewed** it exactly as she was told, but when the woman came to pick it up, she hadn't brought the money to pay for it. Teri rolled her eyes and took a deep breath, but she didn't get upset. She didn't explode, and she didn't scold the lady. But she didn't fold the dress up and give it to her either. Instead, she hung the dress in her store window. Pretty soon, another woman saw it and asked to buy it. Because it was a unique design, she was happy to pay a high price. Teri (2) **sold** it for more than she would have received from the first woman.

Contrasting Sentences

❏ Teri _____ the dress. (for the first woman)

❏ Teri _____ the dress. (to the second woman)

Additional Practice

It's *code / cold.* (CC12-A/a)

Other Words

[d] **owed**, expl**ode**, m**ode**, unl**oad**, epis**ode**, r**oad**

[ld] t**old**, r**olled**, sc**old**, f**old**, b**old**, m**old**

Other Practice Activities

❏ Partner Cards—Listening.
❏ Partner Cards—Speaking.
❏ Story Reading.
❏ Story Dictation.
❏ Cloze Reading.

❏ Story Retelling
from Skeleton.
❏ Free Story Retelling.
❏ Parallel Story.
❏ Mini-drama.

Unit CC13-A [CC] train—[CəC] terrain

Story

Listen to the story as your teacher reads it, or on tape, until you understand the main ideas.

Tracy once traveled through most of Europe. He had a great time on the trip. He saw castles, palaces, and museums, as well as lots of beautiful scenery. The best part was that he didn't have to worry about arranging transportation or buying tickets. Tracy had a pass that allowed him to travel on almost any (1) **train** in any European country for a two-week period. The pass gave him a feeling of freedom. When he wanted to go to a different country, he just went to the station, boarded a train, and showed his pass. The trains were nearly always on time, and they were very reliable. There was only one time when one broke down. All in all, he really liked the train.

As he traveled from city to city, Tracy learned a lot about history and art. He even learned to distinguish baroque architecture from rococo. But after a while, he started to enjoy the breaks between cities. He liked to sit in the train, look out the window, and watch the (2) **terrain** go by—hills and valleys, plains and mountains. He thought of the farmers who had worked the land for many centuries. They were an important part of history, too.

Contrasting Sentences

Listening: Write the appropriate key word in each blank. Later, as you hear each sentence, mark the box, point to the picture, make a gesture, and/or say the rejoinder. Speaking: Choose and say each sentence so that your listener(s) can respond correctly.

❏ Tracy liked the _____. (railroad)

❏ Tracy liked the _____. (land)

Explanations and diagrams for this unit's target sounds are on pages 352–53 in Section 10.

Additional Practice

They *prayed/parade* for a long time. (CC13-b)

Other Words

Many, if not all, of the words listed below are in the story. Find them and circle or underline them each time they occur. Say each marked word aloud—individually and then in its entire sentence. Look for additional words in the story that contain the target sounds. Mark and say them also.

[CC] **gr**eat, **tr**ip, **fr**eedom, coun**tr**y, **br**oke, **pl**ace

[CƏC] pa**lac**es, sce**ner**y, dif**fer**ent, his**tor**y, **bar**oque, cen**tur**ies

Other Practice Activities

❑ Partner Cards—Listening. *Practice until you can point to the right card every time.*

❑ Partner Cards—Speaking. *Practice until you can say the contrasting sentences so accurately that your partner points to the right card every time.*

❑ Story Reading. *Practice reading the story aloud. Mark any difficult words. Then record the story on tape.*

❑ Story Dictation. *Write the story as your teacher reads it or as you listen to it on the audiotape.*

❑ Cloze Reading. *Choose some key words in the story and black them out. Then read the entire story aloud. Do this several times.*

Each time black out more words. Continue until most of the story is blacked out and you can tell it without looking at the page very often.

❑ Story Retelling from Skeleton. *Black out all the remaining words except those you need in order to remind you of the story line. Then, using just this skeleton, tell the story to your partner or class.*

❑ Free Story Retelling. *Retell the whole story from memory, without looking at your book.*

❑ Parallel Story. *Create your own story similar to the one in this unit.*

❑ Mini-drama. *Make up a skit or do a role play based on the story.*

Section 5

Reduction and Blending (RB)

Unit RB1-A [h] saw her—
[ ] ([h] dropped) saw 'er

Story

Listen to the story as your teacher reads it, or on tape, until you understand the main ideas.

Amanda was absent from school for two weeks, and (1) my classmates and I were wondering what had happened to her. Before class, Holly said, "I **saw 'er** yesterday. She was (2) comin' out of a grocery store."

"Did you talk to 'er?" I asked.

"No, 'cause I was on the bus," she answered. "Maybe 'er mother's sick or somethin'." We thought that would explain why Amanda hadn't been to school and was out buying groceries by herself.

Then (3) our teacher, Ms. English, came into the room. She called the class to attention, took attendance, and said, "Amanda is absent again today. Does anyone have any idea what has happened to her?"

Someone volunteered, "Holly **saw her** yesterday at a grocery store. We think Amanda's mother might be sick. Perhaps some of us should go and visit her." Ms. English thought that might be helpful.

Sarah and I volunteered for the job and went to Amanda's home after school. Our suspicions were half right. Amanda's mother was sick, but Amanda was taking care of her and she was getting better. Before that, however, Amanda herself had been sick. I hope I don't catch what they had.

Contrasting Sentences

Listening: Write the appropriate key word(s) in each blank. Later, as you hear each sentence, mark the box, point to the picture, make a gesture, and/or say the rejoinder. Speaking: Choose and say each sentence so that your listener(s) can respond correctly.

❏ Sarah saw _____ yesterday. (relaxed [speaking to classmates])

❏ Sarah saw _____ yesterday. (careful [speaking to teacher])

Explanations and diagrams for this unit's target sounds are on pages 353–54 in Section 10.

Additional Practice

Did you *see him / see 'im*? (RB1-B/b)

Other Examples

The words and phrases listed below are in the story. Find them and circle or underline them. Say each marked word or phrase aloud—individually and then in its entire sentence. Look for additional words in the story that are reduced and/or blended. Mark and say them also.

[h] **h**appened, **H**olly, **h**ave any idea, **h**elpful, Amanda's **h**ome, **h**alf right,

[ ] (possible in casual speech) to **'er**, maybe **'er** mother, by **'er**self, talk to **'er**, visit **'er**, taking care of **'er**

Other Practice Activities

- ❏ Partner Cards—Listening. *Practice until you can point to the right card every time.*
- ❏ Partner Cards—Speaking. *Practice until you can say the contrasting sentences so accurately that your partner points to the right card every time.*
- ❏ Story Reading. *Practice reading the story aloud. Mark any difficult words. Then record the story on tape.*
- ❏ Story Dictation. *Write the story as your teacher reads it or as you listen to it on the audiotape.*
- ❏ Cloze Reading. *Choose some key words in the story and black them out. Then read the entire story aloud. Do this several times.*

Each time black out more words. Continue until most of the story is blacked out and you can tell it without looking at the page very often.
- ❏ Story Retelling from Skeleton. *Black out all the remaining words except those you need in order to remind you of the story line. Then, using just this skeleton, tell the story to your partner or class.*
- ❏ Free Story Retelling. *Retell the whole story from memory, without looking at your book.*
- ❏ Parallel Story. *Create your own story similar to the one in this unit.*
- ❏ Mini-drama. *Make up a skit or do a role play based on the story.*

Unit RB1-B [h] see him— [ ] ([h] dropped) see 'im

Story

My brother Mark, who is a college student, plays the (1) trumpet in the marching band. During football season, the band marches during halftime at all the home games. My (2) family likes to go and watch him. But sometimes it's hard to tell which trumpet player is Mark. The band is large, and there are about ten trumpet players. From where we sit high up in the stadium, they all look alike when they're wearing uniforms.

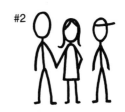

My (3) grandpa, who is getting old, likes football games, and he loves to see Mark march at halftime. However, since his latest operation he has had to stay home and watch the games on TV. He is getting hard of hearing, but he can understand if he turns the volume up really loud.

When we return from the game, Grandpa is there waiting and asks us, "Did you **see 'im**?"

Usually we have to answer, "Well, we saw the band, but we couldn't tell which one was Mark."

Then, speaking clearly and loudly, we ask Grandpa, "Did you **see him**?"

Once he answered, "I sure did. The cameras focused right on 'im." Then we wished we had stayed home and watched the game on TV.

Contrasting Sentences

❏ Did you see _____ ? (Grandpa asking family)

❏ Did you see _____ ? (family asking Grandpa)

Additional Practice

Sarah *saw her / saw 'er* yesterday. (RB1-A/a)

Other Examples

[h] **wh**o is going to college, **h**alftime, **h**ome, it's **h**ard to tell, **h**e's **h**ad to stay, **h**ard of **h**earing

[ ] (possible in casual speech) watch **'im**, and **'e** loves, since **'is** latest operation, speak to **'im**, but **'e** turns the volume up, right on **'im**

Other Practice Activities

❏ Partner Cards—Listening.
❏ Partner Cards—Speaking.
❏ Story Reading.
❏ Story Dictation.
❏ Cloze Reading.

❏ Story Retelling from Skeleton.
❏ Free Story Retelling.
❏ Parallel Story.
❏ Mini-drama.

Unit RB2-A [kən + C] can tell— [kænt] can't tell

Story

Listen to the story as your teacher reads it, or on tape, until you understand the main ideas.

My sister is a very funny girl. She can make people laugh all day long. She knows lots of jokes, and she can tell them very well. (1) She uses funny voices and facial expressions that are so comical that people can't stop laughing. Whenever she's at parties, her friends ask her to tell jokes, and she does. She wants to be a stand-up comedian someday, and she can't pass up the opportunity to practice. But she also warns her friends, "Stop me when you get tired. I **can** tell jokes all night long once I get started."

Today, however, she is different. We are planning to go to a comedy club. It's amateur night, and anyone in the audience can go up on stage and tell jokes. We've been looking forward to this night for weeks, but now my sister says she can't go. She is worried about standing up in front of a group of critical strangers. (2) "I **can't** tell jokes tonight," she insists. "I'm too nervous."

I can't stand it, so I reassure her, "You'll be a hit. I know you can do it." I hope she will calm down so we can go to the club.

Contrasting Sentences

Listening: Write the appropriate key word in each blank. Later, as you hear each sentence, mark the box, point to the picture, make a gesture, and/or say the rejoinder. Speaking: Choose and say each sentence so that your listener(s) can respond correctly.

❏ I _____ tell jokes . . . (all night long once I get started)

❏ I _____ tell jokes . . . (tonight. I'm too nervous.)

Explanations and diagrams for this unit's target sounds are on page 354 in Section 10.

Additional Practice

You *can take / can't take* it with you. (RB2-B/b)

Other Examples

The words and phrases listed below are in the story. Find them and circle or underline them. Say each marked word or phrase aloud—individually and then in its entire sentence. Look for additional words in the story that are reduced and / or blended. Mark and say them also.

[kən] she **can** make people laugh, the audience **can** go up, you **can** do it, we **can** get to the club

[kænt] people **can't** stop, she **can't** pass up, my sister says she **can't** go, I **can't** stand it

Other Practice Activities

❑ Partner Cards—Listening. *Practice until you can point to the right card every time.*
❑ Partner Cards—Speaking. *Practice until you can say the contrasting sentences so accurately that your partner points to the right card every time.*
❑ Story Reading. *Practice reading the story aloud. Mark any difficult words. Then record the story on tape.*
❑ Story Dictation. *Write the story as your teacher reads it or as you listen to it on the audiotape.*
❑ Cloze Reading. *Choose some key words in the story and black them out. Then read the entire story aloud. Do this several times.*

Each time black out more words. Continue until most of the story is blacked out and you can tell it without looking at the page very often.
❑ Story Retelling from Skeleton. *Black out all the remaining words except those you need in order to remind you of the story line. Then, using just this skeleton, tell the story to your partner or class.*
❑ Free Story Retelling. *Retell the whole story from memory, without looking at your book.*
❑ Parallel Story. *Create your own story similar to the one in this unit.*
❑ Mini-drama. *Make up a skit or do a role play based on the story.*

Unit RB2-B [kən + C] can take—
[kænt] can't take

Story

Joe's family was moving, and they had a lot of stuff to pack. When I stopped by to help them, they were separating out the things that they were going to take with them from the things that they were giving away. The parents didn't want to take anything they didn't really need, but Joe's little brother and sister were crying about all the stuff in the give-away pile. "Why can't we take these things, Dad? Can we take them, please?"

The father was trying to be patient. He kept explaining, "We can't take everything. We can take only what fits in the moving van."

As I was helping, I found an old (1) desk lamp in the back of a closet. "What should I do with this nice looking lamp? Which pile should I put it in?" I asked.

#1

Joe's father answered, "You like it? It's yours. You **can** take it with you tonight. Just don't leave it here."

#2

Later, when I was helping Joe pack up the (2) computer, his father laughed and said, "Now *that* you **can't** take with you. Make sure you put it in the right pile!"

Contrasting Sentences

❏ You _____ take it with you. (the lamp)

❏ You _____ take it with you. (the computer)

Additional Practice

I *can tell / can't tell* jokes . . . (RB2-A/a)

Other Examples

[kən] **can** we take, we **can** take only what fits

[kænt] why **can't** we take, we **can't** take everything

Other Practice Activities

❏ Partner Cards—Listening.
❏ Partner Cards—Speaking.
❏ Story Reading.
❏ Story Dictation.
❏ Cloze Reading.

❏ Story Retelling from Skeleton.
❏ Free Story Retelling.
❏ Parallel Story.
❏ Mini-drama.

Unit RB3-A [ɪt ɪz] it is—[ɪts] it's

Story

Listen to the story as your teacher reads it, or on tape, until you understand the main ideas.

I visited Japan with my mother last year. Among the cities we visited, I liked Kyoto best because we stayed at a traditional Japanese inn. In other cities we stayed in modern hotels, but in historic Kyoto we wanted to try something different.

As we expected, everything was totally different. For example, as the (1) innkeeper carefully explained to us, "In a Japanese inn you have to take your shoes off at the door. Also, it is improper to wash yourself in the bathtub. It is only for soaking. You are supposed to wash before you get in."

What I really liked was the dinner and the way it was served. When it's time to eat, the innkeeper comes into your room and politely says, "**It is** time for dinner." Then the employees bring in the dinner. All the food is carefully arranged. It's like a beautiful piece of art.

But when our first dinner was served, my mother was not there to see it. She was at the balcony enjoying the view. (2) "Mom! **It's** time for dinner!" I called. She was impressed with the beautiful dinner too. In fact, before we ate it, she took a picture of it.

Contrasting Sentences

Listening: Write the appropriate key word(s) in each blank. Later, as you hear each sentence, mark the box, point to the picture, make a gesture, and/or say the rejoinder. Speaking: Choose and say each sentence so that your listener(s) can respond correctly.

❏ _____ time for dinner. (the innkeeper)

❏ _____ time for dinner. (the storyteller)

Explanations and diagrams for this unit's target sounds are on page 355 in Section 10.

Additional Practice

For similar types of blending: Do you really think *they'll / they'd* do that? (RB10-A/a), *They've / They'd* eaten all their dinner. (RB11-A/a), *Where'd / Where've* you run to? (RB12-A/a), *Where'd / Where'll* you run to? (RB13-A/a)

Other Examples

The words and phrases listed below are in the story. Find them and circle or underline them. Say each marked word or phrase aloud— individually and then in its entire sentence. Look for additional words in the story that are reduced and / or blended. Mark and say them also.

Unblended: **it is** improper, **it is** only for soaking

Blended: when **it's** time to eat, **it's** like a beautiful piece of art

Other Practice Activities

❏ Partner Cards—Listening. *Practice until you can point to the right card every time.*

❏ Partner Cards—Speaking. *Practice until you can say the contrasting sentences so accurately that your partner points to the right card every time.*

❏ Story Reading. *Practice reading the story aloud. Mark any difficult words. Then record the story on tape.*

❏ Story Dictation. *Write the story as your teacher reads it or as you listen to it on the audiotape.*

❏ Cloze Reading. *Choose some key words in the story and black them out. Then read the entire story aloud. Do this several times.*

Each time black out more words. Continue until most of the story is blacked out and you can tell it without looking at the page very often.

❏ Story Retelling from Skeleton. *Black out all the remaining words except those you need in order to remind you of the story line. Then, using just this skeleton, tell the story to your partner or class.*

❏ Free Story Retelling. *Retell the whole story from memory, without looking at your book.*

❏ Parallel Story. *Create your own story similar to the one in this unit.*

❏ Mini-drama. *Make up a skit or do a role play based on the story.*

Unit RB4-A [wɑnt tuw] want to—[wɑnə] wanna

Story

Listen to the story as your teacher reads it, or on tape, until you understand the main ideas.

Little Jimmy was hungry. He was also tired. Jimmy's parents were shopping, but their tired little son wanted to go home. He repeatedly complained to his parents, (1) "I **wanna** go home! I don't wanna stay here any longer."

Unfortunately for Jimmy, his parents were busy buying food and other things. They tried to ignore him and finish up their shopping as quickly as possible. However, Jimmy just got more and more upset. Finally, feeling totally frustrated, he screamed slowly and clearly, so nearly everyone in the store could hear, (2) "I **want to** go home!" A lot of people stopped their shopping and looked at Jimmy and his parents.

Jimmy's mother quickly opened a box of crackers and gave one to Jimmy. Jimmy's father walked immediately to the checkout line. Before Jimmy could complain again, they were in the car and on their way home. Now it was Jimmy's parents' turn to be upset. "What do you want to do now, Jimmy?" they asked.

Contrasting Sentences

Listening: Write the appropriate key word(s) in each blank. Later, as you hear each sentence, mark the box, point to the picture, make a gesture, and/or say the rejoinder. Speaking: Choose and say each sentence so that your listener(s) can respond correctly.

❏ I _____ go home. (tired and complaining)

❏ I _____ go home. (frustrated and upset)

Explanations and diagrams for this unit's target sounds are on page 355 in Section 10.

Additional Practice

I'm *going to / gonna* study. (RB4-B/b), He's *going to Gallup/gonna gallop*. (RB4-c)

Other Examples

The words and phrases listed below are in the story. Find them and circle or underline them. Say each marked word or phrase aloud—individually and then in its entire sentence. Look for additional words in the story that are reduced and/or blended. Mark and say them also.

Unblended: What do you **want to** do now?

Blended: I don't **wanna** stay here any longer.

Other Practice Activities

❑ Partner Cards—Listening. *Practice until you can point to the right card every time.*

❑ Partner Cards—Speaking. *Practice until you can say the contrasting sentences so accurately that your partner points to the right card every time.*

❑ Story Reading. *Practice reading the story aloud. Mark any difficult words. Then record the story on tape.*

❑ Story Dictation. *Write the story as your teacher reads it or as you listen to it on the audiotape.*

❑ Cloze Reading. *Choose some key words in the story and black them out. Then read the entire story aloud. Do this several times.*

Each time black out more words. Continue until most of the story is blacked out and you can tell it without looking at the page very often.

❑ Story Retelling from Skeleton. *Black out all the remaining words except those you need in order to remind you of the story line. Then, using just this skeleton, tell the story to your partner or class.*

❑ Free Story Retelling. *Retell the whole story from memory, without looking at your book.*

❑ Parallel Story. *Create your own story similar to the one in this unit.*

❑ Mini-drama. *Make up a skit or do a role play based on the story.*

Unit RB4-B [gówiŋ tuw] *going to—* [gə́nə] *gonna*

Story

(1) Peter got a D on his English literature exam. His performance disappointed him very much, and he decided to study hard for the next test. When his (2) teacher, Ms. Ingles, talked to him about his low grade, he said, "I promise I'm **going to** study hard, Ms. Ingles." She had her doubts about that.

Peter started studying as soon as he got home. After a while, the phone rang. It was (3) his friend George. "Hey Pete, do you have any plans for this weekend?" asked George.

Peter answered, "No, not really. Why?"

George said, "Donna and Cindy are going skiing, and we're invited to go with them."

"That sounds fun, but I can't," said Peter.

"Why not?" asked George.

"I got a bad grade on my English test, so I'm **gonna** study," said Peter.

"You're gonna what?" said George. "Don't you know it's the weekend?"

"Don't you know I got a D on my exam?" said Peter, and he hung up. He studied very hard, and he got a B+ on the next test. That made him happy.

Ms. Ingles was happy, too. She told Peter, "I think you're going to succeed after all."

Contrasting Sentences

❏ I'm _____ study. (careful—speaking to teacher)

❏ I'm _____ study. (casual—speaking to friend)

Additional Practice

I *want to* / *wanna* go home. (RB4-A/a), He's *going to Gallup* / *gonna gallop*. (RB4-c)

Other Examples

Unblended: You're **going to** succeed.

Blended: You're **gonna** what?

Other Practice Activities

❏ Partner Cards—Listening.
❏ Partner Cards—Speaking.
❏ Story Reading.
❏ Story Dictation.
❏ Cloze Reading.

❏ Story Retelling
    from Skeleton.
❏ Free Story Retelling.
❏ Parallel Story.
❏ Mini-drama.

Unit RB5-A [dównt nów] don't know—[dənów] dunno

Story

Listen to the story as your teacher reads it, or on tape, until you understand the main ideas.

Dr. Hardy is a vocational counselor in a high school. She helps teenagers decide on what classes to take in school and what careers they want to follow. She finds that students often have a difficult time deciding on careers. When she asks, "What do you want to do in life?" the most common answer is "I dunno. What are my choices?" When they're really confused, the students often (1) get discouraged, look at the floor, and say dejectedly, "I **dunno** what to do."

Dr. Hardy is very good at her job and knows how to find out students' interests and skills. She also knows a lot about different employment options. She makes good suggestions, and, after a few sessions with her, students are (2) filled with excitement. Then, instead of having no ideas about what to do with their lives, they see so many possible options that they end up saying cheerfully, "I **don't know** what to do."

I don't know how Dr. Hardy does it, but I'm glad that she does. She makes a big difference in many students' lives.

Contrasting Sentences

Listening: Write the appropriate key word(s) in each blank. Later, as you hear each sentence, mark the box, point to the picture, make a gesture, and/or say the rejoinder. Speaking: Choose and say each sentence so that your listener(s) can respond correctly.

❏ I _____ what to do. (discouraged)

❏ I _____ what to do. (enthusiastic)

Explanations and diagrams for this unit's target sounds are on page 356 in Section 10.

Additional Practice

For a similar type of reduction: I *want to* / *wanna* go home. (RB4-A/a), I'm *going to* / *gonna* study. (RB4-B/b), He's *going to Gallup* / *gonna gallop.* (RB4-c)

Other Examples

The words and phrases listed below are in the story. Find them and circle or underline them. Say each marked word or phrase aloud—individually and then in its entire sentence. Look for additional words in the story that are reduced and / or blended. Mark and say them also.

Unblended: I **don't know** how she does it.

Blended: I **dunno.** What are my choices?

Other Practice Activities

❏ Partner Cards—Listening. *Practice until you can point to the right card every time.*

❏ Partner Cards—Speaking. *Practice until you can say the contrasting sentences so accurately that your partner points to the right card every time.*

❏ Story Reading. *Practice reading the story aloud. Mark any difficult words. Then record the story on tape.*

❏ Story Dictation. *Write the story as your teacher reads it or as you listen to it on the audiotape.*

❏ Cloze Reading. *Choose some key words in the story and black them out. Then read the entire story aloud. Do this several times.*

Each time black out more words. Continue until most of the story is blacked out and you can tell it without looking at the page very often.

❏ Story Retelling from Skeleton. *Black out all the remaining words except those you need in order to remind you of the story line. Then, using just this skeleton, tell the story to your partner or class.*

❏ Free Story Retelling. *Retell the whole story from memory, without looking at your book.*

❏ Parallel Story. *Create your own story similar to the one in this unit.*

❏ Mini-drama. *Make up a skit or do a role play based on the story.*

Unit RB6-A [hwát dúw yúw] what do you—
[hwádəyə] whaddaya

Story

Listen to the story as your teacher reads it, or on tape, until you understand the main ideas.

Professor Jones frequently secludes himself in his office when he has to write something. He doesn't mind helping students in class or during his office hours, but he hates to be bothered when he's writing.

One evening he was working late on a big report that was due the next day. Yolanda, one of his students from Latin America, saw the light on in his office. She hadn't understood the assignment given earlier that day, so she thought that she would knock on his door and ask him to explain it.

When he heard the knocking, Professor Jones thought, "Now, whodaya think that is?" but he didn't answer. He tried to focus on the report, but Yolanda continued to knock more loudly. Finally, (1) upset by the disturbance, he yelled through the door, **"Whaddaya** want!" Poor Yolanda was frightened by this response from her teacher. Professor Jones then opened the door and saw his student standing there trembling.

"I'm sorry," he said in a more polite and careful way. (2) "I didn't mean to shout. Tell me. **What do you** want?"

All Yolanda could think to say was "Why do you shout?" Then, realizing she had made a mistake by knocking on his door late at night, she turned and ran away. She never knocked on a professor's door at night after that.

Contrasting Sentences

Listening: Write the appropriate key word(s) in each blank. Later, as you hear each sentence, mark the box, point to the picture, make a gesture, and/or say the rejoinder. Speaking: Choose and say each sentence so that your listener(s) can respond correctly.

❏ _____ want? (upset)

❏ _____ want? (polite)

Explanations and diagrams for this unit's target sounds are on page 356 in Section 10.

Additional Practice

For similar types of reduction and blending: *What are you / Whatcha* doing? (RB7-A/a), Can I *get you / getcha* something? (RB7-B/b), I *want to / wanna* go home. (RB4-A/a), I'm *going to / gonna* study. (RB4-B/b), He's *going to Gallup / gonna gallop*. (RB4-c) I *don't know / dunno* what to do. (RB5-A/a)

Other Examples

The words and phrases listed below are in the story. Find them and circle or underline them. Say each marked word or phrase aloud—individually and then in its entire sentence. Look for additional words in the story that are reduced and/or blended. Mark and say them also.

Unblended: **Why do you** shout?

Blended: **Whodaya** think that is?

Other Practice Activities

❏ Partner Cards—Listening. *Practice until you can point to the right card every time.*
❏ Partner Cards—Speaking. *Practice until you can say the contrasting sentences so accurately that your partner points to the right card every time.*
❏ Story Reading. *Practice reading the story aloud. Mark any difficult words. Then record the story on tape.*
❏ Story Dictation. *Write the story as your teacher reads it or as you listen to it on the audiotape.*
❏ Cloze Reading. *Choose some key words in the story and black them out. Then read the entire story aloud. Do this several times.*

Each time black out more words. Continue until most of the story is blacked out and you can tell it without looking at the page very often.
❏ Story Retelling from Skeleton. *Black out all the remaining words except those you need in order to remind you of the story line. Then, using just this skeleton, tell the story to your partner or class.*
❏ Free Story Retelling. *Retell the whole story from memory, without looking at your book.*
❏ Parallel Story. *Create your own story similar to the one in this unit.*
❏ Mini-drama. *Make up a skit or do a role play based on the story.*

Unit RB7-A [t . . . y] *what are you*—[tʃ] *whatcha*

Story

Listen to the story as your teacher reads it, or on tape, until you understand the main ideas.

When Tom was walking along the river, he saw a couple of his friends. He went up to them and said, (1) "Hey! **Whatcha** doin'?"

They answered, "We're fishin'. Why don'tcha join us?" So Tom sat next to them, but they didn't catch any fish. They wouldn't talk either. They didn't want to scare the fish. Tom felt bored, so he left.

Before long, he found two other friends. They were swimming around in the river with their clothes on. They acted like they were looking for something. "Whatcha doin'?" Tom asked.

They saw him and stopped swimming, but they couldn't understand what he was saying. "Huh?" they replied.

"Whatcha doin'?" Tom repeated.

"What?" they responded. They were a little distance from shore, and maybe they had water in their ears.

(2) "**What are you** doing?" Tom shouted, pronouncing each word clearly.

"Oh," one guy explained, "we're looking for my shoe."

"Your shoe?" yelled Tom.

"Yes!" he shouted back. "We were playing soccer. I kicked the ball hard, my shoe came off, and it flew into the river. Why don't you help us?"

"Well, at least these guys aren't boring," thought Tom and jumped into the water.

Contrasting Sentences

Listening: Write the appropriate key word(s) in each blank. Later, as you hear each sentence, mark the box, point to the picture, make a ges-

ture, and / or say the rejoinder. Speaking: Choose and say each sentence so that your listener(s) can respond correctly.

❑ _____ doing? (casual)

❑ _____ doing? (careful)

Explanations and diagrams for this unit's target sounds are on pages 356–57 in Section 10.

Additional Practice

Can I *get you / getcha* something? (RB7-B/b)

For similar types of blending: *Did you / Didja* hear . . . ? (RB8-A/a), I *guess you're / guesshur* happier now. (RB9-A/a)

Other Examples

The words and phrases listed below are in the story. Find them and circle or underline them. Say each marked word or phrase aloud— individually and then in its entire sentence. Look for additional words in the story that are reduced and / or blended. Mark and say them also.

Unblended: **Why don't you** help us?

Blended: **Why don'tcha** join us?

Other Practice Activities

❑ Partner Cards—Listening. *Practice until you can point to the right card every time.*
❑ Partner Cards—Speaking. *Practice until you can say the contrasting sentences so accurately that your partner points to the right card every time.*
❑ Story Reading. *Practice reading the story aloud. Mark any difficult words. Then record the story on tape.*
❑ Story Dictation. *Write the story as your teacher reads it or as you listen to it on the audiotape.*
❑ Cloze Reading. *Choose some key words in the story and black them out. Then read the entire story aloud. Do this several times.*

Each time black out more words. Continue until most of the story is blacked out and you can tell it without looking at the page very often.
❑ Story Retelling from Skeleton. *Black out all the remaining words except those you need in order to remind you of the story line. Then, using just this skeleton, tell the story to your partner or class.*
❑ Free Story Retelling. *Retell the whole story from memory, without looking at your book.*
❑ Parallel Story. *Create your own story similar to the one in this unit.*
❑ Mini-drama. *Make up a skit or do a role play based on the story.*

Unit RB7-B Unblended [t + y] get you—
Blended [tʃ] getcha

Story

To prepare for a big mathematics test, I had a study group at my
house yesterday. (1) After studying for a couple of hours, my
classmates and I all got tired. We were especially frustrated
with one very difficult math problem. We just couldn't figure it
out. So I said, "Let's take a break. You guys must be hungry. Can
I **getcha** something?"

They responded, "Sure! Whatcha got?"

Just then the doorbell rang. At the door was (2) an older
woman, someone I'd never met before, one of my mother's
friends. I said to her, "My mother has gone shopping, but she
should be back soon. Would you care to wait inside?"

"Gladly," she said and came in.

I asked her, "I'm getting some snacks for my friends. Can I
get you something?"

She said, "No, thank you. Don't worry about me."

I explained, "We've been working on a math problem for an
hour, and we still don't get it, so we're taking a break."

Then she smiled and said, "What have you done so far?
Maybe I can help you." It turned out that she was a math pro-
fessor. What luck! I didn't know my mother had such a friend.
Thanks to her, we solved the problem at last.

Contrasting Sentences

❑ Can I _____ something? (to friends)

❑ Can I _____ something? (to older guest)

Additional Practice

What are you / Whatcha doing? (RB7-A/a)

For similar types of blending: *Did you / Didja* hear . . . ? (RB8-A/a),
  I *guess you're / guesshur* happier now. (RB9-A/a)

Other Examples

Unblended: **What have you** done so far?

Blended: **Whatcha** got?

Other Practice Activities

- ❏ Partner Cards—Listening.
- ❏ Partner Cards—Speaking.
- ❏ Story Reading.
- ❏ Story Dictation.
- ❏ Cloze Reading.
- ❏ Story Retelling
  from Skeleton.
- ❏ Free Story Retelling.
- ❏ Parallel Story.
- ❏ Mini-drama.

Unit RB8-A [d + y] did you—[dʒ] didja

Story

Listen to the story as your teacher reads it, or on tape, until you under-stand the main ideas.

One foggy morning, (1) Jerry and I took our neighbor Sidney out on the lake near our town. (2) Sid had never been fishing before. You see, Sid is not much of an outdoors person. But he's very proud and he doesn't think of himself as being deficient in any way. In fact, he thinks of himself as being superior in almost everything. For instance, he thinks he's very educated and shows it by the way he talks. That bothers people, so we decided to teach him a lesson.

In the boat Jerry started, "**Didja** ever hear the story of the monster in this lake?"

Sid smiled, "**Did you** ever hear that monsters don't really exist?" As usual, Sid thought he knew more than we did.

Suddenly Jerry shouted, "Didja hear that?"

"Did you really hear something?" Sid replied.

Jerry said, "There it is again. It's getting closer."

Then I screamed, "Look out behind you!" Sid turned and saw the head of a giant sea monster coming out of the fog. He panicked and jumped right out of the boat.

Jerry laughed, "Hey Sid, didn'tcha read the newspaper yes-terday? They're shooting scenes for a new monster movie here on the lake."

Sid was embarrassed that the monster was only part of a film. He tried to cover up by asking, "Did you really think I believed your silly monster was real?"

I'm afraid Sid didn't learn anything from his experience.

Contrasting Sentences

Listening: Write the appropriate key word(s) in each blank. Later, as you hear each sentence, mark the box, point to the picture, make a ges-

ture, and/or say the rejoinder. Speaking: Choose and say each sentence so that your listener(s) can respond correctly.

❏ _____ ever hear . . . (the story of the monster? Jerry speaking)

❏ _____ ever hear . . . (that monsters don't really exist? Sid speaking)

Explanations and diagrams for this unit's target sounds are on page 357 in Section 10.

Additional Practice

For similar types of blending: *What are you / Whatcha* doing? (RB7-A/a), Can I *get you / getcha* something? (RB7-B/b), I *guess you're / guesshur* happier now. (RB9-A/a)

Other Examples

The words and phrases listed below are in the story. Find them and circle or underline them. Say each marked word or phrase aloud—individually and then in its entire sentence. Look for additional words in the story that are reduced and/or blended. Mark and say them also.

Unblended: **Did you** really hear something? **Did you** really think . . .

Blended: **Didja** hear that? **Didn'tcha** read the newspaper yesterday?

Other Practice Activities

❏ Partner Cards—Listening. *Practice until you can point to the right card every time.*
❏ Partner Cards—Speaking. *Practice until you can say the contrasting sentences so accurately that your partner points to the right card every time.*
❏ Story Reading. *Practice reading the story aloud. Mark any difficult words. Then record the story on tape.*
❏ Story Dictation. *Write the story as your teacher reads it or as you listen to it on the audiotape.*
❏ Cloze Reading. *Choose some key words in the story and black them out. Then read the entire story aloud. Do this several times.*

Each time black out more words. Continue until most of the story is blacked out and you can tell it without looking at the page very often.
❏ Story Retelling from Skeleton. *Black out all the remaining words except those you need in order to remind you of the story line. Then, using just this skeleton, tell the story to your partner or class.*
❏ Free Story Retelling. *Retell the whole story from memory, without looking at your book.*
❏ Parallel Story. *Create your own story similar to the one in this unit.*
❏ Mini-drama. *Make up a skit or do a role play based on the story.*

Unit RB9-A [s + y] guess you're—[ʃ] guesshur

Story

Listen to the story as your teacher reads it, or on tape, until you understand the main ideas.

(1) Yumi is from Japan, but she is studying English in America. Whenever she hears new words or expressions, she takes notes and asks me about them later.

The other day, we went for a walk and ran into (2) my old co-worker Shirley, who had changed jobs. I asked her, "Do you miss your old job?"

She answered, "Oh no. My new job is wonderful! Everyone is super nice. Also, I get paid more, and I do more responsible work. I really love my new job."

I couldn't believe that she was the same person. In her old job, Shirley had always been complaining. So, I said, "I **guesshur** happier now."

"Oh, yes. You're right there," Shirley answered.

After Shirley left us, Yumi looked at her notes and asked me a question. "What did you mean by 'I get sure happier'? I didn't understand the grammar of that sentence."

"Get sure happier?" I couldn't understand that myself. Then I remembered what I had said to Shirley. "Oh, you mean 'I **guess you're** happier,'" I explained, saying each word distinctly.

"Oh, of course!" said Yumi. "I didn't understand because you blended the words together." Then she started repeating, "guesshur, guesshur, guesshur."

Contrasting Sentences

Listening: Write the appropriate key word(s) in each blank. Later, as you hear each sentence, mark the box, point to the picture, make a ges-

ture, and/or say the rejoinder. Speaking: Choose and say each sentence so that your listener(s) can respond correctly.

❏ I _____ happier now. (speaking to Shirley)

❏ I _____ happier now. (speaking to Yumi)

Explanations and diagrams for this unit's target sounds are on pages 357–58 in Section 10.

Additional Practice

For similar types of blending: *What are you / Whatcha doing?* (RB7-A/a), *Can I get you / getcha something?* (RB7-B/b), *Did you / Didja hear…?* (RB8-A/a)

Other Examples

The words and phrases listed below are in the story. Find them and circle or underline them. Say each marked word or phrase aloud—individually and then in its entire sentence. Look for additional words in the story that are reduced and/or blended. Mark and say them also.

Unblended: Oh, **yes. You're** right there.

Blended: Do you **miss your** [mɪʃyər] old job?

Other Practice Activities

❏ Partner Cards—Listening. *Practice until you can point to the right card every time.*
❏ Partner Cards—Speaking. *Practice until you can say the contrasting sentences so accurately that your partner points to the right card every time.*
❏ Story Reading. *Practice reading the story aloud. Mark any difficult words. Then record the story on tape.*
❏ Story Dictation. *Write the story as your teacher reads it or as you listen to it on the audiotape.*
❏ Cloze Reading. *Choose some key words in the story and black them out. Then read the entire story aloud. Do this several times.*

Each time black out more words. Continue until most of the story is blacked out and you can tell it without looking at the page very often.
❏ Story Retelling from Skeleton. *Black out all the remaining words except those you need in order to remind you of the story line. Then, using just this skeleton, tell the story to your partner or class.*
❏ Free Story Retelling. *Retell the whole story from memory, without looking at your book.*
❏ Parallel Story. *Create your own story similar to the one in this unit.*
❏ Mini-drama. *Make up a skit or do a role play based on the story.*

Unit RB10-A Blended *will,* They'll— Blended *would,* They'd

Story

Listen to the story as your teacher reads it, or on tape, until you understand the main ideas.

Larry and Vanessa ran out of the school as soon as class finished today. I asked another classmate why they were in such a hurry. According to her, they were going to (1) dye their hair red today. I was surprised because I thought they were both on the conservative side.

"Dye their hair? Do you really think **they'll** do that?" I asked. "That sounds pretty wild for them."

She said, "Of course, they will. If you think Larry and Vanessa are conservative, you're wrong. Have you seen some of their friends? Blue hair, green hair, pierced bodies . . . "

"Wow, that's a surprise," I responded.

Then she said, "They might even get (2) tattoos next."

"Larry and Vanessa? Tattoos? That's really serious. I can't believe they'd do that. Tattoos are permanent. Do you really think **they'd** do that?" I asked.

My classmate answered, "Anything's possible. We'll see."

I still can't believe that they'd go that far. But I do think they'll dye their hair. I am looking forward to seeing their new hair color tomorrow.

Contrasting Sentences

Listening: Write the appropriate key word(s) in each blank. Later, as you hear each sentence, mark the box, point to the picture, make a gesture, and/or say the rejoinder. Speaking: Choose and say each sentence so that your listener(s) can respond correctly.

❏ Do you really think _____ do that? (Of course they will.)

❏ Do you really think _____ do that? (Anything's possible.)

Explanations and diagrams for this unit's target sounds are on pages 358–59 in Section 10.

Additional Practice

For similar types of blending: *They've / They'd* eaten all their dinner. (RB11-A/a),*Where'd / Where've* you run to? (RB12-A/a), *Where'd / Where'll* you run to? (RB13-A/a)

Other Examples

The words and phrases listed below are in the story. Find them and circle or underline them. Say each marked word or phrase aloud— individually and then in its entire sentence. Look for additional words in the story that are reduced and/or blended. Mark and say them also.

[l] I do think **they'll** dye their hair, **We'll** see

[d] I can't believe **they'd** do that, I still can't believe that **they'd** go that far

Other Practice Activities

❑ Partner Cards—Listening. *Practice until you can point to the right card every time.*

❑ Partner Cards—Speaking. *Practice until you can say the contrasting sentences so accurately that your partner points to the right card every time.*

❑ Story Reading. *Practice reading the story aloud. Mark any difficult words. Then record the story on tape.*

❑ Story Dictation. *Write the story as your teacher reads it or as you listen to it on the audiotape.*

❑ Cloze Reading. *Choose some key words in the story and black them out. Then read the entire story aloud. Do this several times.*

Each time black out more words. Continue until most of the story is blacked out and you can tell it without looking at the page very often.

❑ Story Retelling from Skeleton. *Black out all the remaining words except those you need in order to remind you of the story line. Then, using just this skeleton, tell the story to your partner or class.*

❑ Free Story Retelling. *Retell the whole story from memory, without looking at your book.*

❑ Parallel Story. *Create your own story similar to the one in this unit.*

❑ Mini-drama. *Make up a skit or do a role play based on the story.*

Unit RB11-A Blended *have*, They've— Blended *had*, They'd

Story

Listen to the story as your teacher reads it, or on tape, until you understand the main ideas.

I work for a catering service that makes meals and delivers them to families. Last week, near the end of the day, my boss looked down at her ring and realized that the stone had fallen out. "That stone is very valuable," she announced. "We've got to find it." We looked everywhere but didn't have any success. She finally decided that it must've fallen into one of the dinners that we'd prepared. She'd worked on the dinners for the Phillips and the Navarones.

(1) The Phillips' nanny reported, "I'm sorry. **They've** eaten all their dinner, and nothing unusual has turned up."

At the Navarones' house (2) the babysitter said that **they'd** eaten all their dinner earlier, and they'd not found any sort of stone either.

My boss was very depressed and said, "Well, we've done all that we can. Let's call it quits." She took off her apron to throw it in the dirty laundry. She'd checked the apron pockets before and hadn't found the stone. But, as she checked them one last time, she gave a cry of relief, "I've found it!" Her precious stone was in the bottom corner of one of her apron pockets. It was not lost after all.

Contrasting Sentences

Listening: Write the appropriate key word(s) in each blank. Later, as you hear each sentence, mark the box, point to the picture, make a gesture, and/or say the rejoinder. Speaking: Choose and say each sentence so that your listener(s) can respond correctly.

❑ _____ eaten all their dinner. (Yes, they have.)

❑ _____ eaten all their dinner. (Yes, they had.)

Explanations and diagrams for this unit's target sounds are on pages 358–59 in Section 10.

Additional Practice

For similar types of blending: Do you really think *they'll / they'd* do that? (RB10-A/a),*Where'd / Where've* you run to? (RB12-A/a), *Where'd / Where'll* you run to? (RB13-A/a)

Other Examples

The words and phrases listed below are in the story. Find them and circle or underline them. Say each marked word or phrase aloud—individually and then in its entire sentence. Look for additional words in the story that are reduced and/or blended. Mark and say them also.

[v] **We've** got to find it, It **must've** fallen, **We've** done all, **I've** found it

[d] **We'd** prepared, **She'd** worked on, **They'd** not found the stone, **She'd** checked

Other Practice Activities

❑ Partner Cards—Listening. *Practice until you can point to the right card every time.*

❑ Partner Cards—Speaking. *Practice until you can say the contrasting sentences so accurately that your partner points to the right card every time.*

❑ Story Reading. *Practice reading the story aloud. Mark any difficult words. Then record the story on tape.*

❑ Story Dictation. *Write the story as your teacher reads it or as you listen to it on the audiotape.*

❑ Cloze Reading. *Choose some key words in the story and black them out. Then read the entire story aloud. Do this several times.*

Each time black out more words. Continue until most of the story is blacked out and you can tell it without looking at the page very often.

❑ Story Retelling from Skeleton. *Black out all the remaining words except those you need in order to remind you of the story line. Then, using just this skeleton, tell the story to your partner or class.*

❑ Free Story Retelling. *Retell the whole story from memory, without looking at your book.*

❑ Parallel Story. *Create your own story similar to the one in this unit.*

❑ Mini-drama. *Make up a skit or do a role play based on the story.*

Unit RB12-A Blended *did,* Where'd—
Blended *have,* Where've

Story

Listen to the story as your teacher reads it, or on tape, until you understand the main ideas.

Karen is a long-distance (1) runner. She runs many hours and many miles every week. So much running can be boring, so for variety's sake Karen tries to run different routes. She also runs to various destinations. Sometimes she goes to the library, sometimes the airport, and sometimes even other towns.

Karen runs so much that she is running out of interesting routes and destinations, so she often asks (2) other runners for suggestions. She hopes to learn about good routes that they've run. Of course, before answering they usually ask, **"Where've you run to already?"** They don't want to describe a complicated route to a place only to hear her say, "Oh, I've been there." Coming up with a place that is new for Karen is not easy, but sometimes they tell her of a place that they've run to and she hasn't.

Yesterday, when I passed her place, (3) Karen was just getting home from running. I asked her, **"Where'd** you run to today?"** To my amazement, she had run to a lake five miles away.

When she asked me, "What'd you do today? Where'd you go?" I was embarrassed to tell her that I had spent my day at home watching television.

Contrasting Sentences

Listening: Write the appropriate key word(s) in each blank. Later, as you hear each sentence, mark the box, point to the picture, make a gesture, and/or say the rejoinder. Speaking: Choose and say each sentence so that your listener(s) can respond correctly.

❏ _____ you run to? (already)

❏ _____ you run to? (today)

Explanations and diagrams for this unit's target sounds are on pages 358–59 in Section 10.

Additional Practice

For similar types of blending: Do you really think *they'll/they'd* do that? (RB10-A/a), *They've/They'd* eaten all their dinner. (RB11-A/a), *Where'd/Where'll* you run to? (RB13-A/a)

Other Examples

The words and phrases listed below are in the story. Find them and circle or underline them. Say each marked word or phrase aloud— individually and then in its entire sentence. Look for additional words in the story that are reduced and/or blended. Mark and say them also.

[d] **What'd** you do today? **Where'd** you go?

[v] routes that **they've** run, Oh, **I've** been there

Other Practice Activities

❏ Partner Cards—Listening. *Practice until you can point to the right card every time.*
❏ Partner Cards—Speaking. *Practice until you can say the contrasting sentences so accurately that your partner points to the right card every time.*
❏ Story Reading. *Practice reading the story aloud. Mark any difficult words. Then record the story on tape.*
❏ Story Dictation. *Write the story as your teacher reads it or as you listen to it on the audiotape.*
❏ Cloze Reading. *Choose some key words in the story and black them out. Then read the entire story aloud. Do this several times.*

Each time black out more words. Continue until most of the story is blacked out and you can tell it without looking at the page very often.
❏ Story Retelling from Skeleton. *Black out all the remaining words except those you need in order to remind you of the story line. Then, using just this skeleton, tell the story to your partner or class.*
❏ Free Story Retelling. *Retell the whole story from memory, without looking at your book.*
❏ Parallel Story. *Create your own story similar to the one in this unit.*
❏ Mini-drama. *Make up a skit or do a role play based on the story.*

Unit RB13-A Blended *did,* Where'd— Blended *will,* Where'll

Story

Listen to the story as your teacher reads it, or on tape, until you understand the main ideas.

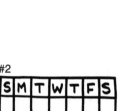

"I saw you (1) jogging yesterday," I told my friend Lucy.

"Jogging?" said Lucy. "Oh, that wasn't really jogging. At least I wasn't doing it for exercise." Then Lucy explained what she'd been doing. "Once a week, my family gets together and we play games after dinner. If you lose, you have to go buy a dessert for everybody. And you have to come back in fifteen minutes. That's why I was running. And you know what else? To keep things from getting boring, you have to go to a different place and buy a different dessert every time."

"That sounds fun," I responded.

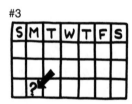

"Well, it is if you win, but not if you lose," said Lucy.

"So, **where'd** you run to (2) yesterday?"

"The ice cream store near the station."

Then I asked her, "**Where'll** you run to if you lose again (3) next week?"

She said, "I don't know where I'll go, but I don't expect to lose two weeks in a row. My luck isn't that bad."

Contrasting Sentences

Listening: Write the appropriate key word(s) in each blank. Later, as you hear each sentence, mark the box, point to the picture, make a gesture, and/or say the rejoinder. Speaking: Choose and say each sentence so that your listener(s) can respond correctly.

❏ _____ you run to? (yesterday)

❏ _____ you run to? (next week)

Explanations and diagrams for this unit's target sounds are on pages 358–59 in Section 10.

Additional Practice

For similar types of blending: Do you really think *they'll / they'd* do that? (RB10-A/a), *They've / They'd* eaten all their dinner. (RB11-A/a), *Where'd / Where've* you run to? (RB12-A/a)

Other Examples

The words and phrases listed below are in the story. Find them and circle or underline them. Say each marked word or phrase aloud—individually and then in its entire sentence. Look for additional words in the story that are reduced and/or blended. Mark and say them also.

[d] Lucy explained what **she'd** been doing

[l] I don't know where **I'll** go.

Other Practice Activities

❏ Partner Cards—Listening. *Practice until you can point to the right card every time.*
❏ Partner Cards—Speaking. *Practice until you can say the contrasting sentences so accurately that your partner points to the right card every time.*
❏ Story Reading. *Practice reading the story aloud. Mark any difficult words. Then record the story on tape.*
❏ Story Dictation. *Write the story as your teacher reads it or as you listen to it on the audiotape.*
❏ Cloze Reading. *Choose some key words in the story and black them out. Then read the entire story aloud. Do this several times.*

Each time black out more words. Continue until most of the story is blacked out and you can tell it without looking at the page very often.

❏ Story Retelling from Skeleton. *Black out all the remaining words except those you need in order to remind you of the story line. Then, using just this skeleton, tell the story to your partner or class.*
❏ Free Story Retelling. *Retell the whole story from memory, without looking at your book.*
❏ Parallel Story. *Create your own story similar to the one in this unit.*
❏ Mini-drama. *Make up a skit or do a role play based on the story.*

Section 6
Word Stress (WS)

Unit WS1-A [S´-S] DESert—[S-S´] desSERT

Story

Listen to the story as your teacher reads it, or on tape, until you understand the main ideas.

My friend Peter and I were driving across the (1) desert on our vacation. We took the back roads to escape the crowds and traffic. Peter loved the **desert** and its beautiful scenery. We were having a great time. Then our car broke down. Suddenly we saw things differently. The desert was very hot and dry, and it didn't seem so pretty anymore.

We were lucky because we had lots of water with us. On the other hand, we were unlucky because nobody came by to help us. We waited there for hours. The longer we were in the desert, the hotter we got. Even though he drank lots of water, Peter got so hot that he started dreaming of swimming pools and ice cream. In the end, we were lucky because a sheriff arrived and helped us get to the next town.

When Peter and I got there, we were very hungry, so we went to a cafe to eat. Peter ordered a (2) large bowl of ice cream. He loved it. Then he had a big dinner. The waitress couldn't believe he wanted **dessert** first. She just didn't understand, but I did.

Contrasting Sentences

Listening: Write the appropriate key word in each blank. Later, as you hear each sentence, mark the box, point to the picture, make a gesture, and/or say the rejoinder. Speaking: Choose and say each sentence so that your listener(s) can respond correctly.

❏ Peter loved the _____. (scenery)

❏ Peter loved the _____. (ice cream)

Explanations and diagrams for this unit's target sounds are on pages 359–60 in Section 10.

Additional Practice

In *1914/1940,* Nancy was born. (WS1-B/b), Please turn to page *fifty/fifteen* now. (WS1-c), I will be *seventy/seventeen* next year. (WS1-d), By the time he reaches *sixty/sixteen,* Ned plans to be a millionaire. (WS1-e)

Other Words

Sort the words listed below into two groups according to the stress pattern. Write the words in the spaces provided. The first two have been done for you. Then, circle or underline these words each time they occur in the story. Say each marked word aloud. Then say the entire sentence. Look for additional words in the story that use the target stress pattern. Mark and say them also.
escape, believe, pretty, cafe, lucky, arrived, hotter, sheriff, dinner, because

[S´-S] véry,

[S-S´] acróss,

Other Practice Activities

❏ Partner Cards—Listening. *Practice until you can point to the right card every time.*

❏ Partner Cards—Speaking. *Practice until you can say the contrasting sentences so accurately that your partner points to the right card every time.*

❏ Story Reading. *Practice reading the story aloud. Mark any difficult words. Then record the story on tape.*

❏ Story Dictation. *Write the story as your teacher reads it or as you listen to it on the audiotape.*

❏ Cloze Reading. *Choose some key words in the story and black them out. Then read the entire story aloud. Do this several times.*

Each time black out more words. Continue until most of the story is blacked out and you can tell it without looking at the page very often.

❏ Story Retelling from Skeleton. *Black out all the remaining words except those you need in order to remind you of the story line. Then, using just this skeleton, tell the story to your partner or class.*

❏ Free Story Retelling. *Retell the whole story from memory, without looking at your book.*

❏ Parallel Story. *Create your own story similar to the one in this unit.*

❏ Mini-drama. *Make up a skit or do a role play based on the story.*

Unit WS1-B [S´-S] FORty—[S-S´] fourTEEN

Story

(1) Nancy was born in **1914.** Twenty-three years later, in 1937, she married, and three years after that, in **1940,** she had (2) a baby girl. Nancy's husband thought the baby looked so much like Nancy that they should give her the same name. Nancy thought that would be cute, so from then on there were two Nancys in the family.

Nancy the mother and Nancy her daughter lived happily for many years. But when young Nancy got older, things changed. She didn't like being named after her mother. She wanted to have her own name and her own identity. She didn't like being called "little Nancy," and she hated it when her mother's friends would say, "Oh, you're just like your mother." As a result, she became rebellious and fought with her mother a lot.

In 1960, Nancy the daughter decided she had had enough. She legally changed her name to Charlene. That turned out to be a good idea. For more than thirty years now, she has had her own identity, and no one has confused Charlene with her mother. As a result, their relationship has been very serene.

Contrasting Sentences

❏ In _____, Nancy was born. (the mother)

❏ In _____, Nancy was born. (the daughter)

Additional Practice

Peter loved the *désert/dessért*. (WS1-A/a), Please turn to page *fifty/fifteen* now. (WS1-c), I will be *seventy/seventeen* next year. (WS1-d), By the time he reaches *sixty/sixteen,* Ned plans to be a millionaire. (WS1-e)

For a similar stress pattern in three-syllable words: Beverly was part of the *cómedy/commíttee.* (WS2-A/a)

Other Words

enough, Charlene, twenty, married, after, baby, between, sixty, decide, machine

[S´-S] Náncy,

[S-S´] confúsed,

Other Practice Activities

❏ Partner Cards—Listening.
❏ Partner Cards—Speaking.
❏ Story Reading.
❏ Story Dictation.
❏ Cloze Reading.

❏ Story Retelling
　from Skeleton.
❏ Free Story Retelling.
❏ Parallel Story.
❏ Mini-drama.

Unit WS2-A [S´-S-S] COMedy— [S-S´-S] comMIttee

Story

Listen to the story as your teacher reads it, or on tape, until you understand the main ideas.

Every year Beverly's high school presents a play. A (1) committee of teachers and students is appointed to assist the director and make sure that everything proceeds smoothly. Along with the director, the committee determines which play will be produced, works out the calendar, and helps choose the actors. In other words, they make sure it is a quality production.

This year Beverly, who is president of the school drama club, was chosen as one of the student representatives on the play **committee.** Since she has always dreamed of being an actor and director, she was very excited. She was honored to be part of the committee.

For the school play this year, the committee chose Shakespeare's (2) comedy, *A Midsummer Night's Dream.* Later, Beverly was very surprised to get a major part in the play. She didn't think she would be part of the **comedy** because she was on the committee. Obviously, other members of the committee thought differently.

Contrasting Sentences

Listening: Write the appropriate key word in each blank. Later, as you hear each sentence, mark the box, point to the picture, make a gesture, and/or say the rejoinder. Speaking: Choose and say each sentence so that your listener(s) can respond correctly.

❑ Beverly was part of the _____. (group in charge)

❑ Beverly was part of the _____. (funny play)

Explanations and diagrams for this unit's target sounds are on pages 360–61 in Section 10.

Additional Practice

For a similar stress pattern in two-syllable words: Peter loved the *désert / dessért.* (WS1-A/a), In *1914 / 1940,* Nancy was born. (WS1-B/b), Please turn to page *fifty / fifteen* now. (WS1-c), I will be *seventy / seventeen* next year. (WS1-d), By the time he reaches *sixty / sixteen,* Ned plans to be a millionaire. (WS1-e)

Other Words

Sort the words listed below into two groups according to the stress pattern. Write the words in the spaces provided. The first two have been done for you. Then, circle or underline these words each time they occur in the story. Say each marked word aloud. Then say the entire sentence. Look for additional words in the story that use the target stress pattern. Mark and say them also.

Beverly, excited, everything, director, quality, production, president, cabinet, appointed, eleven

[S´-S-S] cálendar,

[S-S´-S] detérmines,

Other Practice Activities

❏ Partner Cards—Listening. *Practice until you can point to the right card every time.*

❏ Partner Cards—Speaking. *Practice until you can say the contrasting sentences so accurately that your partner points to the right card every time.*

❏ Story Reading. *Practice reading the story aloud. Mark any difficult words. Then record the story on tape.*

❏ Story Dictation. *Write the story as your teacher reads it or as you listen to it on the audiotape.*

❏ Cloze Reading. *Choose some key words in the story and black them out. Then read the entire story aloud. Do this several times.*

Each time black out more words. Continue until most of the story is blacked out and you can tell it without looking at the page very often.

❏ Story Retelling from Skeleton. *Black out all the remaining words except those you need in order to remind you of the story line. Then, using just this skeleton, tell the story to your partner or class.*

❏ Free Story Retelling. *Retell the whole story from memory, without looking at your book.*

❏ Parallel Story. *Create your own story similar to the one in this unit.*

❏ Mini-drama. *Make up a skit or do a role play based on the story.*

Unit WS3-A [ˋS-Sˊ] ʀᴇ-LEASE—[S-Sˊ] reLEASE

Story

Listen to the story as your teacher reads it, or on tape, until you understand the main ideas.

My friend Joseph is very interested in films. Every few days he talks to the managers of the local movie theater to discuss what new films are going to be (1) released by the film companies during the next week. When there is a new film that he wants to see, Joseph can hardly wait until they **release** it. Then, when it arrives, he watches it as many times as he can.

Because his town and its theater are very small, however, Joseph is often disappointed. Besides taking a long time to arrive, films don't play very long. That means that they are sent back to the company that leases them to the theater before Joseph can see them enough times. He is so disappointed that he occasionally asks the theater managers to (2) **re-lease** the films that he likes the most. The managers appreciate Joseph's enthusiasm, but they don't re-lease films very often. So Joseph has to remember his favorite films and recreate them in his mind.

Contrasting Sentences

Listening: Write the appropriate key word in each blank. Later, as you hear each sentence, mark the box, point to the picture, make a gesture, and/or say the rejoinder. Speaking: Choose and say each sentence so that your listener(s) can respond correctly.

❏ Joseph wants them to _____ the film soon. (send to theaters)

❏ Joseph wants them to _____ the film soon. (lease again)

Explanations and diagrams for this unit's target sounds are on page 361 in Section 10.

Additional Practice

We need to *rè-fórm / refórm* the club. (WS3-B/b), They weren't going to *refúnd / refúnd* the agency. (WS3-C/c), Dad *recóvered / recóvered* the chairs. (WS3-D/d)

Other Words

Sort the words listed below into two groups according to the stress pattern. Write the words in the spaces provided. The first two have been done for you. Then, circle or underline these words each time they occur in the story. Say each marked word aloud. Then say the entire sentence. Look for additional words in the story that use the target stress pattern. Mark and say them also.

recreate, recover, refill, reelect, remember, redirect, recover, redecorate, relax, reject

[`S-S´] rèdelíver,

[S-S´] rehéarse,

Other Practice Activities

❏ Partner Cards—Listening. *Practice until you can point to the right card every time.*

❏ Partner Cards—Speaking. *Practice until you can say the contrasting sentences so accurately that your partner points to the right card every time.*

❏ Story Reading. *Practice reading the story aloud. Mark any difficult words. Then record the story on tape.*

❏ Story Dictation. *Write the story as your teacher reads it or as you listen to it on the audiotape.*

❏ Cloze Reading. *Choose some key words in the story and black them out. Then read the entire story aloud. Do this several times.*

Each time black out more words. Continue until most of the story is blacked out and you can tell it without looking at the page very often.

❏ Story Retelling from Skeleton. *Black out all the remaining words except those you need in order to remind you of the story line. Then, using just this skeleton, tell the story to your partner or class.*

❏ Free Story Retelling. *Retell the whole story from memory, without looking at your book.*

❏ Parallel Story. *Create your own story similar to the one in this unit.*

❏ Mini-drama. *Make up a skit or do a role play based on the story.*

Unit WS3-B [`S-S´] re-FORM— [S-S´] reFORM

Story

When I got to school this morning I found out that the ski club was in trouble. All of the members had received a note that said: "Urgent meeting. Please come. The ski club is in need of major reform."

When I went to the meeting, the club advisor related a sad tale. He reported that the club treasurer had spent most of the club funds for personal purposes. Then, he had moved away without repaying anything and was not expected to return. No one knew how to contact him, and almost no money remained in the club account. The other officers were not even aware that this had happened. They hadn't been having meetings. Besides that, some of our activities had violated school rules.

Because of these problems, our club activities will be restricted until we **reform** the club and make it work properly. We should probably start by (1) electing new officers. If they can't reform the club, we will have to disband it this year and try to (2) **re-form** it next year. Recreating the club from the ground up may be the best approach.

Contrasting Sentences

❏ We need to _____ the club. (correct the problems, now)

❏ We need to _____ the club. (start over, form it again)

Additional Practice

Joseph wants them to *rè-léase / reléase* the film soon. (WS3-A/a), They weren't going to *rèfúnd / refúnd* the agency. (WS3-C/c), Dad *rècóvered / recóvered* the chairs. (WS3-D/d)

Other Words

return, remains, reelect, reported, redeliver, reorganize, restricted, renumber, reinforce, renew

[`S-S´] rècreáte,

[S-S´] reláted,

Other Practice Activities

- ❏ Partner Cards—Listening.
- ❏ Partner Cards—Speaking.
- ❏ Story Reading.
- ❏ Story Dictation.
- ❏ Cloze Reading.

- ❏ Story Retelling from Skeleton.
- ❏ Free Story Retelling.
- ❏ Parallel Story.
- ❏ Mini-drama.

Unit WS3-C [`S-S´] reFUND—[S-S´] reFUND

Story

(1) Mega Star Talent Agency is funded by one of Hollywood's biggest movie studios. The agency's job is to conduct talent searches and supply the studio with new stars who can act, dance, and/or sing. When Mega Star's agents discover new talent, they issue a contract and (2) pay the new star a large amount of money in advance. If the new star later decides to change studios, she or he has to (3) **refund** the money.

Last year, Mega Star had a big problem. They discovered a new female star who seemed perfect for the lead in a new romance movie. After they signed her up and gave her a big advance, she revealed that she was really a man. All the papers carried the sensational story.

The embarrassed studio executives were upset with Mega Star and weren't going to (1) **refund** the agency when its contract was up. Mega Star, in turn, was mad at the impersonator and demanded a refund from him and his agent. But the man and agent refused to give any of it back. Fortunately, everything was resolved when another studio decided to make the impersonator a star in a different movie.

Contrasting Sentences

❏ They weren't going to _____ the agency. (fund it again)

❏ They weren't going to _____ the agency. (give the money back)

Additional Practice

Joseph wants them to *rè-léase/reléase* the film soon. (WS3-A/a), We need to *rè-fórm/refórm* the club. (WS3-B/b), Dad *rècóvered/recóvered* the chairs. (WS3-D/d)

Other Words

resolved, redirect, redecorate, relax, rehearse, reenact, redistribute, refused, reinterpret, rejoice

[`S-S´] rèémphasize,

[S-S´] revéaled,

Other Practice Activities

❏ Partner Cards—Listening.
❏ Partner Cards—Speaking.
❏ Story Reading.
❏ Story Dictation.
❏ Cloze Reading.

❏ Story Retelling from Skeleton.
❏ Free Story Retelling.
❏ Parallel Story.
❏ Mini-drama.

Unit WS3-D [`S-S´-S] RECOVer— [S-S´-S] reCOVer

Story

My dad is a very trusting person. He thinks everyone is honest and good. He is not afraid of thieves, and he always leaves the doors of his house unlocked and things outside.

But last month he got a shock. He left his lawn chairs out on his front porch one evening, and the next morning they were gone. Someone had stolen them.

Dad didn't know who took the chairs, but he went out looking for them. He rejoiced when he found the chairs a few blocks away in a vacant lot. (1) He was relieved to **recover** them, but he was sad to see that the fabric seats had been torn and ruined.

Because the frames of the chairs were still good, Dad decided that he would get some new fabric and **recover** them. He used to do upholstery work, so it was easy for him. He even reinforced the fabric in the places where it had torn before. (2) Now his chairs are as good as new, and he is careful to take them in at night.

Contrasting Sentences

❏ Dad _____ the chairs. (got them back)

❏ Dad _____ the chairs. (put new seats on them)

Additional Practice

Joseph wants them to *rè-léase / reléase* the film soon. (WS3-A/a), We need to *rè-fórm / refórm* the club. (WS3-B/b), They weren't going to *rèfúnd / refúnd* the agency. (WS3-C/c)

Other Words

relieved, refused, redecorate, relax, reemphasize, redo, resolved, rediscover, reeducate, rehearse

[`S-S´] rèínforced,

[S-S´] rejóiced,

Other Practice Activities

❏ Partner Cards—Listening.
❏ Partner Cards—Speaking.
❏ Story Reading.
❏ Story Dictation.
❏ Cloze Reading.

❏ Story Retelling
  from Skeleton.
❏ Free Story Retelling.
❏ Parallel Story.
❏ Mini-drama.

Unit WS4-A [S´-`S] HOT DOG— [`S-S´] HOT DOG

Story

Listen to the story as your teacher reads it, or on tape, until you understand the main ideas.

My uncle likes to train animals to do things. When he is working with dogs, he always has (1) a **hot dog** in his hand. He claims that frankfurters are the best reward to use when you are teaching a dog new tricks. They are perfect because they are cheap and nutritious. Plus, you can cut one of them into many small pieces so the dog thinks that it is getting lots of treats.

Last month, when I went to visit my uncle, his dog performed all sorts of great tricks. But last weekend when I went, things were different. We were having a heat wave, and the temperature was nearly 100 degrees. His dog was (2) so hot that all it would do was sit there with its tongue hanging out. It was a very **hot dog,** and it wouldn't do any tricks at all, not even for a whole hot dog.

Contrasting Sentences

Listening: Write the appropriate key word in each blank. Later, as you hear each sentence, mark the box, point to the picture, make a gesture, and/or say the rejoinder. Speaking: Choose and say each sentence so that your listener(s) can respond correctly.

❑ My uncle has a _____ _____. (Give it to the dog.)

❑ My uncle has a _____ _____. (It won't do any tricks.)

Explanations and diagrams for this unit's target sounds are on pages 361–62 in Section 10.

Additional Practice

I live in the *White Hòuse/whìte hóuse.* (WS4-B/b), There's a *yéllow jàcket/yèllow jácket* on the chair. (WS4-C/c), The students loved their *Énglish tèacher/Ènglish téacher.* (WS4-D/d), He wants to buy the *tóy stòre/tòy stóre.* (WS4-E/e), The doctor was angry because of the *smók-*

ing ròom / smòking róom. (WS4-F/f), There is a *bláckbòard / blàck bóard* on the wall. (WS4-G/g), We need a *shórt stòp / shòrt stóp*. (WS4-H/h)

Other Words

Sort the words listed below into two groups according to the stress pattern. Write the words in the spaces provided. The first two have been done for you. Then, circle or underline these words each time they occur in the story. Say each marked word aloud. Then say the entire sentence. Look for additional words in the story that use the target stress pattern. Mark and say them also.
last month, weekend, apple pie, carport, great tricks, fishhook, driveway, short man, heat wave, new tricks

[S´-`S] shórthànd,

[`S-S´] smàll piéces,

Other Practice Activities

❏ Partner Cards—Listening. *Practice until you can point to the right card every time.*
❏ Partner Cards—Speaking. *Practice until you can say the contrasting sentences so accurately that your partner points to the right card every time.*
❏ Story Reading. *Practice reading the story aloud. Mark any difficult words. Then record the story on tape.*
❏ Story Dictation. *Write the story as your teacher reads it or as you listen to it on the audiotape.*
❏ Cloze Reading. *Choose some key words in the story and black them out. Then read the entire story aloud. Do this several times.*

Each time black out more words. Continue until most of the story is blacked out and you can tell it without looking at the page very often.
❏ Story Retelling from Skeleton. *Black out all the remaining words except those you need in order to remind you of the story line. Then, using just this skeleton, tell the story to your partner or class.*
❏ Free Story Retelling. *Retell the whole story from memory, without looking at your book.*
❏ Parallel Story. *Create your own story similar to the one in this unit.*
❏ Mini-drama. *Make up a skit or do a role play based on the story.*

Unit WS4-B [S´-`S] WHITE HOUSE—[`S-S´] WHITE HOUSE

Story

#1

My neighbor George lives in (1) a **white house** just down the street from me. People always raise their eyebrows when George describes where he lives because the name of our street is Penn-

#2

sylvania Avenue. That's the same as the name of the street in Washington, D.C., where the president of the United States lives. And the president lives in (2) the **White House.** So when George says, "I live in the white house on Pennsylvania Avenue," it sounds almost as if he's claiming to be the president—especially if you're not paying attention.

Of course, George is not really the president of the United States although he does live on Pennsylvania Avenue. And he doesn't really live in the White House. He just lives in a simple white house. He's a very ordinary kind of guy.

Contrasting Sentences

❏ I live in the _____ _____. (George)

❏ I live in the _____ _____. (the president of the United States)

Additional Practice

My uncle has a *hót dòg / hòt dóg.* (WS4-A/a), There's a *yéllow jàcket / yèllow jácket* on the chair. (WS4-C/c), The students loved their *Énglish tèacher / Ènglish téacher.* (WS4-D/d), He wants to buy the *tóy stòre / tòy stóre.* (WS4-E/e), The doctor was angry because of the *smóking ròom / smòking róom.* (WS4-F/f), There is a *bláckbòard / blàck bóard* on the wall. (WS4-G/g), We need a *shórt stòp / shòrt stóp.* (WS4-H/h)

Other Words

[S´-`S] éyebròws, Stóne Àge, píne còne, ápple trèe, Gérman profèssor, cóld crèam

[`S-S´] quìet stréet, stòne wáll, pìne bóx, àpple píe, Gèrman proféssor, còld créam

Other Practice Activities

❏ Partner Cards—Listening.
❏ Partner Cards—Speaking.
❏ Story Reading.
❏ Story Dictation.
❏ Cloze Reading.

❏ Story Retelling from Skeleton.
❏ Free Story Retelling.
❏ Parallel Story.
❏ Mini-drama.

Unit WS4-C [S´-`S] YELlow JACKet—[`S-S´] YELlow JACKet

Story

When I was young, my family lived in the country. In the summers we used to have a terrible time with flying, stinging insects, like bumblebees and (1) **yellow jackets,** on our property. We could be digging a hole in the garden or mowing the lawn, and suddenly there would be a nest of angry bees or wasps chasing us. If we had a barbecue, swarms of yellow jackets would be attracted by the smell. They would fly around our heads, buzz over our plates of food, and land on our chairs. We would do our best to shoo them away.

#1

My brother was especially afraid of these flying, stinging insects. He was so scared they would sting him that he always wore long pants and a (2) jacket while he was outside in the summer. His jacket was bright yellow, and he liked it. He stopped wearing it, though, when he found out that bees are attracted by bright colors. He left it on a chair and never wore it outside again. He didn't want his **yellow jacket** to attract a yellow jacket.

#2

Contrasting Sentences

❑ There's a _____ _____ on the chair. (Shoo it away!)

❑ There's a _____ _____ on the chair. (Please hang it up.)

Additional Practice

My uncle has a *hót dòg / hòt dóg.* (WS4-A/a), I live in the *Whíte Hòuse / whìte hóuse.* (WS4-B/b), The students loved their *Énglish tèacher / Ènglish téacher.* (WS4-D/d), He wants to buy the *tóy stòre / tòy stóre.* (WS4-E/e), The doctor was angry because of the *smók- ing ròom / smòking róom.* (WS4-F/f), There is a *bláckbòard / blàck bóard* on the wall. (WS4-G/g), We need a *shórt stòp / shòrt stóp.* (WS4-H/h)

Other Words

bumblebees, barbecue, outside

[S´-`S] húnting dòg, góldfish, chéering sèction, blúebìrd, bríght yèllow,

[`S-S´] hùnting dóg, gòld físh, chèering séction, blùe bírd, brìght yéllow,

Other Practice Activities

❏ Partner Cards—Listening.
❏ Partner Cards—Speaking.
❏ Story Reading.
❏ Story Dictation.
❏ Cloze Reading.

❏ Story Retelling from Skeleton.
❏ Free Story Retelling.
❏ Parallel Story.
❏ Mini-drama.

Unit WS4-D [S´-`S] ENGlish TEACHer—[`S-S´] ENGlish TEACHer

Story

Ron and Terry were excited to meet their history teacher, Ms. Shelford. She was new this year, and (1) she was from England. They were looking forward to having an **English teacher**—especially for American history. They thought her British perspective would be interesting. All their other teachers were Americans, even their (2) **English teacher,** Ms. Smith. That was not very exciting.

As the school year progressed, however, Ron and Terry found that Ms. Smith was their favorite teacher. Her tests were fair, her writing on the blackboard was clear, and her voice was kind and friendly. Best of all, however, she threw big pizza parties at the end of the semester. The students really loved their English teacher, but Ms. Shelford was not far behind. She was another of their favorites.

Contrasting Sentences

❏ The students loved their _____ _____. (of English)

❏ The students loved their _____ _____. (from England)

Additional Practice

My uncle has a *hót dòg / hòt dóg*. (WS4-A/a), I live in the *Whíte Hòuse / whìte hóuse*. (WS4-B/b), There's a *yéllow jàcket / yèllow jácket* on the chair. (WS4-C/c), He wants to buy the *tóy stòre / tòy stóre*. (WS4-E/e), The doctor was angry because of the *smóking ròom / smòking róom*. (WS4-F/f), There is a *bláckbòard / blàck bóard* on the wall. (WS4-G/g), We need a *shórt stòp / shòrt stóp*. (WS4-H/h)

Other Words

free lunch, large house, hairbrush, weekend, apple pie, freeway, stone wall, post office, big car

[S´-`S] cóld crèam, gréenhòuse,

[`S-S´] còld créam, blàck bóard,

Other Practice Activities

❏ Partner Cards—Listening.
❏ Partner Cards—Speaking.
❏ Story Reading.
❏ Story Dictation.
❏ Cloze Reading.

❏ Story Retelling from Skeleton.
❏ Free Story Retelling.
❏ Parallel Story.
❏ Mini-drama.

Unit WS4-E [S´-`S] TOY STORE— [`S-S´] TOY STORE

Story

Isaac, a boy in my neighborhood, loves toys. He has toys of all kinds—video games, tiny cars, plastic action figures. You name it; he's got it. He especially likes miniature buildings and has a large collection of them—a fire station, a barn, a house, a garage, and several other buildings. He loves to visit the (1) **toy store** at a nearby shopping center to see if he can find new toy

#1

buildings to add to his collection. Of course, while he's there he looks at all the other toys too. He'd like to buy the whole toy store.

Last weekend he saw a (2) miniature grocery store in a toy store and was really excited because he didn't have a **toy store** yet. The only problem was that it was quite expensive, and he didn't have enough money to buy it. He still wants to buy the toy store, but he'll have to save his allowance for a few weeks before he can. Meanwhile, he has been going to the toy store nearly every day to make sure that no one else has bought "his" toy store.

Contrasting Sentences

❏ He wants to buy the _____ _____. (store that sells toys)

❏ He wants to buy the _____ _____. (tiny store to play with)

Additional Practice

My uncle has a *hót dòg / hòt dóg*. (WS4-A/a), I live in the *Whíte Hòuse / whìte hóuse*. (WS4-B/b), There's a *yéllow jàcket / yèllow jácket* on the chair. (WS4-C/c), The students loved their *Énglish tèacher / Ènglish téacher*. (WS4-D/d), The doctor was angry because of the *smóking ròom / smòking róom*. (WS4-F/f), There is a *bláck-bòard / blàck bóard* on the wall. (WS4-G/g), We need a *shórt stòp / shòrt stóp*. (WS4-H/h)

Other Words

tiny cars, toy buildings, video games, action figures, flying saucer, shopping center, cute kid, weekend

[S´-`S] dárkròom, grándfàther, néighborhòod,

[`S-S´] dàrk róom, grànd fáther, gòod mórning,

Other Practice Activities

- ❏ Partner Cards—Listening.
- ❏ Partner Cards—Speaking.
- ❏ Story Reading.
- ❏ Story Dictation.
- ❏ Cloze Reading.

- ❏ Story Retelling from Skeleton.
- ❏ Free Story Retelling.
- ❏ Parallel Story.
- ❏ Mini-drama.

Unit WS4-F [S´-`S] SMOKING ROOM— [`S-S´] SMOKING ROOM

Story

Dr. Heath and Dr. Sikman are both medical doctors, but they are very different. Dr. Heath practices what he preaches. He tries to maintain his own health. He exercises daily and watches what he eats. He doesn't smoke, and he encourages his smoking patients to quit. He is angry that the hospital where he works has a special (1) **smoking room.** He would like the hospital to be smoke free.

Dr. Sikman is the opposite of Dr. Heath. He is overweight and unhealthy. He tells his patients to do many things that he does not do himself, like eating right and not smoking. Dr. Sikman likes having a special room in the hospital for smokers because he himself is one. He visits the smoking room four or five times a day.

One day when Dr. Sikman was going to the smoking room, he saw (2) clouds of black smoke coming from another room nearby. Firefighters were running into it. The fire in the **smoking room** was quickly put out, but the whole area had to be closed for repairs. Dr. Sikman was angry because he no longer had a place to smoke.

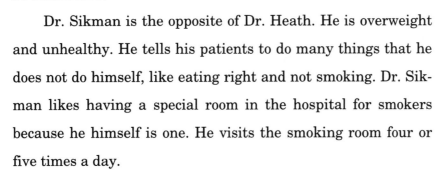

Contrasting Sentences

❑ The doctor was angry because of the _____ _____.
   (Dr. Heath)

❑ The doctor was angry because of the _____ _____.
   (Dr. Sikman)

Additional Practice

My uncle has a *hót dòg/hòt dóg.* (WS4-A/a), I live in the *Whíte Hòuse/whìte hóuse.* (WS4-B/b), There's a *yéllow jàcket/yèllow jácket* on the chair. (WS4-C/c), The students loved their *Énglish tèacher/Ènglish téacher.* (WS4-D/d), He wants to buy the *tóy stòre/tòy stóre.* (WS4-E/e), There is a *bláckbòard/blàck bóard* on the wall. (WS4-G/g), We need a *shórt stòp/shòrt stóp.* (WS4-H/h)

Other Words

medical doctors, smoking patients, special room, freeway, good health, pillbox, race car, daily exercise

[S´-`S] gró wing pàins, héad dòctor,

[`S-S´] grò wing páins, hèad dóctor,

Other Practice Activities

❑ Partner Cards—Listening.
❑ Partner Cards—Speaking.
❑ Story Reading.
❑ Story Dictation.
❑ Cloze Reading.
❑ Story Retelling
   from Skeleton.
❑ Free Story Retelling.
❑ Parallel Story.
❑ Mini-drama.

Unit WS4-G [S´-`S] BLACKBOARD— [`S-S´] BLACK BOARD

Story

#1

There is a (1) **blackboard** on the wall of almost every classroom in the world, but they're not all black anymore. I suppose that many years ago, blackboards were often just large (2) **black boards** hung on the walls of classrooms. In some places that may still be the case, but in most areas blackboards are more up-

#2

to-date. In fact, modern blackboards are often actually green, brown, or even red. That's why the proper term for them is *chalkboard,* not *blackboard.* Still, I tend to call all chalkboards blackboards.

Some classrooms have boards that are white and require special markers instead of chalk. These boards are made from sheets of white plastic, not white boards. At least I have learned to call them whiteboards.

When I call a green or brown chalkboard a blackboard, I realize that it may sound strange to some people. But no matter how hard I try, I can't seem to make myself say *chalkboard* instead of *blackboard.* Old habits are very hard to break.

Contrasting Sentences

❑ There is a _____ on the wall. (a chalkboard)

❑ There is a _____ on the wall. (a board that is black)

Additional Practice

My uncle has a *hót dòg/hòt dóg.* (WS4-A/a), I live in the *Whíte Hòuse/whìte hóuse.* (WS4-B/b), There's a *yéllow jàcket/yèllow jácket* on the chair. (WS4-C/c), The students loved their *Énglish tèacher/Ènglish téacher.* (WS4-D/d), He wants to buy the *tóy stòre/tòy stóre.* (WS4-E/e), The doctor was angry because of the *smóking ròom/smòking róom.* (WS4-F/f), We need a *shórt stòp/shòrt stóp.* (WS4-H/h)

Other Words

high school, chalkboard, old habits, whiteboards, special markers, greenhouse, postcard, white boards, green house, post exchange

[S´-`S] clássròom,

[`S-S´] whìte plástic,

Other Practice Activities

❏ Partner Cards—Listening.
❏ Partner Cards—Speaking.
❏ Story Reading.
❏ Story Dictation.
❏ Cloze Reading.

❏ Story Retelling
   from Skeleton.
❏ Free Story Retelling.
❏ Parallel Story.
❏ Mini-drama.

Unit WS4-H [S´-`S] SHORTstop— [`S-S´] short STOP

Story

Michael was a super basketball player. His professional team won the national championship every year. But Michael always wanted to fulfill his father's dream of his son becoming a professional baseball player. His father had always wanted him to play (1) **shortstop.**

So, Michael decided to quit basketball and join a minor league baseball team. After a few games, Michael realized that he wasn't a very good shortstop. Actually, he was pretty bad, and he knew it, but he didn't want to quit and let his team down.

One day during a long road trip he overheard two teammates talking on the bus. "We need a shortstop," one said to the other, implying that Michael was not doing a good job.

After hearing that, Michael made up his mind to go back to basketball. A while later, the team coach yelled to the bus driver. "We've been traveling a long time. We need to stretch our legs. Let's make a (2) **short stop** soon."

When the bus stopped in the next town, Michael got off, said good-bye, and walked away. His team never heard from him again.

Contrasting Sentences

❏ We need a _____. (Ours is bad.)

❏ We need a _____. (We're tired.)

Additional Practice

My uncle has a *hót dòg/hòt dóg.* (WS4-A/a), I live in the *Whíte Hòuse/whìte hóuse.* (WS4-B/b), There's a *yéllow jàcket/yèllow jácket* on the chair. (WS4-C/c), The students loved their *Énglish tèacher/Ènglish téacher.* (WS4-D/d), He wants to buy the *tóy stòre/tòy stóre.* (WS4-E/e), The doctor was angry because of the *smóking ròom/smòking róom.* (WS4-F/f), There is a *bláckbòard/blàck bóard* on the wall. (WS4-G/g)

Other Words

team coach, baseball player, father's dream, losing team, road trip, bus driver, dark room, teammates

[S´-`S] básketbàll, grándfàther,

[`S-S´] nàtional chámpionship, grànd fáther,

Other Practice Activities

❑ Partner Cards—Listening.
❑ Partner Cards—Speaking.
❑ Story Reading.
❑ Story Dictation.
❑ Cloze Reading.
❑ Story Retelling from Skeleton.
❑ Free Story Retelling.
❑ Parallel Story.
❑ Mini-drama.

Unit WS5-A [Sˊ-ˋS] BEAR ʜᴜɴᴛing— [ˋS-Sˊ] ʙᴇᴀʀ HUNTing

Story

Listen to the story as your teacher reads it, or on tape, until you understand the main ideas.

For years, Mr. Hunter saved his money up to go to Alaska. He loves hunting and fishing, and Alaska offers the best in both. Last year he finally went.

When he arrived, he first went trout fishing. He spent several days on beautiful rivers and lakes and caught some magnificent fish. For many people, that might have been enough, but Mr. Hunter also wanted to get in a little big game hunting before he went home. He hired a guide to take him (1) **bear hunting.** Unfortunately, the guide service cost so much that Mr. Hunter could afford only one day.

The guide took him to a place where bears had been seen recently. There were lots of thickets with berries. With his guide leading, Mr. Hunter spent several hours hiking through those thickets. Finally, they heard a bear feeding. Mr. Hunter was excited. This was his chance to show what a good hunter he was. He wanted to take home a big trophy bear. He crept carefully toward the noise. In a thicket he saw (2) a little **bear hunting** for berries. The bear was so small that Mr. Hunter couldn't shoot it, and, to his disappointment, that was the only bear he saw the whole day.

Contrasting Sentences

Listening: Write the appropriate key word in each blank. Later, as you hear each sentence, mark the box, point to the picture, make a gesture, and / or say the rejoinder. Speaking: Choose and say each sentence so that your listener(s) can respond correctly.

❑ Mr. Hunter saw a little _____ _____ in Alaska.
  (He spent a day hunting for bears.)

❑ Mr. Hunter saw a little _____ _____ in Alaska.
   (The small bear was looking for food.)

Explanations and diagrams for this unit's target sounds are on pages 362–63 in Section 10.

Additional Practice

He watched a *mánhunt / man húnt.* (WS5-B/b)

Other Words

Look for additional words in the story that use the target stress pattern. Mark and say them also.

[S´-`S] tróut fìshing, big gáme hùnting

[`S-S´] gùide léading, bèar féeding

Other Practice Activities

❑ Partner Cards—Listening. *Practice until you can point to the right card every time.*
❑ Partner Cards—Speaking. *Practice until you can say the contrasting sentences so accurately that your partner points to the right card every time.*
❑ Story Reading. *Practice reading the story aloud. Mark any difficult words. Then record the story on tape.*
❑ Story Dictation. *Write the story as your teacher reads it or as you listen to it on the audiotape.*
❑ Cloze Reading. *Choose some key words in the story and black them out. Then read the entire story aloud. Do this several times.*

Each time black out more words. Continue until most of the story is blacked out and you can tell it without looking at the page very often.
❑ Story Retelling from Skeleton. *Black out all the remaining words except those you need in order to remind you of the story line. Then, using just this skeleton, tell the story to your partner or class.*
❑ Free Story Retelling. *Retell the whole story from memory, without looking at your book.*
❑ Parallel Story. *Create your own story similar to the one in this unit.*
❑ Mini-drama. *Make up a skit or do a role play based on the story.*

Unit WS5-B [S´-`S] MANHUNT— [`S-S´] MAN HUNT

Story

I once saw an exciting movie. It was about a doctor who had been falsely accused of murdering his daughter. The crime was really committed by a robber who broke into the doctor's house. The doctor had seen the robber kill his daughter. But the murderer got away, and without enough evidence to defend himself the doctor was convicted of the crime. On his way to prison, the train he was on collided with another one. The train wreck gave him his big chance to escape and go after his daughter's killer.

When the police realized that their prisoner was missing, they organized a large (1) **manhunt.** Police from all over looked for the doctor, but he made it to a wilderness where no people lived. He knew he could not go back to the city for a while, so he stayed there. In order to survive he ate wild plants and hunted small animals. One time he secretly watched (2) a **man hunt** in the same canyon where he was hiding, but the hunter didn't see him.

The doctor was able to avoid being caught by the police. Eventually, he went back to the city, found his daughter's killer, and cleared his own name.

Contrasting Sentences

❏ He watched a _____. (People hunted the man.)

❏ He watched a _____ _____. (The man hunted.)

Additional Practice

Mr. Hunter saw a little *béar hunting / bear húnting* in Alaska. (WS5-A/a)

Other Words

[S´-`S] tráin wrèck, pláne cràsh

[`S-S´] ròbber kíll, polìce séarch

Other Practice Activities

❏ Partner Cards—Listening.
❏ Partner Cards—Speaking.
❏ Story Reading.
❏ Story Dictation.
❏ Cloze Reading.

❏ Story Retelling
  from Skeleton.
❏ Free Story Retelling.
❏ Parallel Story.
❏ Mini-drama.

Section 7

Sentence Stress (SS)

Unit SS1-A told HER—be LATE

Story

Listen to the story as your teacher reads it, or on tape, until you understand the main ideas.

The Smythes are very rich and rather peculiar. They often attend fancy, formal dinners at their neighbors' homes. When it is their turn to host a dinner, they spend thousands of dollars on decorations and catering. They love being hosts, but they hate late arrivals. In fact, they instruct their butler not to allow latecomers in.

Not long ago, the Smythes hosted a dinner. The day before, (1) Mrs. Smythe received a call from one of her neighbors, Mrs. Tyler. Mrs. Tyler explained that Mr. Tyler was on a trip but expected to get back just in time for the dinner at six. She added that they might be (2) a little late. Mrs. Smythe told them to come anyway.

But Mrs. Smythe forgot to tell the butler about the Tylers. The next evening, when they arrived late, he would not let them in. Mrs. Tyler explained, "But we called and explained we'd be late." The butler went to ask Mr. Smythe about it.

When the butler reported that Mr. Smythe did not recall speaking with the Tylers, Mrs. Tyler said, "We told **her** we were going to be late, not him."

The butler then spoke with Mrs. Smythe. She remembered

the call, but she had forgotten if the Tylers were going to arrive early or late. When the butler reported this, Mrs. Tyler screamed, "We told her we were going to be **late,** not early." The Tylers left in a huff and never attended another dinner at the Smythes.

Contrasting Sentences

Listening: Write the appropriate key word in each blank. Later, as you hear each sentence, mark the box, point to the picture, make a gesture, and/or say the rejoinder. Speaking: Choose and say each sentence so that your listener(s) can respond correctly.

❏ We told _____ we were going to be late. (not him)

❏ We told her we were going to be _____. (not early)

Explanations and diagrams for this unit's target sounds are on pages 363–65 in Section 10.

Additional Practice

Mr. *Wébb* rides his bike to *wórk?* (SS1-B/b), I like *chócolate íce* cream. (SS1-C/c), I'm sorry. We ordered *twó hámburgers.* (SS1-D/d), I *thínk* this bag is *míne.* (SS1-E/e), The *cát* caught a *bírd.* (SS1-f), The *dóg* is under the *táble.* (SS1-g)

Other Examples

The phrases listed below are in the story. Find them and circle or underline them. Say each marked phrase aloud—individually and then in its entire sentence. Look for additional sentences in the story that use the target stress pattern(s). Mark and say them also.

[´] When it is THEIR turn . . . , They LOVE being hosts, but they HATE . . . , MRS. Tyler explained that MR. Tyler . . . , The butler then spoke with MRS. Smythe, She reMEMbered the call, but she had forGOTten if . . . , The Tylers left in a huff and NEVer attended . . .

Other Practice Activities

❏ Partner Cards—Listening. *Practice until you can point to the right card every time.*

❏ Partner Cards—Speaking. *Practice until you can say the contrasting sentences so accurately that your partner points to the right card every time.*

❏ Story Reading. *Practice reading the story aloud. Mark any difficult words. Then record the story on tape.*

❏ Story Dictation. *Write the story as your teacher reads it or as you listen to it on the audiotape.*

❏ Cloze Reading. *Choose some key words in the story and black them out. Then read the entire story aloud. Do this several times.*

Each time black out more words. Continue until most of the story is blacked out and you can tell it without looking at the page very often.

❏ Story Retelling from Skeleton. *Black out all the remaining words except those you need in order to remind you of the story line. Then, using just this skeleton, tell the story to your partner or class.*

❏ Free Story Retelling. *Retell the whole story from memory, without looking at your book.*

❏ Parallel Story. *Create your own story similar to the one in this unit.*

❏ Mini-drama. *Make up a skit or do a role play based on the story.*

Unit SS1-B Mr. WEBB?—to WORK?

Story

When Sally and Bob moved into a new house, the realtor told them that their next door neighbor, Mr. Webb, was (1) an old man who lived alone. They were a bit worried that he would get sick or hurt and nobody would know about it. You can imagine their surprise when they saw him riding his bike down the street.

"Is that Mr. **Webb** riding his bike?" said Sally as she and Bob were talking to another neighbor on the sidewalk.

"Yes," said the neighbor. "He rides his bike to and from work every day."

"Mr. Webb rides his bike to **work**?" exclaimed Bob. "You mean he still works?"

"Yes," laughed the neighbor. "He has worked at his (2) shoe repair shop every day for the past fifty years."

"Every day? For fifty years? How old is he?" asked Sally.

"He'll be eighty-eight this year," responded the neighbor.

"Eighty-eight? Wow!" Both Bob and Sally were surprised.
But they were also happy to know that their neighbor was still
living an active life in his old age.

Contrasting Sentences

❑ Mr. _____ rides his bike to work? (the old man?)

❑ Mr. Webb rides his bike to _____? (He's still working?)

Additional Practice

We told *hér* we were going to be *láte.* (SS1-A/a), I like *chócolate íce*
cream. (SS1-C/c), I'm sorry. We ordered *twó hámburgers.* (SS1-D/d), I
thínk this bag is *míne.* (SS1-E/e), The *cát* caught a *bírd.* (SS1-f), The
dóg is under the *táble.* (SS1-g)

Other Examples

[´] Every DAY?, For fifty YEARS?, Èighty-EIGHT?, were sur-
PRISED. BUT they were also HAPPY

Other Practice Activities

❑ Partner Cards—Listening.
❑ Partner Cards—Speaking.
❑ Story Reading.
❑ Story Dictation.
❑ Cloze Reading.

❑ Story Retelling
  from Skeleton.
❑ Free Story Retelling.
❑ Parallel Story.
❑ Mini-drama.

Unit SS1-C CHOColate—ICE cream

Story

Jennifer is particular in a strange way. She eats only one kind of
dessert—(1) chocolate ice cream. She won't eat cake, pudding,
cookies, or pie. It's because her parents spoiled her when she
was a little girl. Whenever they didn't give her chocolate ice
cream, she screamed and kicked, and eventually they would give
in.

#1

Now that she's older, Jennifer doesn't throw tantrums anymore, but when her friends offer her any dessert except chocolate ice cream she gets offended and won't talk to them for days. "If you were a real friend," she says, "then you'd give me what I like."

Once Jennifer was out eating with her friend Jeff. When they finished their dinner, Jeff ordered two dishes of (2) chocolate mousse—the specialty of the house.

#2

Jennifer quickly kicked Jeff under the table and said, "I want **ice cream**!"

Jeff changed the order to "One mousse, one ice cream." The server returned shortly with a bowl of chocolate mousse and a (3) bowl of vanilla ice cream.

#3

Jennifer became very angry. She left the restaurant in a huff, but before she did she yelled back, "I like **chocolate** ice cream, not vanilla!"

Contrasting Sentences

❑ I like chocolate _____ _____. (not mousse)

❑ I like _____ ice cream. (not vanilla)

Additional Practice

We told *her* we were going to be *láte*. (SS1-A/a), Mr. *Wébb* rides his bike to *wórk*? (SS1-B/b), I'm sorry. We ordered *twó hámburgers*. (SS1-D/d), I *thínk* this bag is *míne*. (SS1-E/e), The *cát* caught a *bírd*. (SS1-f), The *dóg* is under the *táble*. (SS1-g)

Other Examples

[´] doesn't throw TANtrums anymore, but . . . she gets ofFENDed, if you were a REAL friend, then you'd give me what I LIKE

Other Practice Activities

❏ Partner Cards—Listening.
❏ Partner Cards—Speaking.
❏ Story Reading.
❏ Story Dictation.
❏ Cloze Reading.

❏ Story Retelling
  from Skeleton.
❏ Free Story Retelling.
❏ Parallel Story.
❏ Mini-drama.

Unit SS1-D TWO—HAMburgers

Story

On warm summer evenings Nate and Dan love to go out to a fast food restaurant near their home and eat hamburgers. One evening, when they placed their usual order of two hamburgers, they noticed several new workers at the restaurant. They also noticed that the manager was not there. The restaurant was crowded, and the new workers seemed nervous.

When Nate and Dan received their bag of food and opened it, they noticed something had gone wrong. There was (1) only one hamburger inside. Nate explained to the worker that they had ordered **two** hamburgers.

#1

The worker apologized and took the bag back. In a few minutes, he returned. But when Dan opened the bag this time he found (2) two hot dogs! The workers had mixed up the order again. Dan had to explain that they had ordered two **hamburgers,** not hot dogs.

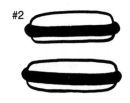

#2

Fortunately, at that moment, the manager arrived. Dan told him, "Your new workers are all confused," and asked, "Can you get our order straight?"

Contrasting Sentences

❏ I'm sorry. We ordered _____ hamburgers. (not just one)

❏ I'm sorry. We ordered two _____. (not hot dogs)

Additional Practice

We told *hér* we were going to be *láte*. (SS1-A/a), Mr. *Wébb* rides his bike to *wórk*? (SS1-B/b), I like *chócolate íce* cream. (SS1-C/c), I *thínk* this bag is *míne*. (SS1-E/e), The *cát* caught a *bírd*. (SS1-f), The *dóg* is under the *táble*. (SS1-g)

Other Examples

[´] They also noticed that the MANager was not, something had gone WRONG, can YOU get our order straight?

Other Practice Activities

❏ Partner Cards—Listening.
❏ Partner Cards—Speaking.
❏ Story Reading.
❏ Story Dictation.
❏ Cloze Reading.

❏ Story Retelling from Skeleton.
❏ Free Story Retelling.
❏ Parallel Story.
❏ Mini-drama.

Unit SS1-E I THINK—It's MINE

Story

Jack was "salesman of the year" and won a Florida vacation and some new luggage. On the day of his flight, he was late getting to the airport. He didn't even have time to mark all of his bags at check-in.

When he arrived in Florida, Jack went to the baggage claim and was surprised to see several bags that looked like his. He had left his claim tickets on the airplane and didn't know what to do.

He grabbed one of the bags, but (1) a man stepped up to him and said, "I think that bag is **mine**." Jack apologized and gave it to him.

#1

Jack was more cautious after that. Finally, there was just one bag left that looked like his. Jack decided that it had to be his bag, but before he could reach it a woman took it. Jack called to her, "Excuse me, I believe that bag is mine!"

She answered, "No, it's mine, not yours!"

A security guard came up and asked, "How do you know it's yours? There's no name tag on it. "

#2

"Well," Jack answered, (2) "I'm not certain, but I **think** that bag is mine. It looks just like my bag."

They finally resolved the problem by opening the bag and looking at its contents. To Jack's relief, it was his. The airline had lost the woman's bag.

Contrasting Sentences

❑ I think that bag is _____. (not yours)

❑ I _____ that bag is mine. (But I'm not certain.)

Additional Practice

We told *hér* we were going to be *láte.* (SS1-A/a), Mr. *Wébb* rides his bike to *wórk?* (SS1-B/b), I like *chócolate íce* cream. (SS1-C/c), I'm sorry. We ordered *twó hámburgers.* (SS1-D/d), The *cát* caught a *bírd.* (SS1-f), The *dóg* is under the *táble.* (SS1-g)

Other Examples

[´] there was just ONE bag left, Jack decided that it HAD to be his bag, I believe that bag is MINE, it's MINE, not yóurs, How do you KNOW it's yours? It LOOKS just like my bag

Other Practice Activities

❑ Partner Cards—Listening.
❑ Partner Cards—Speaking.
❑ Story Reading.
❑ Story Dictation.
❑ Cloze Reading.

❑ Story Retelling from Skeleton.
❑ Free Story Retelling.
❑ Parallel Story.
❑ Mini-drama.

Unit SS2-A had STUDied—HAD studied

Story

Listen to the story as your teacher reads it, or on tape, until you understand the main ideas.

Sam was the top student in his accounting class, and Bert was the worst. Sam always studied hard for the tests and received the highest score in the class. Bert never studied for anything and usually received the lowest score.

On one particular test, however, an unusual thing happened. Bert received the second highest score in the class. Only Sam's score was higher.

After class several students gathered outside the classroom to discuss the results. One said, "Can you believe Bert got such a high score? It can't be because he studied. He never studies. He must have cheated."

Hearing this, Sam stood up for Bert and said, "No, he didn't cheat. He really did know the answers. (1) He studied hard. I know because I studied with him."

Bert explained that he had decided to turn over a new leaf. He had **studied** for the test for several hours.

Everyone was (2) amazed with the "new" Bert. He really **had** studied for the test, and apparently it paid off.

Contrasting Sentences

Listening: Write the appropriate key word in each blank. Later, as you hear each sentence, mark the box, point to the picture, make a gesture, and/or say the rejoinder. Speaking: Choose and say each sentence so that your listener(s) can respond correctly.

❏ He had _____ for the test. (He's turning over a new leaf.)

❏ He _____ studied for the test. (I can't believe it.)

Explanations and diagrams for this unit's target sounds are on page 365 in Section 10.

Additional Practice

You *cán* do it. (SS2-B/b), These microwave dinners *áre* pretty good. (SS2-C/c)

Other Examples

The phrases listed below are in the story. Find them and circle or underline them. Say each marked phrase aloud—individually and then in its entire sentence. Look for additional sentences in the story that use the target stress pattern(s). Mark and say them also.

[´] it CAN'T be because he studied, he MUST have cheated, he DIDn't cheat, he really DID know the answers

Other Practice Activities

❑ Partner Cards—Listening. *Practice until you can point to the right card every time.*

❑ Partner Cards—Speaking. *Practice until you can say the contrasting sentences so accurately that your partner points to the right card every time.*

❑ Story Reading. *Practice reading the story aloud. Mark any difficult words. Then record the story on tape.*

❑ Story Dictation. *Write the story as your teacher reads it or as you listen to it on the audiotape.*

❑ Cloze Reading. *Choose some key words in the story and black them out. Then read the entire story aloud. Do this several times.*

Each time black out more words. Continue until most of the story is blacked out and you can tell it without looking at the page very often.

❑ Story Retelling from Skeleton. *Black out all the remaining words except those you need in order to remind you of the story line. Then, using just this skeleton, tell the story to your partner or class.*

❑ Free Story Retelling. *Retell the whole story from memory, without looking at your book.*

❑ Parallel Story. *Create your own story similar to the one in this unit.*

❑ Mini-drama. *Make up a skit or do a role play based on the story.*

Unit SS2-B can DO it (statement)— CAN do it (affirmation)

Story

Zina was the kind of person who never succeeded at anything she did. It wasn't because she lacked talent. She was a good athlete and very smart. She just didn't have the self-confidence to succeed. Whenever she faced a problem or test she would say to herself, "You can't do it, you're too dumb," or "You can't do it you're too clumsy." What she needed was some encouragement from a friend. (1) She needed someone who would say, "You **can** do it, and you will."

One day Zina met Andrew in one of her classes. Andrew was just the opposite of Zina. He was "Mr. Success." He acted successful, he dressed for success, and he always said positive things.

Have you ever heard the expression "opposites attract"? Well it seemed to be true in Zina and Andrew's case because they hit it off right away. What's more, Andrew really helped Zina overcome her negative feelings. His positive attitude rubbed off on her. Whenever Zina felt like giving up, (2) Andrew would chant, "You can **do** it, you can do it, if you put your mind to it." Eventually, Zina convinced herself she really could succeed, and she did.

Contrasting Sentences

❏ You _____ do it. (And you *will*.)

❏ You can _____ it. (If you put your mind to it.)

Additional Practice

He *hád* studied for the test. (SS2-A/a), These microwave dinners *áre* pretty good. (SS2-C/c)

Other Examples

[´] it WASn't because, she just DIDn't have the self-confidence, and you WILL, Zina convinced herself she really COULD succeed

Other Practice Activities

❏ Partner Cards—Listening.
❏ Partner Cards—Speaking.
❏ Story Reading.
❏ Story Dictation.
❏ Cloze Reading.

❏ Story Retelling
   from Skeleton.
❏ Free Story Retelling.
❏ Parallel Story.
❏ Mini-drama.

Unit SS2-C are GOOD (statement)— ARE good (surprise)

Story

Rick and Joe were roommates but as different as night and day. Rick was always well dressed, well groomed, and clean cut. Joe, on the other hand, wore wrinkled clothes, had scraggly hair, and never shaved more than once a week.

When it came to food, Rick always ate the best money can buy. Joe, on the other hand, ate microwave dinners.

Rick hated microwave dinners. He didn't even like to watch (1) Joe eating them. Joe always told him, "These microwave dinners are pretty good," but Rick wouldn't even try them.

One day Joe decided to trick Rick. He invited him to eat a special dinner with him that night. Joe first cooked the microwave dinners and then put the food into fancy dishes. He made sure to get rid of any microwave evidence. When Rick arrived and saw the food in nice dishes, he got excited. He thought Joe was a changed man. (2) He sat down with Joe and ate all of the food.

"I love this food! I really do," said Rick. "It's the best I've ever eaten."

At that point Joe couldn't keep his secret any longer. He said, "Rick, I must tell you something. The food you have just eaten was from microwave dinners."

Rick was shocked and angry at first, but in the end he smiled and admitted, "You were right. These microwave dinners are pretty good."

Contrasting Sentences

❑ These microwave dinners are pretty _____. (You should try them.)

❑ These microwave dinners _____ pretty good. (It's really true!)

Additional Practice

He *hád* studied for the test. (SS2-A/a), You *cán* do it. (SS2-B/b)

Other Examples

[´] I really DO, I MUST tell you something

Other Practice Activities

❑ Partner Cards—Listening.
❑ Partner Cards—Speaking.
❑ Story Reading.
❑ Story Dictation.
❑ Cloze Reading.

❑ Story Retelling from Skeleton.
❑ Free Story Retelling.
❑ Parallel Story.
❑ Mini-drama.

Section 8
Intonation (I)

Unit I1-A [231(↘)] . . . dark already.—
[23 ↗] . . . dark already?

Story

Listen to the story as your teacher reads it, or on tape, until you understand the main ideas.

Jerry and Tom loved to hike in the mountains near their home. One afternoon as they were hiking they found a large cave. Inside the cave they found many dark tunnels. They decided to explore several of them. They got out their flashlights and wandered through the cave.

They were having so much fun that they didn't realize how much time had passed. When they reached the main entrance again, Tom, who was walking in front of Jerry, looked out, saw (1) the moon in the sky, and said, "Oh, oh. It's **dark already.**"

Jerry responded in (2) disbelief, "It's **dark already?** I can't believe it. We weren't in the cave that long." But when Jerry saw that it really was dark outside, he was very surprised. "How long were we in there? We must have totally lost track of time," he said.

Tom asked, "Did you bring a watch? Do you know what time it is?"

Jerry answered, "Do I know what time it is? No, but I'm sure it's time to get out of here. Let's head home!" They both hiked down the mountain as fast as they could.

Contrasting Sentences

Listening: Write the appropriate word in each blank. Later, as you hear each sentence, mark the box, point to the picture, make a gesture, and/or say the rejoinder. Speaking: Choose and say each sentence so that your listener(s) can respond correctly.

❑ It's dark _____. (Look at the moon.)

❑ It's dark _____? (Are you sure?)

Explanations and diagrams for this unit's target sounds are on pages 365–68 in Section 10.

Additional Practice

It's due *today.* / *today?* (I1-B/b), Susan's in love *with Sam.* / *with Sam?* (I1-C/c)

Other Examples

The sentences below are in the story. Find them and circle or underline them. Say each marked sentence aloud. Look for any additional sentences in the story that use the target stress patterns. Mark and say them also.

[231] I can't belíeve it. We weren't in the cave thát long. How long were we ín there? Let's head hóme!

3	líeve		thát		ín		hó-
2 I can't be-		We weren't in the cave		How long were we		Let's head \	
1		it.		long.		there?		me!

[23 ↗] Did you bring a wátch? Do you know what tíme it is? Do I know what tíme it is?

3		wátch? ↗		tíme it is? ↗		tíme it is? ↗
2 Did you bring a		Do you know what		Do I know what		
1						

Other Practice Activities

❏ Partner Cards—Listening. *Practice until you can point to the right card every time.*

❏ Partner Cards—Speaking. *Practice until you can say the contrasting sentences so accurately that your partner points to the right card every time.*

❏ Story Reading. *Practice reading the story aloud. Mark any difficult words. Then record the story on tape.*

❏ Story Dictation. *Write the story as your teacher reads it or as you listen to it on the audiotape.*

❏ Cloze Reading. *Choose some key words in the story and black them out. Then read the entire story aloud. Do this several times.*

Each time black out more words. Continue until most of the story is blacked out and you can tell it without looking at the page very often.

❏ Story Retelling from Skeleton. *Black out all the remaining words except those you need in order to remind you of the story line. Then, using just this skeleton, tell the story to your partner or class.*

❏ Free Story Retelling. *Retell the whole story from memory, without looking at your book.*

❏ Parallel Story. *Create your own story similar to the one in this unit.*

❏ Mini-drama. *Make up a skit or do a role play based on the story.*

Unit I1-B [231(↘)] . . . today.—[23↗] . . . today?

Story

Mr. White told his students that their term paper would be due a week before the final exam. Sandy, the best student in the class, finished her paper long before the due date. John, on the other hand, waited until the second-to-last week of class to even begin writing his paper.

When the due date arrived, John still had to type and proofread his paper. He wasn't worried, however, because he thought he had until the final exam to turn his paper in. His carefree attitude changed when he met Sandy in the hall a couple of hours before class.

"Did you finish your paper?" Sandy asked. "It's due (1) **today.**"

John panicked. (2) "It's due **today?** Oh no, I'll never get it done."

Sandy, who had already finished all of her assignments, told John that she would help him finish his paper. "You'll help me? Really? That's great!" he said. They went to work on John's paper and barely met the deadline. "How can I ever thank you enough?" said John.

Contrasting Sentences

❑ It's due _____. (in a couple of hours—Sandy's statement)

❑ It's due _____? (Really?—John's question)

Additional Practice

It's *dark already. / dark already?* (I1-A/a), Susan's in love *with Sam. / with Sam?* (I1-C/c)

Other Examples

[231↘] I'll nèver get it dóne. That's gréat! How can I èver thank you enóugh? They bárely met the déadline.

3	nèv-		dó-		gré-			èv-		nó		báre-		déad
2	I'll	er get it	\	That's	\	How can I	er thank you e-		\	They		ly	met the	\
1			ne.		at!				ugh?					line.

[23↗] Did you finish your páper? You'll hélp me?   Réally?

3			páper?↗		hélp me?↗	Réally?↗
2	Did you finish your			You'll		
1						

Other Practice Activities

❑ Partner Cards—Listening.
❑ Partner Cards—Speaking.
❑ Story Reading.
❑ Story Dictation.
❑ Cloze Reading.

❑ Story Retelling from Skeleton.
❑ Free Story Retelling.
❑ Parallel Story.
❑ Mini-drama.

Unit I1-C [231(↘)] . . . with Sam.—
[23↗] . . . with Sam?

Story

Julie and Bob work in an office. There, their favorite pastime is to spread rumors about the personal lives of their co-workers. One day Julie overheard two other workers, Susan and Sam, talking in the copy room. Susan had asked Sam to go to a local concert with her. Sam told Susan that he couldn't think of anyone that he would rather go with than her. (1) Susan let Sam know she felt the same way.

Upon hearing this, Julie ran back to Bob's desk to inform him of the new information. "Susan's in love **with Sam,**" explained Julie.

(2) "Susan's in love **with Sam?** Are you sure?" exclaimed Bob, amazed at this new information.

"Yes, and they're going to the concert together tonight."

"To the concert tonight? That's exciting! Let's go tell Terry," said Bob. In a few hours the secret was spread to all their co-workers, and everyone knew about the new office romance.

Contrasting Sentences

❏ Susan's in love with _____. (I just heard them talking.— Julie's information)

❏ Susan's in love with _____? (Really?—Bob's amazement)

Additional Practice

It's *dark already.* / *dark already?* (I1-A/a), It's due *today.* / *today?* (I1-B/b)

Other Examples

[231↘] They're going to the cóncert together toníght. That's exciting! Let's go tell Térry.

```
3                  cón-           ní          cí-              Tér
2 They're going to the    cert  together to- \    That's ex- \    Let's go tell \
1                                      ght.       ting!           ry.
```

[23 ↗] Are you súre? To the cóncert toníght?

```
3            súre? ↗                          níght? ↗
2      Are you              To the cóncert to-
1
```

Other Practice Activities

❑ Partner Cards—Listening.
❑ Partner Cards—Speaking.
❑ Story Reading.
❑ Story Dictation.
❑ Cloze Reading.

❑ Story Retelling
 from Skeleton.
❑ Free Story Retelling.
❑ Parallel Story.
❑ Mini-drama.

Unit I2-A [23 ↗] What?—[31 ↘] What?

Story

Listen to the story as your teacher reads it, or on tape, until you understand the main ideas.

Eric didn't read much. He would much rather play basketball than read a book. It wasn't that he couldn't read. He did it for school assignments, and he read the sports section of the newspaper. He just didn't like to read other things. His parents tried to encourage him to read more, but nothing worked. That's why his mother was (1) shocked one day during summer vacation when Eric casually told her, (2) "I'm reading a good book."

"**What?**" she said in disbelief. "Are you OK?"

"Sure. I just got tired of nothing but sports and decided to read something. The book turned out to be pretty good."

Eric's mother was so surprised that she called her husband at work. "Eric's reading a book!" she said.

His response was the same as hers. "What? Did I hear you correctly? Eric?" He just couldn't believe it either. But by the time he came home later that day he had gotten used to the idea. (3) So, when Eric told him, "Hey Dad, I'm reading a good book," he calmly replied, "**What?**"

"Oh, the title is *Tom Sawyer*," Eric explained. "You ought to read it some time."

Eric's dad just smiled.

Contrasting Sentences

Listening: Write the appropriate word in each blank. Later, as you hear each sentence, mark the box, point to the picture, make a gesture, and/or say the rejoinder. Speaking: Choose and say each sentence so that your listener(s) can respond correctly.

❏ _____? (Did I hear correctly?)

❏ _____? (Tell me the title.)

Explanations and diagrams for this unit's target sounds are on page 368 in Section 10.

Additional Practice

I've got a problem. *What? / What?* (I2-B/b)

Other Examples

The sentences below are in the story. Find them and circle or underline them. Say each marked sentence aloud. Look for any additional sentences in the story that use the target stress patterns. Mark and say them also.

[31 ↘] Eric didn't réad much. Súre. The book turned out to be pretty góod.

```
3          réad     Sú-                                    gó-
2 Eric didn't         \        The book turned out to be pretty    \
1              much.   re.                                  od.
```

[23 ↗] Are you OK? Did I héar you correctly? Éric?

```
3          K?↗      héar you correctly? ↗  Éric? ↗
2 Are you O      Did I
1
```

Other Practice Activities

❑ Partner Cards—Listening. *Practice until you can point to the right card every time.*

❑ Partner Cards—Speaking. *Practice until you can say the contrasting sentences so accurately that your partner points to the right card every time.*

❑ Story Reading. *Practice reading the story aloud. Mark any difficult words. Then record the story on tape.*

❑ Story Dictation. *Write the story as your teacher reads it or as you listen to it on the audiotape.*

❑ Cloze Reading. *Choose some key words in the story and black them out. Then read the entire story aloud. Do this several times.*

Each time black out more words. Continue until most of the story is blacked out and you can tell it without looking at the page very often.

❑ Story Retelling from Skeleton. *Black out all the remaining words except those you need in order to remind you of the story line. Then, using just this skeleton, tell the story to your partner or class.*

❑ Free Story Retelling. *Retell the whole story from memory, without looking at your book.*

❑ Parallel Story. *Create your own story similar to the one in this unit.*

❑ Mini-drama. *Make up a skit or do a role play based on the story.*

Unit I2-B [23 ↗] What?—[31 ↘] What?

Story

Ed and Don worked together, side by side, in a factory. Lots of machines were running all the time, so it was a pretty noisy place. Still, they talked as they worked. Sometimes they almost had to shout, but they talked a lot—about politics, sports, their families, etc. Usually, Don did most of the talking and Ed listened.

One day Don said, "I've got a problem."

"What?" said Ed. (1) "I didn't hear you. The noise is terrible today."

"I said, I've got a problem," repeated Don.

"What?" asked Ed. (2) "Tell me more about it." He really was a good listener.

"Well," said Don, "it's Don Junior, my son."

"Who?" asked Ed. "You'll have to speak up."

"Sorry," apologized Don. "It's Don, my son, he's started hanging out with kids I don't like. You should have seen who he was with last night."

"Who?" asked Ed. "Anybody I know?"

"Probably not, but it was a rough-looking group." He continued talking while Ed listened. After about an hour, they still hadn't solved the problem, but Don felt a lot better anyway. It really helps to have a friend to talk to.

Contrasting Sentences

❏ _____? (I didn't hear you.)

❏ _____? (Tell me more about it.)

Additional Practice

I'm reading a good book. *What?/What?* (I2-A/a)

Other Examples

[31 ↘] Whó? I didn't héar you. The noise is térrible today. Sórry.

3	Wh-		héar		tér-		Sór-
2		\	I didn't	\	The noise is	\	\
1	ó?		you.		rible today.		ry.

[23 ↗] Who? Anybody I knów?

3	o? ↗		ów?
2	Wh-	Anybody I kn-	
1			

Other Practice Activities

❏ Partner Cards—Listening.
❏ Partner Cards—Speaking.
❏ Story Reading.
❏ Story Dictation.
❏ Cloze Reading.

❏ Story Retelling from Skeleton.
❏ Free Story Retelling.
❏ Parallel Story.
❏ Mini-drama.

Unit I3-A [23 ↗] will he?—[31] will he?

Story

Listen to the story as your teacher reads it, or on tape, until you understand the main ideas.

Frank works in the suicide division of the San Francisco Police Department. Several times a month he is called to the Golden Gate Bridge to deal with suicidal people who are threatening to jump into the icy waters far below.

One day, Frank was called to talk to a young man who was about to jump off the bridge. This man had just failed his college entrance exam. He felt tremendous pressure from his family to get into a good university, and now he was ashamed to face them. He wanted to die, but he didn't really want to jump either.

When Frank arrived on the scene, he heard (1) several bystanders saying, "He won't jump, **will he?**" They hoped not, but they weren't sure.

(2) Several experienced police officers, observing the look on the young man's face, suspected that he wouldn't really jump. When they saw Frank, they predicted, "He won't jump, **will he?**"

Frank looked at the young man's face and agreed with them. "No, I don't think he will." And he was right. Frank was able to convince him to come down. Later, the young man received counseling, retook the exam, and passed it.

Contrasting Sentences

Listening: Write the appropriate word in each blank. Later, as you hear each sentence, mark the box, point to the picture, make a gesture, and / or say the rejoinder. Speaking: Choose and say each sentence so that your listener(s) can respond correctly.

❑ He won't jump, _____ _____? (uncertain bystanders)

❑ He won't jump, _____ _____? (experienced police)

Explanations and diagrams for this unit's target sounds are on page 369 in Section 10.

Additional Practice

Cindy can do it, *can't she? / can't she?* (I3-B/b)

Other Examples

The sentences below are not in the story, but they use the target stress patterns. Practice saying them also.

[23↗] Frank's a good policeman, isn't he? He knows his stuff, doesn't he?

3   he?↗   he?↗

2 Frank's a good policeman, isn't   He knows his stuff, doesn't

1

[31] Frank's a good policeman, isn't he? He knows his stuff, doesn't he?

3   is-   does-

2 Frank's a good policeman, \   He knows his stuff, \

1   n't he?   n't he?

Other Practice Activities

❏ Partner Cards—Listening. *Practice until you can point to the right card every time.*
❏ Partner Cards—Speaking. *Practice until you can say the contrasting sentences so accurately that your partner points to the right card every time.*
❏ Story Reading. *Practice reading the story aloud. Mark any difficult words. Then record the story on tape.*
❏ Story Dictation. *Write the story as your teacher reads it or as you listen to it on the audiotape.*
❏ Cloze Reading. *Choose some key words in the story and black them out. Then read the entire story aloud. Do this several times.*

Each time black out more words. Continue until most of the story is blacked out and you can tell it without looking at the page very often.

❏ Story Retelling from Skeleton. *Black out all the remaining words except those you need in order to remind you of the story line. Then, using just this skeleton, tell the story to your partner or class.*
❏ Free Story Retelling. *Retell the whole story from memory, without looking at your book.*
❏ Parallel Story. *Create your own story similar to the one in this unit.*
❏ Mini-drama. *Make up a skit or do a role play based on the story.*

Unit I3-B [23 ↗] can't she?—[31] can't she?

Story

Cindy was a shy and timid person. Whenever she was given a difficult task at the bank where she worked, her co-workers hoped she would be able to do it, but they weren't sure. "Cindy can do it, **can't she?**" (1) they wondered.

One day, much to the surprise of her co-workers, Cindy quit her job and went off to the Amazon. When she reappeared two years later, she looked much the same. She got her old job back, and many people doubted that she had really gone to the jungles at all. They still questioned her ability to complete tasks.

Then, one day the bank was robbed. Three men pulled out guns and told everyone to put their hands in the air. Cindy, surprising everyone, quickly grabbed a stapler and threw it at one of the men. It hit him on the head and knocked him out. She then jumped up on the counter, grabbed hold of the hanging light and gave a wild yell as she swung herself into the remaining robbers, knocking both down.

After that no one questioned Cindy's ability to do anything. "Cindy can do it, **can't she?**" (2) has been the response from her co-workers ever since.

Contrasting Sentences

❏ Cindy can do it, _____. (I hope so.)

❏ Cindy can do it, _____. (She can do anything!)

Additional Practice

He won't jump, *will he? / will he?* (I3-A/a)

Other Examples

[23 ↗] Cindy learned a lot in the jungle, didn't she? Her actions surprised everyone, didn't they?

3   she? ↗   they? ↗

2 Cindy learned a lot in the jungle, didn't   Her actions surprised everyone, didn't

1

[31] Cindy learned a lot in the jungle, didn't she? Her actions surprised everyone, didn't they?

3   didn't   didn't

2 Cindy learned a lot in the jungle,   \   Her actions surprised everyone,   \

1   she?   they?

Other Practice Activities

- ❏ Partner Cards—Listening.
- ❏ Partner Cards—Speaking.
- ❏ Story Reading.
- ❏ Story Dictation.
- ❏ Cloze Reading.
- ❏ Story Retelling from Skeleton.
- ❏ Free Story Retelling.
- ❏ Parallel Story.
- ❏ Mini-drama.

Unit I4-A [231‖23 ↗] Studying?— [231‖231 ↘] Studying.

Story

Listen to the story as your teacher reads it, or on tape, until you understand the main ideas.

Sam never studied. At least that's what his roommates thought. Whenever they saw him, he was playing video games or watching TV. But the amazing thing was that he didn't fail his classes. In fact, he did very well, and his roommates couldn't figure out why.

Well, Sam's secret was that he needed only a few hours of sleep each night. When all of his roommates were in bed, Sam would do his studying at the kitchen table, go to sleep at 4:00 or 5:00 A.M., and then wake up in time for class.

One night, Art, one of Sam's roommates, woke up in the middle of the night and noticed the kitchen light on. Thinking that maybe someone had left it on by mistake, he got up to turn it off. As he walked around the corner he saw (1) Sam diligently reading his textbook. Somewhat shocked at the sight, Art asked, "What are you doing? **Studying?**"

"Yes, I am," replied Sam. (2) "What are you doing?"

"Studying," answered Art.

"Really?" asked Sam.

"No, not really. I'm just kidding. I'm going back to bed," Art mumbled.

Contrasting Sentences

Listening: Write the appropriate word in each blank. Later, as you hear each sentence, mark the box, point to the picture, make a gesture, and/or say the rejoinder. Speaking: Choose and say each sentence so that your listener(s) can respond correctly.

❑ What are you doing? _____? (Yes.)

❑ What are you doing? _____. (Really?)

Explanations and diagrams for this unit's target sounds are on pages 370–71 in Section 10.

Additional Practice

What's that? *A bird?/A bird.* (I4-B/b), When are you leaving? *Tomorrow?/tomorrow?* (I4-C/c)

Other Examples

The sentences below are not in the story, but they use the target stress patterns. Practice saying them also.

[231‖23↗] What are you studying? Ancient history? What grade are you getting? An A?

3		stud-		tory?↗	grade		A?↗
2 What are you	\		Ancient his-	What		An	
1		ying?			are you getting?		

[231‖231↘] What are you studying? Ancient history. What grade are you getting? An A.

3		stud-		his-		grade		A	
2 What are you	\		Ancient	\	What			An	\
1		ying?			tory.		are you getting?		↘.

Other Practice Activities

❑ Partner Cards—Listening. *Practice until you can point to the right card every time.*
❑ Partner Cards—Speaking. *Practice until you can say the contrasting sentences so accurately that your partner points to the right card every time.*
❑ Story Reading. *Practice reading the story aloud. Mark any difficult words. Then record the story on tape.*
❑ Story Dictation. *Write the story as your teacher reads it or as you listen to it on the audiotape.*
❑ Cloze Reading. *Choose some key words in the story and black them out. Then read the entire story aloud. Do this several times.*

Each time black out more words. Continue until most of the story is blacked out and you can tell it without looking at the page very often.
❑ Story Retelling from Skeleton. *Black out all the remaining words except those you need in order to remind you of the story line. Then, using just this skeleton, tell the story to your partner or class.*
❑ Free Story Retelling. *Retell the whole story from memory, without looking at your book.*
❑ Parallel Story. *Create your own story similar to the one in this unit.*
❑ Mini-drama. *Make up a skit or do a role play based on the story.*

Unit I4-B [231∥23 ↗] A bird?— [231∥231 ↘] A bird.

Story

#1

(1) Mr. Park's (2) second grade class loves to go on field trips. They go to government offices, museums, farms, etc. Wherever they go, the young children get excited and ask a lot of questions.

#2

Yesterday they went to the zoo and saw many different types of animals. For many of them it was the first time they had been to a zoo, so many animals were new to them.

#3

When they came to the (3) ostrich pen, several children stared in wonder. They had never seen an ostrich before. It looked like a bird, but it was so big that they weren't sure. Several students asked Mr. Park, "What's that? **A bird?**"

Mr. Park replied, "Yes students, **a bird.** See? It has a bill and lays eggs."

Later they saw a beaver and asked, "What's that?"

Mr. Park explained, "A beaver. It's a mammal. It has fur."

A few minutes later, some of the second graders saw a platypus. It had a bill like a duck's, but it had fur like a beaver's. They asked, "What's that animal? A bird? Why does it have fur?" Others wondered, "What's that strange creature? A mammal? Why does it have a bill?" They were very confused.

Mr. Park explained, "It's a platypus," but that's as far as he went.

Contrasting Sentences

❏ What's that? A _____? (students asking)

❏ What's that? A _____. (teacher answering)

Additional Practice

What are you doing? *Studying?/Studying.* (I4-A/a), When are you leaving? *Tomorrow?/tomorrow?* (I4-C/c)

Other Examples

[231‖23↗] What's that animal? A bird? What's that strange creature? A mammal?

3		that		bird?↗		that			mammal?↗
2 What's			A		What's			A	
1		animal?				strange creature?			

[231‖231↘] What's that animal? A platypus. Why does it have a bill? I don't know.

3		that		platy-			bi-		don't
2 What's			A	＼	Why does it have a		＼	I	
1		animal?		pus.			ll?		know.

Other Practice Activities

❑ Partner Cards—Listening.
❑ Partner Cards—Speaking.
❑ Story Reading.
❑ Story Dictation.
❑ Cloze Reading.

❑ Story Retelling
   from Skeleton.
❑ Free Story Retelling.
❑ Parallel Story.
❑ Mini-drama.

Unit I4-C [231‖23↗] Tomorrow?— [231↘]... tomorrow?

Story

Even though I am now an adult, my father likes to know all about what I am doing. He's always asking me about my plans for the future.

For example, last spring he remembered that I had previously said I wanted to vacation in the western United States the next summer, so he asked me, "Where are you going on your vacation this summer? The Grand Canyon?"

"No, I don't think so," I replied. "I've already been there."

The next time he asked, he was more open in his question, but by then I had decided. When he asked, "Where are you going this summer?" I answered, "Yellowstone."

Of course, that information alone did not satisfy his interest. He continued to ask me questions about my trip. One day, when he saw me packing up, he asked, (1) "When are you leaving? **Tomorrow?**"

"Yeah, tomorrow," I told him, but even that information was not enough for him.

He asked, "When are you leaving **tomorrow?**" (2)

"Oh, about ten o'clock in the morning," I explained. But I knew that I would soon hear more questions, like, "How long will you be gone?" and "How are you traveling?"

Contrasting Sentences

❏ When are you leaving? _____? (Yeah, tomorrow.)

❏ When are you leaving _____? (About ten o'clock.)

Additional Practice

What are you doing? *Studying? / Studying.* (I4-A/a), What's that? *A bird? / A bird.* (I4-B/b)

Other Examples

[231‖23↗] Where are you going on your vacation this summer? The Grand Canyon?

3		ca-		Canyon?↗
2 Where are you going on your va- \			The Grand	
1		tion this summer?		

[231‖231↘] Where are you going this summer? Yellowstone. How long will you be gone? About ten days.

3	go-	Yel-		go-	ten
2 Where are you \		\	How long will you be \		About
1	ing this summer?	lowstone.		ne?	days.

Other Practice Activities

- ❏ Partner Cards—Listening.
- ❏ Partner Cards—Speaking.
- ❏ Story Reading.
- ❏ Story Dictation.
- ❏ Cloze Reading.
- ❏ Story Retelling from Skeleton.
- ❏ Free Story Retelling.
- ❏ Parallel Story.
- ❏ Mini-drama.

Unit I5-A [23 ↗] chicken . . .—
[231 ↘] chicken.

Story

Listen to the story as your teacher reads it, or on tape, until you understand the main ideas.

The Mandarin Gourmet restaurant was very busy one evening. Mr. Allred had to wait nearly an hour for a table. When he was finally seated and able to place his order, Mr. Allred could tell that the waiter was in a big hurry. But Mr. Allred, upset at having to wait so long to be seated, decided to take his time ordering. He looked at the menu carefully. (1) "I'll have fried rice," he said, pausing thoughtfully, "and cashew **chicken . . .**"

While Mr. Allred paused, the waiter said, "Yes, sir!" and started walking away.

Mr. Allred called out, "Hey, I'm not finished ordering. Come back here. You made me wait; now I'm going to make you wait." The waiter hurried back to Mr. Allred's table and waited for him to finish. Mr. Allred said, "No, I think I'll have chow mein and beef broccoli . . . and . . . maybe something else." After a lot more thinking and looking at the menu, Mr. Allred finally decided to have the items he had originally ordered. He announced, (2) "I'll have fried rice and cashew **chicken.**" Very frustrated at this point, the waiter turned around, let out a sigh, and rushed off to the kitchen.

Contrasting Sentences

Listening: Write the appropriate word in each blank. Later, as you hear each sentence, mark the box, point to the picture, make a gesture, and/or say the rejoinder. Speaking: Choose and say each sentence so that your listener(s) can respond correctly.

❏ I'll have fried rice and cashew _____ . . . (not finished ordering)

❏ I'll have fried rice and cashew _____. (finished ordering)

Explanations and diagrams for this unit's target sounds are on page 371 in Section 10.

Additional Practice

He bought *a new house, boat, and truck. / a new houseboat and truck.* (I5-B/b), I'm taking *Spanish, history, and art. / Spanish history and art.* (I5-c)

Other Examples

The sentences below are in the story. Find them and circle or underline them. Say each marked sentence aloud.

[23 ↗] I think I'll have chow mein and beef broccoli . . . and . . .

3		mein ↗		broccoli ↗	
2 I think I'll have chow		and beef . . .		and . . .	
1					

[231 ↘] The waiter turned around, let out a big sigh, and rushed off to the kitchen.

3		round, ↗		sigh, ↗	rushed off to the kitch-	
2 The waiter turned a-		let out a		and		↘
1						en. ↘

Other Practice Activities

❏ Partner Cards—Listening. *Practice until you can point to the right card every time.*

❏ Partner Cards—Speaking. *Practice until you can say the contrasting sentences so accurately that your partner points to the right card every time.*

❏ Story Reading. *Practice reading the story aloud. Mark any difficult words. Then record the story on tape.*

❏ Story Dictation. *Write the story as your teacher reads it or as you listen to it on the audiotape.*

❏ Cloze Reading. *Choose some key words in the story and black them out. Then read the entire story aloud. Do this several times.*

Each time black out more words. Continue until most of the story is blacked out and you can tell it without looking at the page very often.

❏ Story Retelling from Skeleton. *Black out all the remaining words except those you need in order to remind you of the story line. Then, using just this skeleton, tell the story to your partner or class.*

❏ Free Story Retelling. *Retell the whole story from memory, without looking at your book.*

❏ Parallel Story. *Create your own story similar to the one in this unit.*

❏ Mini-drama. *Make up a skit or do a role play based on the story.*

Unit I5-B [23 ↗ ‖23 ↗] a new house, boat . . . — [231 ↗] a new houseboat

Story

The Smiths and the Jones were neighbors. Both families had three children, lived in large homes, and took long summer vacations. The Jones family was very rich. Mr. Jones owned a large import/export company and made over a million dollars a year. In contrast, Mr. Smith's salary as a schoolteacher was not even close to Mr. Jones's salary. Nevertheless, he still wanted to have everything the Jones family had.

When the Jones family had a swimming pool put in last summer, Mr. Smith had to have one too. Mr. Jones paid cash for his pool, but Mr. Smith had to take out a loan. This summer Mr. Jones is planning to buy a new **house** in a resort community next to a lake. (1) He has already bought a new **boat** and a truck to pull the boat. When Mr. Smith saw the new boat and truck in the Jones's driveway, he felt that he had to outdo the Joneses. (2) So he went out and bought a new **houseboat** and truck.

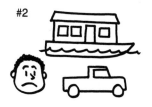

Sadly, however, Mr. Smith just couldn't keep up with the Joneses. In the end, he couldn't make all his loan payments, the bank foreclosed, and Mr. Smith lost everything.

Contrasting Sentences

❏ He bought a new _____, _____, and truck. (Mr. Jones, 3 things)

❏ He bought a new _____ and truck. (Mr. Smith, 2 things)

Additional Practice

I'll have fried rice and *cashew chicken . . . / cashew chicken.* (I5-A/a),
I'm taking *Spanish, history, and art. / Spanish history and art.* (I5-c)

Other Examples

[23 ↗](& [231 ↘]) Both families had three children, lived in large
  homes, and took long summer vacations.

3		three children,		homes,		long summer va-
2 Both families had			lived in large		and took	
1						cations.

[231 ↗](& [231 ↘]) He couldn't make all his loan payments, the
  bank foreclosed, and Mr. Smith lost everything.

3		loan		closed ↗,		eve-
2 He couldn't make all his		ments, ↗, the bank fore-		and Mr. Smith lost	↘	
1		pay-				rything.

Other Practice Activities

❑ Partner Cards—Listening.
❑ Partner Cards—Speaking.
❑ Story Reading.
❑ Story Dictation.
❑ Cloze Reading.

❑ Story Retelling
  from Skeleton.
❑ Free Story Retelling.
❑ Parallel Story.
❑ Mini-drama.

Unit I6-A [23 ↗ ‖231] a pen, or a pencil?—
[23 ↗] a pen or a pencil?

Story

Listen to the story as your teacher reads it, or on tape, until you understand the main ideas.

A few months ago, Sarah graduated from high school and started looking for a job. Her friend Roger told her that she needed to make a resumé listing her goals and previous experience. Sarah had never done that before, so she asked him several questions.

Sarah didn't type very well, so the first question she asked was "Can I use **a pen or a pencil?**" Roger told her that writing a resumé by hand was not neat enough. He told her that a resumé should always be (1) typed or done on a word processor.

When Sarah's resumé was finally complete, she went off job hunting. At the first office, she handed the secretary a copy of her resumé but was told that she still needed to fill out a job application. "Should I use **a pen, or a pencil?**" Sarah asked the secretary. The secretary replied, (2) "A pen. And make sure it has black ink. Blue ink doesn't copy well, and pencil smudges."

Sarah's effort and care paid off. Two weeks later she got a call from the office where she had applied. She was hired! She was so happy that she called Roger and treated him to dinner and a movie.

Contrasting Sentences

Listening: Write the appropriate words in each blank. Later, as you hear each sentence, mark the box, point to the picture, make a gesture, and/or say the rejoinder. Speaking: Choose and say each sentence so that your listener(s) can respond correctly.

❑ Should I use a _____? (No, it's better if you type it.)

❑ Should I use a _____? (A black pen, please.)

Explanations and diagrams for this unit's target sounds are on pages 371–73 in Section 10.

Additional Practice

Do you want *soup, or salad? / soup or salad?* (I6-B/b), Will you travel by *train, or plane? / train or plane?* (I6-C/c), *Friday, or Saturday? / Friday or Saturday?* (I6-d)

Other Examples

The sentences below are not in the story, but they use the target stress patterns. Practice saying them also.

[23 ↗ ‖231] Can you start work on Friday, or Saturday?

3   Friday, ↗ ‖   Sat-

2 Can you start work on   or   \

1   urday?

[23 ↗] Can you start work on Friday or Saturday?

3   Friday or Saturday? ↗

2 Can you start work on

1

Other Practice Activities

❏ Partner Cards—Listening. *Practice until you can point to the right card every time.*
❏ Partner Cards—Speaking. *Practice until you can say the contrasting sentences so accurately that your partner points to the right card every time.*
❏ Story Reading. *Practice reading the story aloud. Mark any difficult words. Then record the story on tape.*
❏ Story Dictation. *Write the story as your teacher reads it or as you listen to it on the audiotape.*
❏ Cloze Reading. *Choose some key words in the story and black them out. Then read the entire story aloud. Do this several times. Each time black out more words. Continue*

until most of the story is blacked out and you can tell it without looking at the page very often.
❏ Story Retelling from Skeleton. *Black out all the remaining words except those you need in order to remind you of the story line. Then, using just this skeleton, tell the story to your partner or class.*
❏ Free Story Retelling. *Retell the whole story from memory, without looking at your book.*
❏ Parallel Story. *Create your own story similar to the one in this unit.*
❏ Mini-drama. *Make up a skit or do a role play based on the story.*

Unit I6-B [23 ↗ ‖231] soup, or salad?— [23 ↗] soup or salad?

Story

Linda and her friend Donna love to eat at the local Italian restaurant every Wednesday. Wednesday is their favorite day because the restaurant offers all-you-can-eat soup, salad, and breadsticks for a special low price.

Last Wednesday, when Donna ordered her usual all-you-can-eat special, she was surprised when the server asked her, (1) "Do you want **soup, or salad?**"

"Don't I get both?" she responded with surprise. The server explained to her that the restaurant was no longer able to provide both soup and salad with breadsticks. She had to make a choice. Donna muttered, "I'll have salad, then."

The server then turned to Linda. She was especially hungry, so she ordered the full spaghetti dinner. It came with several soup and salad options, so the server asked, "Do you want **soup or salad?**"

Linda responded, "Yes, what are my choices?" (2) When she learned that she could have any combination of soup, salad, and even breadsticks, she ordered them all. Donna decided she would order the full dinner next time.

Contrasting Sentences

❑ Do you want _____? (Salad, please.)

❑ Do you want _____? (Yes, what are my choices?)

Additional Practice

Should I use a *pen, or a pencil?*/*pen or a pencil?* (I6-A/a), Will you travel by *train, or plane?*/*train or plane?* (I6-C/c), Can you start work on *Friday, or Saturday?*/*Friday or Saturday?* (I6-d)

Other Examples

[23 ↗ ‖231] Will you be paying by cash, or credit card?

3   cash, ↗ ‖

2 Will you be paying by   or cred-

1   it card?

[23 ↗] Would you like some coffee or tea?

3   coffee or tea? ↗

2 Would you like some

1

Other Practice Activities

- ❏ Partner Cards—Listening.
- ❏ Partner Cards—Speaking.
- ❏ Story Reading.
- ❏ Story Dictation.
- ❏ Cloze Reading.
- ❏ Story Retelling from Skeleton.
- ❏ Free Story Retelling.
- ❏ Parallel Story.
- ❏ Mini-drama.

Unit I6-C [23 ↗ ‖231] by train, or plane?— [23 ↗] by train or plane?

Story

The Stevens are retired and take long trips every summer. In the past they visited many historical sites around the United States by traveling in their large mobile home. When they told people about their extensive travel plans they were often asked, "Will you travel by **train or plane?**" Their reply was always, (1) "No, we have a mobile home, and we just take our time."

#1

Last year, however, when returning from their New York trip, they had a serious accident on the highway. Fortunately, the Stevens escaped with only minor injuries, but their mobile home was destroyed. They decided not to replace it. Driving long distances was just too dangerous for them.

Since the Stevens no longer have their mobile home and don't want to drive much, they have decided to try a different mode of travel this year. They want to visit the Grand Canyon, but since both of them are afraid to travel in airplanes and since trains have a better safety record, they have decided to travel by train. So now, when people who know about their accident and travel plans ask them, "Will you travel by **plane, or train?**" their response is (2) "By train. It's safer."

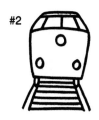
#2

Contrasting Sentences

❏ Will you travel by _____? (No, we have a mobile home.)

❏ Will you travel by _____? (By train. It's safer.)

Additional Practice

Should I use a *pen, or a pencil? / pen or a pencil?* (I6-A/a), Do you want *soup, or salad? / soup or salad?* (I6-B/b), Can you start work on *Friday, or Saturday? / Friday or Saturday?* (I6-d)

Other Examples

[23 ↗ ‖231] When you visit the Grand Canyon, will you go to the north rim, or the south rim?

3   north rim, ↗ ‖   south

2 When you visit the Grand Canyon, will you go to the   or the   \

1   rim?

[23 ↗] When you're there, will you also visit Bryce Canyon or Zion National Park?

3   Bryce Canyon or Zion National Park? ↗

2 When you're there, will you also visit

1

Other Practice Activities

- ❏ Partner Cards—Listening.
- ❏ Partner Cards—Speaking.
- ❏ Story Reading.
- ❏ Story Dictation.
- ❏ Cloze Reading.
- ❏ Story Retelling from Skeleton.
- ❏ Free Story Retelling.
- ❏ Parallel Story.
- ❏ Mini-drama.

Unit I7-A [23 ↗ ‖231] soup 'r salad?— [23 ↗] "Super Salad"?

Story

Listen to the story as your teacher reads it, or on tape, until you understand the main ideas.

Paul and Lisa were excited to try out the new "Super Steak" restaurant in town. On their way into the steakhouse, they saw a very large sign that read, "Try our New **Super Salad,** today!" They were curious as to what a "Super Salad" was, so they asked their server when they were ordering their meal. The server explained that the Super Salad was (1) a gallon-size bowl of green salad that was big enough to feed a whole family, yet it was offered at a low price.

Deciding that the Super Salad was too big for them, Paul and Lisa ordered steaks. The server then explained that (2) soup 'r salad was included in their meal. The soup of the day was French onion, and the salad was tossed green salad. She then asked them if they would like (2) the **soup 'r salad.** Paul responded, "I'll have the salad, please, but not the Super Salad. It's way too large for even the two of us."

Contrasting Sentences

Listening: Write the appropriate words in each blank. Later, as you hear each sentence, mark the box, point to the picture, make a gesture, and/or say the rejoinder. Speaking: Choose and say each sentence so that your listener(s) can respond correctly.

❑ Would you like the _____? (Salad, please.)

❑ Would you like the _____? (No, thanks! It's way too large.)

Explanations and diagrams for this unit's target sounds are on pages 373–74 in Section 10.

Additional Practice

For alternative questions: Should I use a *pen, or a pencil? / pen or a pencil?* (I6-A/a), Would you like *soup, or salad? / soup or salad?* (I6-B/b), Will you travel by *train, or plane? / train or plane?* (I6-C/c), Can you start work on *Friday, or Saturday? / Friday or Saturday?* (I6-d)

For *yes/no* questions: It's *dark already. / dark already?* (I1-A/a), It's due *today. / today?* (I1-B/b), Susan's in love *with Sam. / with Sam?* (I1-C/c)

Other Examples

The sentences below are not in the story, but they use the target stress patterns. Practice saying them also.

[23 ↗ ‖231] Shall we eat out, or stay at home?

3   out, ↗ ‖   ho-

2 Shall we eat   or stay at   \

1   me?

[23 ↗] Shall we eat at the new "Super Steak"?

3   "Super Steak"? ↗

2 Shall we eat at the new

1

Other Practice Activities

❏ Partner Cards—Listening. *Practice until you can point to the right card every time.*
❏ Partner Cards—Speaking. *Practice until you can say the contrasting sentences so accurately that your partner points to the right card every time.*
❏ Story Reading. *Practice reading the story aloud. Mark any difficult words. Then record the story on tape.*
❏ Story Dictation. *Write the story as your teacher reads it or as you listen to it on the audiotape.*
❏ Cloze Reading. *Choose some key words in the story and black them out. Then read the entire story aloud. Do this several times.*

Each time black out more words. Continue until most of the story is blacked out and you can tell it without looking at the page very often.
❏ Story Retelling from Skeleton. *Black out all the remaining words except those you need in order to remind you of the story line. Then, using just this skeleton, tell the story to your partner or class.*
❏ Free Story Retelling. *Retell the whole story from memory, without looking at your book.*
❏ Parallel Story. *Create your own story similar to the one in this unit.*
❏ Mini-drama. *Make up a skit or do a role play based on the story.*

Unit I8-A [23 ↗|231] gold 'n' jewelry— [231] golden jewelry

Story

Listen to the story as your teacher reads it, or on tape, until you understand the main ideas.

Ray and Earl were thieves who stole from rich people. They would often go to expensive department stores to find victims. One day, as they were looking for people who seemed rich, a woman with lots of (1) **golden jewelry** walked by. Ray and Earl looked at each other and nodded. They both knew that she was their next victim. When the woman left the store, they stopped her at gunpoint and made her give them her golden bracelet. They also took her golden necklace and earrings. In addition, they took her purse. Then they ran away.

When they reached a hiding place, Ray and Earl stopped and looked in the purse. They were surprised to see that the woman had been carrying (2) several rare, old twenty dollar gold coins. They were worth around a thousand dollars each! In the purse there was also a diamond necklace.

When they saw the **gold 'n' jewelry,** Ray and Earl thought they were very lucky, but they weren't as lucky as they thought. The woman was really an undercover police officer, and the purse had a radio transmitter hidden inside. Within minutes, Ray and Earl were surrounded by police and under arrest.

Contrasting Sentences

Listening: Write the appropriate words in each blank. Later, as you hear each sentence, mark the box, point to the picture, make a gesture, and/or say the rejoinder. Speaking: Choose and say each sentence so that your listener(s) can respond correctly.

❏ The lady had lots of _____. (jewelry made of gold)

❏ The lady had lots of _____. (precious metal and jewels)

Explanations and diagrams for this unit's target sounds are on page 374 in Section 10.

Additional Practice

The fire was started by *wood 'n' matches / wooden matches.* (I8-B/b), I love *pie 'n' apples / pineapples.* (I8-C/c), Sarah didn't want *red or orange / redder orange.* (I8-D/d)

Other Examples

Some of the sentences below are in the story. Find them and circle or underline them. Say each marked and/or listed sentence aloud.

[23↗|231] They also took her golden necklace 'n' earrings. They were surrounded by police 'n' under arrest.

```
3                    necklace↗|  ear-                        lice↗|       re-
2 They also took her golden       'n'   \    They were surrounded by po-    'n' under ar-  \
1                              rings.                                       st.
```

[231] They made her give them her golden bracelet. The police recovered the stolen goods.

```
3                    brace-                              go-
2 They made her give them her golden    \    The police recovered the stolen    \
1                              let.                              ods.
```

Other Practice Activities

❑ Partner Cards—Listening. *Practice until you can point to the right card every time.*

❑ Partner Cards—Speaking. *Practice until you can say the contrasting sentences so accurately that your partner points to the right card every time.*

❑ Story Reading. *Practice reading the story aloud. Mark any difficult words. Then record the story on tape.*

❑ Story Dictation. *Write the story as your teacher reads it or as you listen to it on the audiotape.*

❑ Cloze Reading. *Choose some key words in the story and black them out. Then read the entire story aloud. Do this several times.*

Each time black out more words. Continue until most of the story is blacked out and you can tell it without looking at the page very often.

❑ Story Retelling from Skeleton. *Black out all the remaining words except those you need in order to remind you of the story line. Then, using just this skeleton, tell the story to your partner or class.*

❑ Free Story Retelling. *Retell the whole story from memory, without looking at your book.*

❑ Parallel Story. *Create your own story similar to the one in this unit.*

❑ Mini-drama. *Make up a skit or do a role play based on the story.*

Unit I8-B [23 ↗ |231] wood 'n' matches— [231] wooden matches

Story

My brother Larry works for the Alaskan government. He is a veteran firefighter. In his lifetime he has seen many destructive fires—in Alaska and other states. His main job now is to investigate how bad forest fires get started. Some forest fires are started by lightning, but most are started by people using (1) **wood and matches** carelessly. For instance, many people build campfires and then fail to extinguish them when they leave their campgrounds.

#1

Just last year, a big forest fire was started by the young children of some campers. The children were playing with matches in a grassy field near their camp. The grass was dry and caught on fire. The fire then spread to the forest and burned hundreds of acres. When the forest fire was finally put out, Larry was called in to investigate. In the field where the fire had started, he found a box of (2) **wooden matches** along with some other things the children had left there. The campers whose children had been playing with matches were fined over ten thousand dollars!

#2

Contrasting Sentences

❏ The fire was started by _____. (People should put their campfires out.)

❏ The fire was started by _____. (Children shouldn't play with them.)

Additional Practice

The lady had lots of *gold 'n' jewelry / golden jewelry.* (I8-A/a), I love *pie 'n' apples / pineapples.* (I8-C/c), Sarah didn't want *red or orange / redder orange.* (I8-D/d)

Other Examples

[23 ↗ |231] He has seen many fires—in Alaska 'n' other states. The grass was dry 'n' caught on fire.

3		laska ↗|	o-	dry ↗|	fi-
2 He has seen many fires—in A-		'n' \	The grass was	'n' caught on	\
1			ther states.		re.

[231] My brother works for the Alaskan government. He is a veteran firefighter.

3	gov-	fire-
2 My brother works for the Alaskan	He is a veteran	
1	ernment.	fighter.

Other Practice Activities

❏ Partner Cards—Listening.
❏ Partner Cards—Speaking.
❏ Story Reading.
❏ Story Dictation.
❏ Cloze Reading.
❏ Story Retelling from Skeleton.
❏ Free Story Retelling.
❏ Parallel Story.
❏ Mini-drama.

Unit I8-C [23 ↗ |231] pie 'n' apples— [31] pineapples

Story

Susan and John joined their best friends, Alice and Tony, on a cruise to celebrate their golden wedding anniversary. One afternoon, while the two couples were eating, they began discussing their favorite things. They talked about their favorite colors, cars, places, and movies. When the topic moved to food, trouble began. You see, Susan and John thought they knew each other very well after 50 years of marriage.

Susan said their favorite thing to eat was (1) pineapples, especially in cake and ice cream. John was surprised because he didn't like **pineapples.** When he said so, Susan started crying and ran back to her room, upset that all these years John had secretly disliked her pineapple desserts.

Tony told John that he didn't like pineapples either, but he loved apples—especially when they were made into pie. He couldn't imagine anyone not liking apple pie. When his wife, Alice, heard him say that, she became upset. She hated (2) pie of any kind, and apples were not her favorite fruit. **Pie 'n' apples** were not what she liked. How could she and her husband be so incompatible?

Contrasting Sentences

❑ I love _____. (Especially in cake and ice cream!)

❑ I love _____. (They're a perfect combination!)

Additional Practice

The lady had lots of *gold 'n' jewelry / golden jewelry.* (I8-A/a), The fire was started by *wood 'n' matches / wooden matches.* (I8-B/b), Sarah didn't want *red or orange / redder orange.* (I8-D/d)

Other Examples

[23 ↗ |231] I'd like some cake 'n' ice cream.

3   cake ↗ | ice

2 I'd like some   'n'   \

1   cream.

[231] It was their golden anniversary.

3   ver-

2 It was their golden anni-   \

1   sary.

Other Practice Activities

- ❏ Partner Cards—Listening.
- ❏ Partner Cards—Speaking.
- ❏ Story Reading.
- ❏ Story Dictation.
- ❏ Cloze Reading.
- ❏ Story Retelling from Skeleton.
- ❏ Free Story Retelling.
- ❏ Parallel Story.
- ❏ Mini-drama.

Unit I8-D [23 ↗ |231] red or orange— [231] redder orange

Story

Samantha the interior decorator was helping her client Sarah decide on what color of curtains she should put in her newly remodeled bedroom. Sarah was having a hard time deciding which color best matched her reddish-orange carpet.

"Should I use (1) **red, or orange**?" she asked Samantha.

"Red would work quite well," suggested Samantha.

"But it doesn't highlight the orange in the carpet," responded Sarah.

"OK, let's go with orange then," said Samantha, feeling a bit frustrated with Sarah's inability to decide.

"That won't work either because it doesn't go with the red in the carpet," argued Sarah.

"How about (2) a **redder orange**?"

"No, I'm afraid that will make the room seem dark. I want it to have a brighter feeling."

Samantha finally came up with the idea of using striped material for the curtains. On a light background there would be red, orange, and red-orange stripes. The stripes would give the room the lighter feeling that Sarah wanted, and they would harmonize with all the colors in the carpet.

"You're a genius, Samantha!" said Sarah. "That's why I always hire you to help me with my decorating."

Contrasting Sentences

❑ Sarah didn't want _____. (Neither one worked.)

❑ Sarah didn't want _____? (It was too dark.)

Additional Practice

The lady had lots of *gold 'n' jewelry / golden jewelry.* (18-A/a), The fire was started by *wood 'n' matches / wooden matches.* (18-B/b), I love *pie 'n' apples / pineapples.* (18-C/c)

Other Examples

[23 ↗|231] Sarah didn't want the room to be too light or too dark.

3			light↗|	da-	
2 Sarah didn't want the room to be too				or too	\\
1					rk.

[231] The stripes gave the room a lighter feeling.

3		light-	
2 The stripes gave the room a	\\		
1		er feeling.	

Other Practice Activities

❑ Partner Cards—Listening.
❑ Partner Cards—Speaking.
❑ Story Reading.
❑ Story Dictation.
❑ Cloze Reading.

❑ Story Retelling from Skeleton.
❑ Free Story Retelling.
❑ Parallel Story.
❑ Mini-drama.

Section 9

Segmentation (S)

Unit S1-A [231↗ ‖1↗ ‖231] "Elizabeth," said John, "was . . ."—[231↗ |231] Elizabeth said, "John was . . ."

Story

Listen to the story as your teacher reads it, or on tape, until you understand the main ideas.

Elizabeth and John's friends were waiting for them outside the Tasty Freeze. They had been waiting for over an hour and were running out of patience. Their plan had been to meet at 7:00, eat, and then go to the movie at 8:30. It was now 8:00, and there was no sign of their two friends.

Finally John's car arrived. When both John and Elizabeth jumped out, all of their friends cried, "Where have you been?"

First John declared, "It's not my fault." He acted very innocent. "Elizabeth," said John, "was late." He explained that (1) Elizabeth made him wait in the car for 45 minutes while she was fixing her hair.

"Wait a minute," objected Elizabeth. "That's not true at all." She said, (2) "John was the one who was late." She started getting angry. "He picked me up nearly an hour later than scheduled, and he told me," she explained, "that his car had broken down."

They all looked at John. He smiled weakly, lifted his still greasy hands, and said, "Sorry."

Contrasting Sentences

Listening: Write the appropriate word in each blank. Later, as you hear each sentence, mark the box, point to the picture, make a gesture, and / or say the rejoinder. Speaking: Choose and say each sentence so that your listener(s) can respond correctly.

❑ "Elizabeth," _____ _____, "was late." (Elizabeth was late.)

❑ Elizabeth _____, "_____ was late." (John was late.)

Explanations and diagrams for this unit's target sounds are on pages 375–76 in Section 10.

Additional Practice

"Jerry," explained Susan, "was / Jerry explained, "Susan was in the car also." (S1-B/b), "Alexander," thought Simon "is / Alexander thought, "Simon is wrong this time." (S1-C/c)

Other Examples

The sentences below are in the story. Find them and circle or underline them. Say each marked sentence aloud. Look for any additional sentences in the story that use the target stress patterns. Mark and say them also.

[231↗‖1↗‖231] "And he tóld me," she explained, "that his cár had broken down."

3	told		cár
2	"And he		"that his
1	me,"↗‖ she explained,↗‖		had broken down."

[231↗|231] First Jóhn declared, "It's not mý fault."

3	Jóhn		mý
2	First		"It's not
1	declared,↗|		fault."

Other Practice Activities

❏ Partner Cards—Listening. *Practice until you can point to the right card every time.*

❏ Partner Cards—Speaking. *Practice until you can say the contrasting sentences so accurately that your partner points to the right card every time.*

❏ Story Reading. *Practice reading the story aloud. Mark any difficult words. Then record the story on tape.*

❏ Story Dictation. *Write the story as your teacher reads it or as you listen to it on the audiotape.*

❏ Cloze Reading. *Choose some key words in the story and black them out. Then read the entire story aloud. Do this several times.*

Each time black out more words. Continue until most of the story is blacked out and you can tell it without looking at the page very often.

❏ Story Retelling from Skeleton. *Black out all the remaining words except those you need in order to remind you of the story line. Then, using just this skeleton, tell the story to your partner or class.*

❏ Free Story Retelling. *Retell the whole story from memory, without looking at your book.*

❏ Parallel Story. *Create your own story similar to the one in this unit.*

❏ Mini-drama. *Make up a skit or do a role play based on the story.*

Unit S1-B [231 ↗ ‖ 1 ↗ ‖ 231] "Jerry," explained Susan, "was . . ."—[231 ↗ |231] Jerry explained, "Susan was . . ."

Story

One winter morning Jerry and his new bride, Susan, were late for work. As they were speeding down an icy road, Jerry lost control of the car. It skidded off the road and rolled down the hillside. It finally came to a stop in some thick bushes. Both Jerry and Susan were seriously injured. Unconscious, they were rushed to the hospital.

When Jerry regained consciousness he didn't see his wife, so he asked, (1) "Where's Susan?" He was afraid that she hadn't been found in the wreck, so he explained, "Susan was in the car also!"

A nurse comforted Jerry and told him, "Susan is in another room. She's fine."

At about the same time, Susan also regained consciousness

and thought immediately of her husband. (2) "Jerry," explained Susan, "was in the car also! Where is he?"

"Your husband," the doctor told Susan, "is recovering nicely." He explained that they would both be out of the hospital in a week.

When they were released from the hospital, they decided that riding the bus to work would be much safer than driving— especially in the winter.

Contrasting Sentences

❏ "Jerry," _____ _____, "was in the car also." (Where is he?)

❏ Jerry _____, "_____ was in the car also." (Where is she?)

Additional Practice

"Elizabeth," said John, "was / Elizabeth said, "John was late." (S1-A/a), "Alexander," thought Simon "is / Alexander thought, "Simon is wrong this time." (S1-C/c)

Other Examples

[231 ↗ ‖1 ↗ ‖231] "Your húsband," the doctor told Susan, "is recovering nícely."

```
3     hús-                                          níce-

2 "Your    \                        "is recovering    \

1          band," ↗ ‖ the doctor told Susan, ↗ ‖            ly."
```

[231 ↗ |231] A núrse told him, "Susan is in anóther room."

```
3   núrse                       óth-

2 A              "Susan is in an-    \

1       told him, ↗ |                er room."
```

Other Practice Activities

❏ Partner Cards—Listening.
❏ Partner Cards—Speaking.
❏ Story Reading.
❏ Story Dictation.
❏ Cloze Reading.

❏ Story Retelling
  from Skeleton.
❏ Free Story Retelling.
❏ Parallel Story.
❏ Mini-drama.

Unit S1-C [231 ↗ ‖1 ↗ ‖231] "Alexander," thought Simon, "is . . ."—[231 ↗ |231] Alexander thought, "Simon is . . ."

Story

(1) Alexander was a creative designer for a children's toy company. His mind was always working. Often he would think of wonderful new toy ideas as he traveled to work. When he got there, he would present these ideas to (2) Simon, his boss, a very practical man. Most of the time, Simon liked Alexander's ideas, and he produced and marketed them successfully. Sometimes, however, Alexander's ideas were not so successful. Simon had to be cautious.

On his way to work one day, Alexander saw an advertisement for a new dinosaur movie. Suddenly, he had an idea for a new toy. When he arrived at work, he rushed to Simon and said, "I've got a great idea. Let's make a life-size, inflatable, human-eating dinosaur."

"Life-size?" questioned Simon. "That will be huge!" He responded, "I'm afraid it's not practical."

"No. That's the appeal," answered Alexander. "The children," he explained, "will love it because it's so big."

"Alexander," thought Simon, "is wrong this time." He couldn't be convinced to produce the huge dinosaur toy.

Alexander, on the other hand, knew it was a good idea.

Alexander thought, "Simon is wrong this time." He walked

away sadly.

Which one do you think was right?

Contrasting Sentences

❏ "Alexander," _____ _____, "is wrong this time."
   (Alexander is wrong.)

❏ Alexander _____, "_____ is wrong this time."
   (Simon is wrong.)

Additional Practice

"Elizabeth," said John, "was / Elizabeth said, "John was late." (S1-A/a), "Jerry," explained Susan, "was / Jerry explained, "Susan was in the car also." (S1-B/b)

Other Examples

[231↗‖1↗‖231] "The chíldren," Alexander explained, "will lóve
   it."

3	chíl-			lóve	
2	"The	\		"will	\
1		dren," ↗‖	Alexander explained, ↗‖		it."

[231↗∣231] Alexánder said, "I've got a great idéa." Símon
   responded, "I'm afraid it's not práctical."

3	án-		é	Sí		prác-
2	Alex- \	"I've got a great id- \	\		"I'm afraid it's not	\
1	der said, ↗∣		a."	mon responded, ↗∣		tical."

Other Practice Activities

❏ Partner Cards—Listening.
❏ Partner Cards—Speaking.
❏ Story Reading.
❏ Story Dictation.
❏ Cloze Reading.

❏ Story Retelling
   from Skeleton.
❏ Free Story Retelling.
❏ Parallel Story.
❏ Mini-drama.

Unit S2-A [232‖12] . . . eat, Henry.— [231] . . . eat Henry.

Story

Listen to the story as your teacher reads it, or on tape, until you understand the main ideas.

(1) Henry was a peculiar person. He rented a house in the country where he lived by himself. His only companions were three animals. Henry liked his animals, and he really liked his name. In fact he liked it so much that he named all of his animals after himself. His cat was Henry the cat, his dog was Henry the dog, and he even named his (2) rooster Henry.

#1

#2

When Henry (the man) lost his job, he had to leave his house and move in with his Uncle Jack. At least his uncle lived in the country also, so Henry was able to take his animals with him. The animals were fine during the summer because they stayed outside. But when winter came, no one wanted a rooster inside the house. Henry's relatives decided to kill the rooster and eat it. One night they called Henry to the dinner table, saying, **"We're going to eat, Henry."**

When they were all at the table, Henry's Uncle Jack announced, "Tonight we have a surprise. **We're going to eat Henry."** Then he uncovered a plate of fried chicken. Henry excused himself from the table and went to bed hungry and heartbroken. At least he still had Henry the cat and Henry the dog.

Contrasting Sentences

Listening: Write the appropriate word in each blank. Later, as you hear each sentence, mark the box, point to the picture, make a gesture, and / or say the rejoinder. Speaking: Choose and say each sentence so that your listener(s) can respond correctly.

❑ We're going to _____, _____. (Come and sit down at the table.)

❑ We're going to _____ _____. (the rooster)

Explanations and diagrams for this unit's target sounds are on pages 376–77 in Section 10.

Additional Practice

Make sure to *wash, Suzy / wash Suzy*. (S2-B/b)

Other Examples

The sentences below are not in the story, but they follow the target pausing, stress, and intonation patterns. Practice saying them also.

[232‖12] I need to move in with yóur family, Uncle Jack.

3   yóur

2 I need to move in with family,‖ Jack.

1   Uncle

[231] Henry had to move in with his Uncle Jáck's family.

3   Jáck's

2 Henry had to move in with his Uncle \

1   family.

Other Practice Activities

❑ Partner Cards—Listening. *Practice until you can point to the right card every time.*

❑ Partner Cards—Speaking. *Practice until you can say the contrasting sentences so accurately that your partner points to the right card every time.*

❑ Story Reading. *Practice reading the story aloud. Mark any difficult words. Then record the story on tape.*

❑ Story Dictation. *Write the story as your teacher reads it or as you listen to it on the audiotape.*

❑ Cloze Reading. *Choose some key words in the story and black them out. Then read the entire story aloud. Do this several times.*

Each time black out more words. Continue until most of the story is blacked out and you can tell it without looking at the page very often.

❑ Story Retelling from Skeleton. *Black out all the remaining words except those you need in order to remind you of the story line. Then, using just this skeleton, tell the story to your partner or class.*

❑ Free Story Retelling. *Retell the whole story from memory, without looking at your book.*

❑ Parallel Story. *Create your own story similar to the one in this unit.*

❑ Mini-drama. *Make up a skit or do a role play based on the story.*

Unit S2-B [232‖12] . . . wash, Suzy.— [231] . . . wash Suzy.

Story

My brother has a daughter whose name is Susan, but because she is just a little girl we call her (1) Suzy. Suzy is three years old, and she is proud that she can do many things by herself. But she still needs someone to watch and help her. My brother usually takes good care of his little girl, but sometimes he has to leave her with someone. Last week, he left her with our mother.

Suzy loves to visit (2) her grandmother because Grandma always fixes Suzy her favorite food—spaghetti. Suzy loves spaghetti, and she can eat it all by herself. When she does, however, she gets it all over her face and hands. She looks cute covered with spaghetti sauce, but if she doesn't wash thoroughly afterward she gets a rash. Her skin is very tender.

Last week, when my brother left Suzy, she was happily eating spaghetti. Her face and hands were dirty with sauce, so as he left my brother told her, "**Make sure to wash, Suzy.** You don't want to get a rash." Then he whispered to my mother, "**Make sure to wash Suzy.** She doesn't always get clean enough by herself."

Contrasting Sentences

❏ Make sure to _____, _____. (You don't want to get a rash.)

❏ Make sure to _____ _____. (She doesn't get clean enough by herself.)

Additional Practice

We're going to *eat, Henry / eat Henry.* (S2-A/a)

Other Examples

[232‖12] Please fix me spaghétti, Grandmá. I've already cóoked it, Suzy.

3		ghét-			cóoked	
2 Please fix me spa-		ti,‖	má. I've already		it,‖	zy.
1			Grand-		Su-	

[231] Suzy loves to visit her grándmother. Her name's Súsan, but we call her Súzy.

3		gránd-		Sú-		Sú-
2 Suzy loves to visit her		\	Her name's	san, but we call her		\
1		mother.				zy.

Other Practice Activities

❏ Partner Cards—Listening.
❏ Partner Cards—Speaking.
❏ Story Reading.
❏ Story Dictation.
❏ Cloze Reading.

❏ Story Retelling from Skeleton.
❏ Free Story Retelling.
❏ Parallel Story.
❏ Mini-drama.

Unit S3-A [23|3 ↗] ... met, Mr. Smith?— [23] ... met Mr. Smith?

Story

Listen to the story as your teacher reads it, or on tape, until you understand the main ideas.

Alice works for a big corporation that puts on a big party for its employees every year during the holiday season. (1) Alice and her husband, Ted, usually have a lot of fun at these parties, and they make new friends.

At last year's party, Ted saw (2) a man who looked familiar to him. He asked his wife, "Do you know who that is, Alice?" She told him all that she knew. The man's name was Smith, and he was an important executive in the corporation.

"Have we met Mr. Smith?" Ted asked Alice. "He looks familiar."

Alice said, "Does he? I don't think so. This is the first time I've seen him."

Ted knew that he had met Mr. Smith before, but he couldn't remember where or when. It was really bothering him. Finally, he walked up to Mr. Smith and introduced himself. Then he asked, **"Have we met, Mr. Smith?** You look familiar."

Mr. Smith looked at Ted closely and said "Teddy? Is that you, Teddy? I'm Ron, Ronnie Smith. We were in the same class in fourth grade. We played baseball together. Don't you remember?"

Ted looked carefully at Mr. Smith's face and immediately recognized Ronnie, his old childhood friend.

Contrasting Sentences

Listening: Write the appropriate word in each blank. Later, as you hear each sentence, mark the box, point to the picture, make a gesture, and/or say the rejoinder. Speaking: Choose and say each sentence so that your listener(s) can respond correctly.

❏ Have we _____, Mr. Smith? (You look familiar.)

❏ Have we _____Mr. Smith? (He looks familiar.)

Explanations and diagrams for this unit's target sounds are on page 377 in Section 10.

Additional Practice

Can you *understand, Dr. Erickson? / understand Dr. Erickson?* (S3-B/b), Shall we *call, Tina? / call Tina?* (S3-c)

Other Examples

The sentences below are in the story. Find them and circle or underline them. Say each marked sentence aloud. Look for any additional sentences in the story that follow the target pausing, stress, and intonation patterns. Mark and say them also.

[23|3 ↗] Do you know who that is, Alice? Is that you, Teddy?

```
3                      is,| Alice? ↗      you,| Teddy? ↗

2 Do you know who that          Is that

1
```

[23] Does he? Don't you remember?

```
3      he?              member?

2 Does     Don't you re-

1
```

Other Practice Activities

❏ Partner Cards—Listening. *Practice until you can point to the right card every time.*

❏ Partner Cards—Speaking. *Practice until you can say the contrasting sentences so accurately that your partner points to the right card every time.*

❏ Story Reading. *Practice reading the story aloud. Mark any difficult words. Then record the story on tape.*

❏ Story Dictation. *Write the story as your teacher reads it or as you listen to it on the audiotape.*

❏ Cloze Reading. *Choose some key words in the story and black them out. Then read the entire story aloud. Do this several times.*

Each time black out more words. Continue until most of the story is blacked out and you can tell it without looking at the page very often.

❏ Story Retelling from Skeleton. *Black out all the remaining words except those you need in order to remind you of the story line. Then, using just this skeleton, tell the story to your partner or class.*

❏ Free Story Retelling. *Retell the whole story from memory, without looking at your book.*

❏ Parallel Story. *Create your own story similar to the one in this unit.*

❏ Mini-drama. *Make up a skit or do a role play based on the story.*

Unit S3-B [23|3 ↗] . . . understand, Dr. Erickson?—[23] . . . understand Dr. Erickson?

Story

(1) Dr. Erickson was a wonderful doctor who had recently come to the United States from another country to practice medicine. The only problem was that her English skills were less than perfect. Sometimes she had trouble understanding her patients, and her patients had difficulty understanding her.

On one particular day, Dr. Erickson was examining a girl who had severe stomach pains. The girl kept asking, "Can you help me, doctor? My tummy really hurts." Dr. Erickson did not know what a tummy was, so she gave her patient a puzzled look. The girl pointed to her stomach and said, **"Can you understand, Dr. Erickson?** It's my tummy." Dr. Erickson understood and was very helpful. She diagnosed the problem and explained what the girl needed to do.

Later, scheduling her follow-up appointment, the girl asked (2) the receptionist, **"Can you understand Dr. Erickson?** Her accent is very strong."

The receptionist smiled and said, "Did you have trouble understanding the doctor today? Don't worry. You'll get used to her accent in no time at all."

Contrasting Sentences

❏ Can you _____, _____? (It's my tummy.)

❏ Can you _____ _____? (Her accent is strong.)

Additional Practice

Have we *met, Mr. Smith? / met Mr. Smith?* (S3-A/a), Shall we *call, Tina? / call Tina?* (S3-c)

Other Examples

[23|3 ↗] Can you hélp me, doctor?

3   hélp me,| doctor? ↗

2 Can you

1

[23] Did you have tróuble understanding the doctor today?

3   tróuble understanding the doctor today?

2 Did you have

1

Other Practice Activities

- ❏ Partner Cards—Listening.
- ❏ Partner Cards—Speaking.
- ❏ Story Reading.
- ❏ Story Dictation.
- ❏ Cloze Reading.
- ❏ Story Retelling from Skeleton.
- ❏ Free Story Retelling.
- ❏ Parallel Story.
- ❏ Mini-drama.

Unit S4-A [231 ↗ ‖231] What's (2 + 4) 3?— [231 ↗ ‖231] What's 2 + (4 x 3)?

Story

Listen to the story as your teacher reads it, or on tape, until you understand the main ideas.

Ms. Jones is an elementary school teacher. She is quizzing her students in preparation for the interschool arithmetic competition. The students have to do multistep arithmetic problems quickly, in their heads.

"OK, Bobby, (1) **what's two plus four, times three?**" she says.

"Eighteen," he responds.

"That's right! Now, Kathy, (2) **what's two, plus four times three?**" she asks.

"Fourteen," Kathy answers.

"Good. Now what's twenty-one plus three, times two? Ellen."

Ellen thinks for a few seconds and then says, "Forty-eight."

"Let's do one more. What's twenty-one, plus three times two? Naomi."

"That's easy," Naomi says immediately, "Twenty-seven."

"Right again," says Ms. Jones. "I think you guys are ready."

#1

$(2+4)3 = 18$

#2

$2+(4 \times 3) = 14$

Contrasting Sentences

Listening: Write the appropriate word in each blank. Later, as you hear each sentence, mark the box, point to the picture, make a gesture, and/or say the rejoinder. Speaking: Choose and say each sentence so that your listener(s) can respond correctly.

❑ What's _____ _____ _____, times three? (18)

❑ What's _____, _____ _____ times three? (14)

Explanations and diagrams for this unit's target sounds are on pages 377–78 in Section 10.

Additional Practice

What's *five minus two,* /*five, minus two* times two? (S4-B/b), What's *twenty-one plus three,* /*twenty-one, plus three* times two? (S4-c)

Other Examples

The sentences below are in the story. Find them and circle or underline them. Say each marked sentence aloud. Look for any additional sentences in the story that contain the target stress patterns. Mark and say them also.

[231 ↗ ‖231] What's twenty-one plus three, times two?

3	twenty-one plus	tw-
2 What's	times	\
1	three, ↗ ‖	o?

[231 ↗ ‖231] What's twenty-one, plus three times two?

3	twenty-	three times
2 What's \	plus	\
1	one, ↗ ‖	two?

Other Practice Activities

❏ Partner Cards—Listening. *Practice until you can point to the right card every time.*

❏ Partner Cards—Speaking. *Practice until you can say the contrasting sentences so accurately that your partner points to the right card every time.*

❏ Story Reading. *Practice reading the story aloud. Mark any difficult words. Then record the story on tape.*

❏ Story Dictation. *Write the story as your teacher reads it or as you listen to it on the audiotape.*

❏ Cloze Reading. *Choose some key words in the story and black them out. Then read the entire story aloud. Do this several times.*

Each time black out more words. Continue until most of the story is blacked out and you can tell it without looking at the page very often.

❏ Story Retelling from Skeleton. *Black out all the remaining words except those you need in order to remind you of the story line. Then, using just this skeleton, tell the story to your partner or class.*

❏ Free Story Retelling. *Retell the whole story from memory, without looking at your book.*

❏ Parallel Story. *Create your own story similar to the one in this unit.*

❏ Mini-drama. *Make up a skit or do a role play based on the story.*

Unit S4-B [231 ↗ ‖231] What's (5 – 2) 2?— [231 ↗ ‖231] What's 5 – (2 x 2)?

Story

Sherry asked her big brother Dennis to help her practice her math problems. He agreed to drill her for a while by asking her questions of the type that would be on her test.

(1) **"What's five minus two, times two?"** he asked.

Sherry answered, "Six."

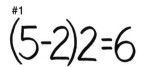
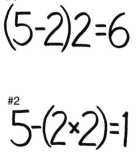

"Good. Here's another one. (2) **What's five, minus two times two?"**

"That's easy. One."

"Exactly! You're really getting the hang of it. Now here's a harder one. What's twenty-one, times nine minus seven?"

Sherry had to think a little bit, but she answered, "Forty-two?"

"Right!" Dennis congratulated her. "Here's the most difficult one of all. What's twenty-one times nine, minus seven?"

For this one, Sherry needed a paper and pencil, but she finally got it right. "One hundred eighty-two!"

"Good job!" said Dennis. "But now I have to go do my own homework. If you need more practice, you'll have to use flash cards."

Contrasting Sentences

❏ What's _____ _____ _____, times two? (6)

❏ What's _____, _____ _____ times two? (1)

Additional Practice

What's *five minus two, / five, minus two* times two? (S4-B/b), What's *twenty-one plus three, / twenty-one, plus three* times two? (S4-c)

Other Examples

[231 ↗ ‖231] What's twenty-one times nine, minus seven?

3		twenty-one times			sev-
2 What's			\	minus	\
1			nine, ↗ ‖		en?

[231 ↗ ‖231] What's twenty-one, times nine minus seven?

3		twenty-		nine minus	
2 What's	\	times		\	
1		one, ↗ ‖		seven?	

Other Practice Activities

- ❑ Partner Cards—Listening.
- ❑ Partner Cards—Speaking.
- ❑ Story Reading.
- ❑ Story Dictation.
- ❑ Cloze Reading.
- ❑ Story Retelling from Skeleton.
- ❑ Free Story Retelling.
- ❑ Parallel Story.
- ❑ Mini-drama.

Section 10
Phonological Explanations

This section provides explanations of how the various sounds that *Pronunciation Matters* units focus on are made. If you cannot produce these sounds correctly through simple imitation of your teacher's model or the one on the audio recordings, or if you cannot figure out what you are doing wrong when you mispronounce a sound, you may want to go through the step-by-step explanations provided in this section.

Teachers may also use these explanations as resource material when explaining the production of sounds to individual students or larger groups.

Hints for Checking Your Pronunciation

Often it is difficult to tell whether your articulators (lips, tongue, teeth, jaw, etc.) are in the proper position because they are difficult to see or sense. The same is true of stress and the pitch of your voice. Most of us are not used to paying attention to such things. For these reasons, in many of the phonological explanations in this section, references are made to "hints" that will help you know if you are making a sound properly.

Hints 1–12 below are techniques that provide visual or tactile feedback. Such guidance may make it easier for you to check your pronunciation by noting the position of your articulators or your manner of articulation. Hints 13–15 help you temporarily ignore vowels and consonants so you can concentrate on stress, intonation, and pausing.

Hint 1. While pronouncing a vowel or consonant, **"freeze" or "lock" your tongue in position. Then inhale** (breathe in, instead of out). You should feel a cool spot at the point of articulation, where the articulators (tongue, lips, teeth, palate, etc.) are closest. This trick is especially useful for checking vowels and consonants made with two articulators near one another or touching, such as [iy], [l], [r], [k], and [g].

Hint 2. Place the **tips of your fingers on your cheeks** just behind the corners of your mouth to feel whether your cheek muscles are tensed and your lips are spread or rounded. (See Hint 4 for another way to check lip spreading and rounding.) This trick is especially useful for checking vowels made with spread or rounded lips, such as [iy], [ɪ], [uw], and [ʊ].

Hint 3. Place the **tips of your fingers on your upper and lower lips** to feel how rounded and/or protruding they are. (See Hint 4 for another way to check lip rounding.) This trick is especially useful for vowels such as [ow], [uw], and [ʊ].

Hint 4. Hold a **small mirror in front of your mouth** (or look in a larger mirror) to see how spread, rounded, or protruding your lips are. This trick is especially useful for checking vowels such as [iy], [ɪ], [ow], [uw], and [ʊ]. (See Hints 2 and 3 for other ways to check lip spreading, rounding, and protrusion.) Using a mirror in this way, you can also check on the location of your tongue when making the interdental consonant sounds [θ] and [ð]. The tip of your tongue should be visible between your upper and lower teeth.

Hint 5. Place your **thumb beneath your chin and press upward firmly** while pronouncing a sound in order to feel whether your tongue muscles are tensed or relaxed. As they are tensed, your thumb will be pushed downward. This trick is useful for distinguishing between vowels that are tense, such as [iy], [ey], [ow], and [uw], and those that are relaxed, such as [ɪ], [ɛ], [ɑ], and [ʊ]. It is also useful for checking the [r] pronunciation in [ɑ]-[ɑr] and [ə]-[ər]. The movement of your tongue when pronouncing the [r] will push your thumb downward.

Hint 6. Place the **tip of your finger lightly on the front of and/or between your upper and lower front teeth.** With your fingertip you will be able to feel the slight differences in how open your jaw is while pronouncing similar vowel sounds, such as [iy], [ɪ], [ɛ], and [æ]. Also, when you pronounce a dipthong like [ey] or [ow] properly, your mouth will open or close slightly and you will feel your teeth move. Using your fingertip in this way, you can also check on the proper location of your tongue when making the interdental consonant sounds [θ] and [ð]. You should be able to feel the tip of your tongue between your upper and lower teeth.

Hint 7. Place your **fingertips lightly on the front of your throat** to feel the vibration, or voicing, when you pronounce voiced consonants like [z], [b], [v], and [g]. Keep your fingers in the same place while producing the voiceless counterparts ([s], [p], [f], and [k]). You should feel no vibration from these voiceless consonants. (See Hint 8 for another way to check voicing.)

Hint 8. Use your fingertip to **plug one ear** in order to hear the voicing in consonants like [z], [b], [v], and [g] more clearly. For an even stronger effect, you can **plug both ears.** (See Hint 7 for another way to check voicing.)

Hint 9. Hold your **index finger horizontally** and place it **lightly between your lips or next to your upper lip.** This trick is useful for distinguishing between bilabial consonants (made with your upper and lower lips touching), such as [b] and [p], and labiodentals (made with your lower lip touching your upper teeth), such as [v] and [f].

Hint 10. Place a clean **pen or pencil horizontally across the inside of your mouth, between your upper and lower teeth.** Then, when you pronounce consonants such as [l], [r], and [n], notice the position of the tip of your tongue. For [l] it will be below the pencil, for [r] it will be above the pencil, and for [n] it will probably be pushing against the pencil.

Hint 11. Hold a **small strip of paper** (approximately 4 inches long and 1/2 inch wide) **about 1/2 inch in front of your mouth.** (A strip of facial tissue is especially sensitive, but plain notebook paper will do.) When you pronounce an aspirated consonant, like the [p] in *pin,* the paper will move. When you pronounce an unaspirated consonant, like the [b] in *bin* or the [p] in *spin,* the paper will not move. (For an even more dramatic effect, see Hint 12.)

Hint 12. Hold a **lighted match or candle in front of your mouth** when practicing aspirated and unaspirated consonants (see explanation in Hint 11). When you produce the puff of air that distinguishes these two types of consonants, the flame will flicker or even be blown out. When you pronounce an unaspirated consonant correctly, the flame will remain steady and barely move.

Hint 13. **Clap your hands together,** once for each syllable, as you say or hum a word, phrase, or sentence. Clap very softly for non-stressed syllables, normally for lightly stressed syllables, and loudly for strongly stressed syllables. If clapping is not appropriate where you are practicing, try **tapping on your table or desktop with your finger or a pencil.** Use the same soft or loud technique for nonstressed, lightly stressed, and strongly stressed syllables. This trick is good for practicing both stress and rhythm.

Hint 14. Instead of speaking normally, **hum or play a kazoo** (a toy humming instrument) as you say a sentence. This trick will mask out the consonant and vowel sounds and make your intonation much more obvious. It can be used together with Hint 15.

Hint 15. Hold your hand horizontally in front of you at about chin level. Then, as you say or hum a word, phrase, or sentence, **move your hand up or down** to match the rising or falling intonation.

Phonological Explanations for Vowels
(Section 2)

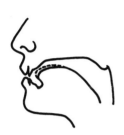

[iy], V1

- Bunch or arch the **front** part of your tongue **high** up in the front part of your mouth. The tip should almost (but not quite) touch the biting edges of your front teeth (Hint 1).
- Your jaw should be **nearly closed.** Your upper and lower teeth should almost touch.
- **Spread your lips** as if you were smiling (Hints 2 and 4).
- Move the front part of your tongue **forward and up.**
- The muscles in your cheeks and beneath your chin should be **tensed** (Hints 2 and 5).
- This vowel tends to be **a bit longer** than [ɪ].

[ɪ], V1/2

- Bunch or arch the **front** part of your tongue high in the front part of your mouth but **not as high** as for [iy]. The tip should almost (but not quite) touch the biting edges of your front teeth (Hint 1).
- Your jaw should be **open more** than it was for [iy] but still nearly closed (Hint 6).
- **Spread your lips** as if you were smiling but **less** than for [iy] (Hints 2 and 4).
- Your tongue should **not move** while you are making this sound.
- The muscles in your **cheeks** should be somewhat **tensed** (Hint 2), but those **beneath your chin** should be relatively **relaxed** (Hint 5).

[ɛ], V2/3/4

- Position your **tongue slightly lower** and your **jaw more open** than they are for [ɪ] (Hint 6). This makes a larger passage for the air to travel through.
- You may touch the back of your lower front teeth with the tip of your tongue.

- This sound is not a dipthong. **Do not move your tongue and jaw** while making it (Hint 6).
- Your **lips should be open and relaxed** (not spread and not rounded) (Hints 2 and 4).
- The muscles beneath your chin should be relatively relaxed (Hint 5).

[ey], V3

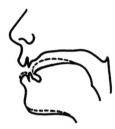

- This vowel is actually a **dipthong,** a glide between two sounds (Hint 6). For this reason, it tends to be a little **longer** than other, simple vowels, such as [ɛ] and [ɪ].
- Begin with your tongue and jaw in the same position they are in for [ɛ] (Hint 1).
- Glide into the [ɪ] position by moving your tongue **upward** and **forward.**
- Your jaw should also **close slightly** (Hint 6).
- Your lips should be slightly spread but open and relaxed at the start. They will spread and close more at the end of this vowel (Hints 2 and 4).
- The muscles beneath your chin should be a bit **tense** (Hint 5).

[æ], V4/5

- Position your **tongue slightly lower** and your **jaw more open** than they are for [ɛ] (Hint 6; for [æ] the opening may be wide enough for your finger) but **not as low or as wide** as they are for [ɑ].
- Your tongue should be **slightly arched** and in the bottom of your mouth (Hint 4). (This makes an even larger passage for the air.)
- You may touch the back of your lower front teeth with the tip of your tongue (Hint 1).
- This sound is not a dipthong. Do not move your tongue and jaw while making it (Hint 6).
- Your lips should be open and relaxed (not spread and not rounded) (Hints 2 and 4).
- The muscles beneath your chin should be relatively **relaxed** (Hint 5).

[ɑ], V5/6/7/8

- Let your tongue lie low and flat in the bottom of your mouth, below the tops of your bottom teeth (Hint 4).
- Your mouth should be wide open and your lips relaxed (not spread and not rounded) (Hint 4). Remember, [ɑ] is the most open of all English

vowels (Hint 4; for [ɑ] your finger should easily fit between your front teeth).
- The muscles beneath your chin should be relaxed (Hint 5).
- This is like the "ahhh" sound that the doctor asks you to make when he or she is examining your throat.

[ɑr], V6

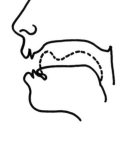

- Begin with your tongue low in your mouth, below the tops of your bottom teeth, and your mouth open as with plain [ɑ] (Hint 4).
- **Immediately move into the much longer [r]** sound by
  1. **Sliding the whole tongue backward** along the lower tooth ridge;
  2. **Arching the middle of the tongue upward;** and
  3. **Curling the tip of your tongue backward** toward the area just behind your upper gum (alveolar) ridge (Hints 1 and 10).
- Be careful not to touch your gum (alveolar) ridge with your tongue tip.
- The muscles beneath your chin may become more tense as you move into the [r] sound (Hint 5).

[ə], V7/9/10

- Open your mouth but **not as wide** as for [ɑ] (Hints 4 and 6).
- Relax your tongue in "**neutral position**" in **the middle** of your mouth.
- The tip of your tongue may rest against your lower front teeth. The sides may touch the lower tooth ridge lightly.
- Your lips should be **relaxed, not rounded** (as for [ʊ]) (Hints 2 and 4).
- The muscles beneath your chin should be relaxed (Hint 5).
- [ə] is the most frequently used vowel in English. It typically appears in unstressed syllables and can be represented by any of the vowel letters—*a, e, i, o,* or *u.* It is also the sound English speakers often make when they are thinking what to say next. When it occurs alone this way, it is often spelled *uh.*

[ow], V8

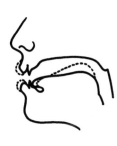

- In English, this vowel is actually a **dipthong** (a combination of two sounds).
- Begin by "bunching up" (**arching**) **the back of your tongue** (Hint 1).
- Tightly **round your lips** into a circle and extend them forward (Hints 3 and 4).
- Glide to the second sound by moving your tongue **upward and**

backward to the [ʊ] position. Your jaw should also **close slightly** (Hint 6).

- Keep your lips **tightly rounded** and extend them even **farther forward.** (Hints 3 and 4).
- The muscles beneath your chin should be **strongly tensed** (see Hint 5).
- Because it is a glide between two sounds, this dipthong is **longer** than other, simple vowels.

[ər], V9

- Begin with your mouth open, your lips relaxed, and your tongue in "neutral" position, as with plain [ə] (Hint 4).
- Immediately move into the **much longer** [r] sound by
  1. Sliding your whole **tongue backward** along the lower tooth ridge;
  2. **Arching the middle of your tongue** upward; and
  3. **Curling the tip of your tongue backward** toward the area just behind your upper gum (alveolar) ridge (Hints 1 and 10).
- Be careful to **not touch** your gum (alveolar) ridge with your tongue tip.
- The muscles beneath your chin may become **more tense** as you move into the [r] sound (Hint 5).

[ʊ], V10/11

- "Bunch up" (**arch**) **the back of your tongue** toward your palate (but not as much as for [uw]) (Hint 1).
- The tip of your tongue should be low and near (or lightly touching) the bottoms of your lower front teeth.
- Your **jaws should be quite close together** (see Hint 6).
- **Round your lips a little** and extend them **slightly forward** (but not nearly as much as for [u]) (Hints 3 and 4). Leave them open. Your teeth will probably still be **clearly visible** (Hint 4).
- The muscles beneath your chin should be rather **relaxed** (see Hint 5).

[uw], V11

- "Bunch up" (**arch**) **the back of your tongue steeply** so that it almost touches your palate (**higher** than for [ʊ]) (Hint 1).
- Your jaws should be **very close together,** closer than for [ʊ], so that your upper and lower teeth almost touch (see Hint 6).

- **Round your lips tightly** and **extend them forward** (Hints 3 and 4). Your teeth will probably be **only slightly visible** (Hint 4).
- The muscles beneath your chin should be strongly **tensed** (see Hint 5).

Phonological Explanations for Consonants (Section 3)

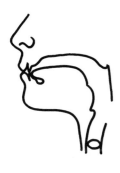

[p], C1/2

- Place your **upper and lower lips** together (Hints 4 and 9). Doing this will stop the air flow.
- Do not make any vibration with your vocal chords (Hints 7 and 8). This consonant is **voiceless.**
- When [p] is the **first** sound in a word or syllable, stop the air flow, build up a little pressure, and then release it with a slight **puff of air** (called "aspiration") (Hints 11 and 12).
- When [p] comes somewhere in the **middle** of a syllable (after another consonant, such as [s]), do not stop the air flow long enough to build up pressure. Release the stop with **no aspiration** (Hints 11 and 12).
- When [p] comes at the **end** of a strongly stressed syllable, **shorten** the preceding **vowel** (i.e., take less time to say the vowel than you would if it were followed by a voiced consonant; compare the lengths of *cap* and *cab*).
- Although **word-final** [p] may be released, it is often **unreleased**—especially when it is followed by another consonant. To make it unreleased, end the [p] sound when your lips come together. Do not open them until you begin the next word and do not release any puff of air.

[b], C1/3

- Place your **upper and lower lips** lightly together (Hints 4 and 9). Doing this will stop the air flow.
- Make your vocal chords vibrate (Hints 7 and 8). This consonant is **voiced.**
- When [b] is the **first** sound in a word or syllable or comes somewhere in the **middle,** stop the air flow and then release it gently. Do **not** make a slight **puff of air** (called "aspiration") (Hints 11 and 12).
- When [b] comes at the **end** of a strongly stressed syllable, **lengthen** the preceding **vowel** (i.e., take a little more time to say

the vowel than you would if it were followed by a voiceless consonant; compare the lengths of *cap* and *cab*).

- Although **word-final** [b] may be released, it is often **un-released**—especially when it is followed by another consonant. To make it unreleased, end the [b] sound when your lips come together. Do not open them until you begin the next word and do not release any puff of air.

[w], C4

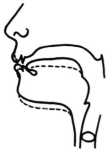

- **Round your lips** to form a circle so tight that it almost stops the air flow (Hints 1, 3, and 4).
- **Open and spread the lips** as you release the air. The amount of opening and spreading will depend on what sound follows.
- Make your **vocal chords vibrate** as the air escapes.

[f], C2/5/6

- Touch your **upper teeth** lightly to the top of your **lower lip** (Hints 1, 4, and 9).
- Gently **force air between** your teeth and lip while they remain lightly in contact. You should **feel a little air escaping** when you hold your hand up to your mouth.
- Do not allow your vocal chords to vibrate (Hints 7 and 8). This consonant is **voiceless.**
- When [f] is the **first** sound in a word or syllable, release the consonant gently by lowering the lip slightly. There should be **no puff of air** (Hints 11 and 12).
- When [f] comes in the **middle** of a word or syllable, close the opening between your upper teeth and lower lip briefly and gently and then open it. Do not stop the air flow or build up pressure. There should be **no puff of air** (Hints 11 and 12).
- When [f] comes at the **end** of a strongly stressed syllable, **shorten** the preceding **vowel** (i.e., take less time to say the vowel than you would if it were followed by a voiced consonant; compare the lengths of *safe* and *save*).
- Although **word-final** [f] may be released, it is often **unreleased**—especially when it is followed by another consonant. To make it unreleased, end the [f] sound by raising your lower lip and closing the opening. Do not open it again until you begin the next word and do not release any puff of air.

[v], C3/4/5

- Touch your **upper teeth** lightly to the top of your **lower lip** (Hints 1, 4, and 9).
- Gently **force air between** your teeth and lip while they remain lightly in contact. You should **feel a little air escaping** when you hold your hand up to your mouth.
- Make your vocal chords vibrate (Hints 7 and 8). This consonant is **voiced.**
- When [v] is the **first** sound in a word or syllable, release the consonant gently by lowering the lip slightly. There should be **no puff of air** (Hints 11 and 12).
- When [v] comes in the **middle** of a word or syllable, close the opening between your upper teeth and lower lip briefly and gently and then open it. Do not stop the air flow or build up pressure. There should be **no puff of air** (Hints 11 and 12).
- When [v] comes at the **end** of a stressed syllable, **lengthen** the preceding **vowel** (i.e., take more time to say the vowel than you would if it were followed by a voiceless consonant; compare the lengths of *safe* and *save*).
- Although **word-final** [v] may be released, it is often **unreleased**—especially when it is followed by another consonant. To make it unreleased, end the [v] sound by raising your lower lip and closing the opening. Do not open it again until you begin the next word and **do not release any puff of air.**

[θ], C6/7/8/9

- Close your mouth so that your upper and lower **teeth** are **almost touching** but leave your **lips open** (Hint 6).

- Place the **tip** of your tongue lightly **between your slightly open upper and lower teeth** (Hints 1 and 6). The tip should be barely visible if you look at your mouth in a mirror (Hint 4).
- Gently **force air between** your teeth and tongue while they remain lightly in contact. Do not pull your tongue in or press it out. You should **feel a little air escaping** when you hold your hand up to your mouth.
- Let the rest of your **tongue lie flat** in your mouth.
- Do not allow your vocal chords to vibrate (Hints 7 and 8). This consonant is **voiceless.**
- When [θ] is the **first** sound in a word or syllable, build up a small amount of pressure and release the consonant by pulling the tip of the tongue back. There should be **a slight puff of air** (Hints 11 and 12).
- When [θ] comes in the **middle** of a word or syllable, place the tip of

your tongue into the opening between your upper and lower teeth briefly and then pull it back. Do not stop the air flow completely but build up a small amount of pressure. There should be **a slight puff of air** (Hints 11 and 12).

- When [θ] comes at the **end** of a strongly stressed syllable, **shorten** the preceding **vowel** (i.e., take less time to say the vowel than you would if it were followed by a voiced consonant).
- Although **word-final** [θ] may be released, it is often **unreleased**—especially when it is followed by another consonant. To make it unreleased, end the [θ] sound by extending the tip of your tongue into the opening between your upper and lower teeth and almost closing the opening. Do not open it again until you begin the next word and do not release any puff of air.

[ð], C7/10/11

- Close your mouth so that your upper and lower **teeth** are **almost touching** but leave your **lips open** (Hint 6).
- Place the **tip** of your tongue lightly **between your slightly open upper and lower teeth** (Hints 1 and 6). The tip should be barely visible if you look at your mouth in a mirror (Hint 4).
- Gently **force air between** your teeth and tongue while they remain lightly in contact. Do not pull your tongue in or press it out. You should **feel only a very small amount of air escaping** when you hold your hand up to your mouth.
- Let the rest of your **tongue lie flat** in your mouth.
- Make your vocal chords vibrate (Hints 7 and 8). This consonant is **voiced.**
- When [ð] is the **first** sound in a word or syllable, build up a small amount of pressure and release the consonant very gently by pulling the tip of the tongue back. There should be **no puff of air** (Hints 11 and 12).
- When [ð] comes in the **middle** of a word or syllable, place the tip of your tongue into the opening between your upper and lower teeth briefly and then pull it back. Do not stop the air flow and do not build up any pressure. There should be **no puff of air** (Hints 11 and 12).
- When [θ] comes at the **end** of a strongly stressed syllable, **lengthen** the preceding **vowel** (i.e., take more time to say the vowel than you would if it were followed by a voiceless consonant).
- Although **word-final** [ð] may be released, it is often **unreleased**—especially when it is followed by another consonant. To make it unreleased, end the [ð] sound by extending the tip of your tongue into the opening between your upper and lower teeth

and almost closing the opening. Do not release any puff of air although air may continue to escape and your vocal chords may still vibrate.

[t], C8/12

- Close your mouth so that your upper and lower **teeth** are **almost touching** but leave your **lips open** (Hint 6).
- **Firmly** place the **tip** of your tongue just behind and above your front teeth so that it is touching the **gum (alveolar) ridge** (Hint 1). The sides of your tongue should be resting against the inner edges of your back teeth. Doing this will stop the air flow.
- Do not make any vibration with your vocal chords (Hints 7 and 8). This consonant is **voiceless.**
- When [t] is the **first** sound in a word or syllable, stop the air flow, build up a little pressure, and then release it by dropping your tongue. (Don't push it forward or pull it down.) Initial [t] is pronounced with a slight **puff of air** (called "aspiration") (Hints 11 and 12).
- When [t] comes somewhere in the **middle** of a syllable (after another consonant, such as [s], as in *stop*), do not stop the air flow long enough to build up pressure. Release the stop with **no aspiration** (Hints 11 and 12).
- When [t] comes **between two voiced sounds** (usually two vowels, but sometimes one is a consonant, like [r]) and the **preceding syllable is stressed and following one isn't** (e.g., *píty, excíted,* or *héarty*), pronounce the [t] as a **quick flap,** without aspiration (Hints 11 and 12) and without stopping the vibration of your vocal chords. (In this case, the [t] will sound very much like a [d].)
- When [t] comes at the **end** of a strongly stressed syllable, **shorten** the preceding **vowel** (i.e., take less time to say the vowel than you would if it were followed by a voiced consonant; compare the lengths of *but* and *bud*).
- Although **word-final** [t] may be released, it is often **unreleased—** especially when it is followed by another consonant. To make it unreleased, end the [t] sound when your tongue touches your gum ridge. Hold it there until you begin the next sound and do not release any puff of air.

[d], C10/12

- Close your mouth so that your upper and lower **teeth** are **almost touching** but leave your **lips open** (Hint 6).
- **Gently** place the **tip** of your tongue just behind and above your front teeth so that it is touching the **gum (alveolar) ridge** (Hint 1). The sides of your tongue should be resting against the inner edges of your back teeth. Doing this will stop the air flow.

- Make your vocal chords vibrate (Hints 7 and 8). This consonant is **voiced.**
- When [d] is the **first** sound in a word or syllable, stop the air flow, build up a little pressure, and then release it by dropping your tongue. (Don't push it forward or pull it down.) Initial [d] is pronounced with a very gentle **puff of air** (called "aspiration") that is **not nearly as strong** as the one produced when you say initial [t] (Hints 11 and 12).
- When [d] comes somewhere in the **middle** of a syllable (after another consonant, such as [n], as in *ending*), do not stop the air flow long enough to build up pressure. Release the stop with **no aspiration** (Hints 11 and 12).
- When [d] comes **between two voiced sounds** (usually two vowels, but sometimes one is a consonant like [r]) and the **preceding syllable is stressed and following one isn't** (e.g., *decíded* or *hárdy*), pronounce the [d] as a **quick flap,** without aspiration (Hints 11 and 12) and without stopping the vibration of your vocal chords. (In this case, the [d] will sound very much like a flapped [t].)
- When [d] comes at the **end** of a strongly stressed syllable, **lengthen** the preceding **vowel** (i.e., take more time to say the vowel than you would if it were followed by a voiceless consonant; compare the lengths of *but* and *bud*).
- Although **word-final** [d] may be released, it is often **unreleased**—especially when it is followed by another consonant. To make it unreleased, end the [d] sound when your tongue touches your gum ridge. Hold it there until you begin the next sound and do not release any puff of air (unless you wish to express anger or frustration).

[n], C13

- Close your mouth so that your upper and lower **teeth** are **almost touching** but leave your **lips open** (Hint 6).
- **Gently** place the **tip** of your tongue just behind and above your front teeth so that it is touching the **gum (alveolar) ridge** (Hint 10).
- Rest the **sides** of your tongue against the **inner edges of your upper back teeth** (Hint 1). At the same time, lower the back of the roof of your mouth, or palate (technically called the "soft palate," or "velum").
- These two actions will divert the air flow through your **nose** (nasal passage).
- Make your vocal chords vibrate (Hints 7 and 8). This consonant is **voiced.**
- Because [n] is a nasal, no air should come out of your mouth when you are saying it.

- When [n] comes at the **end** of a strongly stressed syllable, **lengthen** the preceding **vowel** (i.e., take more time to say the vowel than you would if it were followed by a voiceless consonant).
- Although **word-final** [n] may be released, it is often **unreleased**—especially when it is followed by another consonant. To make it unreleased, end the [n] sound with your tongue touching your gum ridge. Hold it there until you begin the next sound.
- An English syllable containing [n] has a **special "syllabic" pronunciation** when (1) the preceding syllable ends in a [t] or [d] sound and (2) the syllable containing [n] is not stressed (e.g., *hidden*). To produce this special pronunciation, **do not remove the tip of your tongue from the gum ridge** after starting the [t] or [d] sound. Simply **divert the air flow through your nasal passage.** You will go directly from the [t] or [d] sound to the [n] sound without producing a vowel.

[l], C13/14

- Close your mouth so that your upper and lower **teeth** are **almost touching** but leave your **lips open** (Hint 6).
- **Firmly** place the **tip** of your tongue just behind and above your front teeth so that it is touching the **gum (alveolar) ridge** (Hint 10).
- Hold or curl the **sides of your tongue** so they do **not contact** your teeth (Hint 1).
- As you produce the sound, allow the air to pass down and **around the sides** of your tongue near your molar teeth.
- Make your vocal chords vibrate (Hints 7 and 8). This consonant is **voiced.**
- When [l] comes at the **end** of a strongly stressed syllable, **lengthen** the preceding **vowel** (i.e., take more time to say the vowel than you would if it were followed by a voiceless consonant).
- Although **word-final** [l] may be released, it is often **unreleased**—especially when it is followed by another consonant. To make it unreleased, end the [l] sound with your tongue touching your gum ridge. Hold it there until you begin the next sound.
- An English syllable containing [l] has a **special "syllabic" pronunciation** when (1) the preceding syllable ends in a [t], [d], or [n] sound and (2) the syllable containing [l] is not stressed (e.g., *little* or *funnel*). To produce this special pronunciation, **do not remove the tip of your tongue from the gum ridge** after starting the [t], [d], or [n] sound. Simply **divert the air flow around the sides of your tongue.** You will go directly from the [t], [d], or [n] sound to the [l] sound without producing a vowel.
- When [l] comes **after a high, tense, front vowel** like [iy] or [ey], a brief [ə] sound is often produced between the vowel and the [l].

[r], C14

- Close your mouth so that your upper and lower **teeth** are **almost touching** but leave your **lips open** (Hint 6).
- Place the tip of your tongue **close to** the gum (alveolar) ridge (just behind your upper front teeth) but don't let it touch (Hint 1).
- **Lift and curl the tip of your tongue back** toward the roof of your mouth but do not let it touch anything (Hint 10).
- The **sides** of your tongue should touch and slide along the inner edges of your **upper back teeth.**
- Open your lips slightly.
- Allow the air to flow **over and around the tip** of your tongue.
- Make your vocal chords vibrate (Hints 7 and 8). This consonant is **voiced.**
- When [r] comes **after a high, tense, front vowel** like [iy] or [ey], a brief [ə] sound is often produced between the vowel and the [r].

[s], C9/15/16

- Close your mouth so that your upper and lower **teeth** are **almost touching** but leave your **lips open** (Hint 6).
- **Gently** touch the **tip** of your tongue just **behind your upper front teeth and below the gum (alveolar) ridge** (Hint 1).
- Rest the **sides** of your tongue against the inner edges of your back **teeth.**
- Force air **over the top of your tongue** and **behind your teeth** in a smooth, steady stream, making a hissing sound (like a snake makes). This [s] sound can be made continuously until you run out of breath.
- Do not make any vibration with your vocal chords (Hints 7 and 8). This consonant is **voiceless.**
- Do not stop the air flow at any time and do not make a puff of air. You should, however, be able to feel a strong stream of air escaping from the mouth.
- When [s] comes at the **end** of a strongly stressed syllable, **shorten** the preceding **vowel** (i.e., take less time to say the vowel than you would if it were followed by a voiced consonant; compare the lengths of *bus* and *buzz*).
- Although **word-final** [s] may be released, it is often **unreleased**—especially when it is followed by another consonant. To make it unreleased, end the [s] sound with your tongue touching the back of your teeth. Hold it there until you begin the next sound.
- At the **end** of words, [s] is often **lengthened.** You can hear the air escaping for a relatively long time.

[z], C11/15

- Close your mouth so that your upper and lower **teeth** are **almost touching** but leave your **lips open** (Hint 6).
- **Gently** touch the **tip** of your tongue just **behind your upper front teeth and below the gum (alveolar) ridge** (Hint 1).
- Rest the **sides** of your tongue against the inner edges of your back **teeth.**
- Force air **over the top of your tongue** and **behind your teeth** in a smooth, steady stream, making a buzzing sound (like a bee makes). This [z] sound can be made continuously until you run out of breath.
- **Vibrate** your vocal chords (Hints 7 and 8). This consonant is **voiced.**
- Do not stop the air flow at any time and do not make a puff of air. You may be able to feel a small stream of air escaping from the mouth, but it should not be nearly as strong as the one for [s].
- When [z] comes at the **end** of a strongly stressed syllable, **lengthen** the preceding **vowel** (i.e., take more time to say the vowel than you would if it were followed by a voiceless consonant; compare the lengths of *bus* and *buzz*).
- Although **word-final** [z] may be released, it is often **unreleased**—especially when it is followed by another consonant. To make it unreleased, end the [z] sound with your tongue touching the back of your teeth. Hold it there until you begin the next sound.
- At the **end** of words, [z] is often **lengthened.** In such cases, the vibrating of your vocal chords may end before the air stops escaping. This may cause the [z] sound to change to a quick [s] at the very end.

[ʃ], C16/17/18

- Close your mouth so that your upper and lower **teeth** are **almost touching** (Hint 6).
- Extend and round your lips slightly (Hints 3 and 4).
- **Gently** touch the **tip** of your tongue just **above and behind your gum (alveolar) ridge** (Hint 1). The proper point is just a little behind the place for [s] and slightly in front of the one for [t].
- Rest the **sides** of your tongue against the inner edges of your back **teeth.**
- Force air **over the top of your tongue** and **behind your teeth** in a smooth, steady stream. This [ʃ] sound can be made continuously until you run out of breath.
- In most English-speaking North American cultures, this is the sound used to tell someone to be quiet.

- Do not make any vibration with your vocal chords (Hints 7 and 8). This consonant is **voiceless.**
- Do not stop the air flow at any time and do not make a puff of air. You should, however, be able to feel a strong stream of air escaping from the mouth.
- When [ʃ] comes at the **end** of a word, **shorten** the preceding **vowel** (i.e., take less time to say the vowel than you would if it were followed by a voiced consonant).
- Although **word-final** [ʃ] may be released, it is often **unreleased—**especially when it is followed by another consonant. To make it unreleased, end the [ʃ] sound with your tongue still touching just above your gum ridge. Hold it there until you begin the next sound.
- At the end of words, [ʃ] is often lengthened. You can hear the air escaping for a relatively long time.

[ʒ], C17

- Close your mouth so that your upper and lower **teeth** are **almost touching** (Hint 6).
- Extend and round your lips slightly (Hints 3 and 4).
- **Gently** touch the **tip** of your tongue just **above and behind your gum (alveolar) ridge** (Hint 1). The proper point is just a little behind the place for [z] and slightly in front of the one for [d].
- Rest the **sides** of your tongue against the inner edges of your back **teeth.**
- Force air **over the top of your tongue** and **behind your teeth** in a smooth, steady stream. This [ʒ] sound can be made continuously until you run out of breath.
- Vibrate your vocal chords (Hints 7 and 8). This consonant is **voiced.**
- Do not stop the air flow at any time and do not make a puff of air. You should be able to feel a stream of air escaping from the mouth but not as strong as the one for [ʃ].
- When [ʒ] comes at the **end** of a strongly stressed syllable, **shorten** the preceding **vowel** (i.e., take less time to say the vowel than you would if it were followed by a voiced consonant).
- Although **word-final** [ʒ] may be released, it is often **unreleased**—especially when it is followed by another consonant. To make it unreleased, end the [ʒ] sound with your tongue still touching just above your gum ridge. Hold it there until you begin the next sound.

[tʃ], C18/19

- As the phonetic symbol indicates, [tʃ] is actually two sounds. It is a combination of [t] and [ʃ], made in quick sequence.
- Close your mouth so that your upper and lower **teeth** are **almost touching** but leave your **lips open** (Hint 6).
- **Firmly** place the **tip** of your tongue just behind and above your front teeth so that it is touching the **gum (alveolar) ridge** (Hint 1). The sides of your tongue should be resting against the inner edges of your back teeth. Doing this will stop the air flow.
- Build up a little pressure and then release it by lowering your tongue and pulling it back slightly (Hint 1).
- Force air **over the top of your tongue** and **behind your teeth** in a quick, explosive stream. You should be able to feel the air escaping from your mouth (Hints 11 and 12).
- Do not make any vibration with your vocal chords (Hints 7 and 8). This consonant is **voiceless.**
- When [tʃ] comes somewhere in the **middle** of a syllable do not stop the air flow long enough to build up much pressure. Release the stop with **very little aspiration** (Hints 11 and 12).
- When [tʃ] comes at the **end** of a strongly stressed syllable, **shorten** the preceding **vowel** (i.e., take less time to say the vowel than you would if it were followed by a voiced consonant; compare the lengths of *batch* and *badge*).
- When [tʃ] comes at the **end** of a word, you should still **release** it. The final sound is made by air escaping as the tongue tip pulls away from the gum ridge. This aspiration, however, is not as explosive as it is when [tʃ] is pronounced at the start of a word.

[dʒ], C19/20

- As the phonetic symbol indicates, [dʒ] is actually two sounds. It is a combination of [d] and [ʒ], made in quick sequence.
- Close your mouth so that your upper and lower **teeth** are **almost touching** but leave your **lips open** (Hint 6).
- **Gently** place the **tip** of your tongue just behind and above your front teeth so that it is touching the **gum (alveolar) ridge** (Hint 1). The sides of your tongue should be resting against the inner edges of your back teeth. Doing this will stop the air flow.
- Build up a little pressure and then release it by lowering your tongue and pulling it back slightly (Hint 1).
- Extend and round your lips slightly (Hints 3 and 4).
- Force air **over the top of your tongue** and **behind your teeth** in a quick, explosive stream. Although it is not as strong as it is for [tʃ], you should still be able to feel the air escaping from your mouth (Hints 11 and 12).

- Make your vocal chords vibrate (Hints 7 and 8). This consonant is **voiced.**
- When [dʒ] comes somewhere in the **middle** of a syllable, do not stop the air flow long enough to build up much pressure. Release the stop with **almost no aspiration** (Hints 11 and 12).
- When [dʒ] comes at the **end** of a strongly stressed syllable, **lengthen** the preceding **vowel** (i.e., take more time to say the vowel than you would if it were followed by a voiceless consonant; compare the lengths of *batch* and *badge*).
- When [dʒ] comes at the **end** of a word, you should still **release** it. The final sound is made by air escaping as the tongue tip pulls away from the gum ridge. This aspiration, however, is not as explosive as it is when [tʃ] is pronounced at the end of a word.

[y], C20/21

- This consonant is a **glide.** It starts in one position and then smoothly moves into the position of the following vowel.
- Close your mouth so that your upper and lower **teeth** are **almost touching** but leave your **lips open** (Hint 6).
- Rest the **tip** of your tongue behind your lower front teeth.
- Rest the **sides** of your tongue against the inner edges of your back **teeth.**
- Bunch or arch the **front** part of your tongue **high up** in the front part of your mouth—even higher than for the vowel [iy]. The top of your tongue should **almost touch** the front of the roof of your mouth (called the "palate") (Hint 1).
- Force air through the small space **between the top of your tongue and your palate** in a smooth, steady stream, producing a little bit of friction. Do not stop the air flow at any time and do not make a puff of air.
- Make your vocal chords vibrate (Hints 7 and 8). This consonant is **voiced.**
- **Glide** from this initial position to the position of whatever vowel follows [y]. If that vowel is [iy] then the glide will be very short. If that vowel is [uw] then the glide will be very large and obvious.
- Your **lips** can be spread, open, or rounded. They generally adopt the position of the lips in the vowel that follows [y].

[k], C22

- Open your mouth a little so that your upper and lower **teeth** are **slightly apart.** Leave your **lips open** (Hint 4).
- Do not make any vibration with your vocal chords (Hints 7 and 8). This consonant is **voiceless.**
- **Bunch (arch) the back of your tongue upward** and press it firmly against the back part of the roof of your mouth (called the

"soft palate") (Hint 1). (The exact point of contact varies according to the vowel that follows [k].)

- When [k] comes at the **start** of a word or strongly stressed syllable, build up a little **air pressure** in your throat behind your tongue. Then **release** it by dropping your arched tongue suddenly.
- A **puff of air** (called "aspiration") should come out of your mouth (Hints 11 and 12).
- When [k] comes somewhere in the **middle** of a syllable (after another consonant, such as [s], as in *skip*), do not stop the air flow long enough to build up pressure. Release the stop with **no aspiration** (Hints 11 and 12).
- When [k] comes at the **end** of a strongly stressed syllable, **shorten** the preceding **vowel** (i.e., take less time to say the vowel than you would if it were followed by a voiced consonant; compare the lengths of *back* and *bag*).
- Although **word-final** [k] may be released, it is often **unreleased**—especially when it is followed by another consonant. To make it unreleased, stop the [k] sound when your tongue touches your palate and stops the air flow. Do not release the air pressure until you begin the next word.
- If a word that **begins** with a [k] sound **immediately follows** a word that **ends** with [k] (as in "spea**k c**arefully"), pronounce **only one** [k] but make it **longer than ordinary,** releasing the [k] into the start of the second word.

[g], C22

- Open your mouth a little so that your upper and lower **teeth** are **slightly apart.** Leave your **lips open** (Hint 4).
- Make your vocal chords vibrate (Hints 7 and 8). This consonant is **voiced.**
- **Bunch (arch) the back of your tongue upward** and press it firmly against the back part of the roof of your mouth (called the "soft palate") (Hint 1). (The exact point of contact varies according to the vowel that follows [g].)
- When [g] comes at the **start** of a word or strongly stressed syllable, build up a little **air pressure** in your throat behind your tongue. Then **release** it by dropping your arched tongue suddenly.
- A **puff of air** (called "aspiration") should come out of your mouth. It should be noticeable but not as strong as for [k] (Hints 11 and 12).
- When [g] comes at the **end** of a strongly stressed syllable, **lengthen** the preceding **vowel** (i.e., take less time to say the vowel than you would if it were followed by a voiced consonant; compare the lengths of *back* and *bag*).
- Although **word-final** [g] may be released, it is often

unreleased—especially when it is followed by another consonant. To make it unreleased, stop the [g] sound when your tongue touches your palate and stops the air flow. **Do not release** the air pressure until you begin the next word.

- If a word that **begins** with a [g] sound **immediately follows** a word that **ends** with [g] (as in "bi**g g**uy"), do not release the first one. Rather, pronounce **only one** [g] but make it **longer than ordinary,** releasing the [g] into the start of the second word.

Phonological Explanations for Consonant Clusters (Section 4)

- Every English syllable has at least one vowel. This vowel may also have one or more consonants before or after it. In fact, English syllables may have **up to three initial consonants** before the vowel and **up to four final consonants** after the vowel (e.g., *strengths,* pronounced [strɛŋkθs]).
- In many other languages, the syllable structure is much simpler. Speakers of these languages who are learning English often have trouble producing clusters of consonants in English.
- Mispronouncing consonant clusters (either by inserting a vowel or improperly dropping one of the consonants) can change the meaning of a word. For example, *sport* may become *support,* or *screamed* may become *schemed.*
- In the phonetic representations in this book, the symbol [C] stands for any consonant.

Initial [C + l] - [C + r], CC1
- The basic production of [r] and [l] is explained on pages 341–2. When [r] and [l] occur **immediately after other consonants,** however, the resulting clusters become especially difficult for many learners of English to pronounce.
- English allows many initial clusters of the [C + l] or [C + r] type, and they are very common. In fact, over a third of all the different initial consonant clusters permitted in English are of this type. They are [bl], [fl], [gl], [kl], [pl], [sl], [br], [dr], [fr], [gr], [kr], [pr], [ʃr], [tr], [θr], [skl], [spl], [spr], and [str].
- In initial clusters of **three consonants** ending in [r] or [l], the first consonant is always [s], and the second consonant is either [p], [t], or [k]. Practicing the **two-consonant** clusters [sp], [st], and [sk] is a useful preliminary step in mastering these three-consonant clusters.
- To overcome difficulties with **two-consonant** clusters ending in [r] and [l], practice by **inserting a vowel** such as [ə] between the

two consonants. In this way, for example, [greyt] *(great)* will become [gəreyt]. Although this pronunciation is **not natural** for English speakers and may be confusing if used in normal speech, it is useful for **practice purposes.** It may be much easier for you to produce the consonants when they are separated this way. As you master the separate consonant pronunciations, gradually shorten and then eliminate the inserted [ə].

Initial [s + C]-[ɛs + C], CC2/3/4/5

- This cluster is especially difficult for many speakers of Spanish or Farsi. The difficulty results from the transfer of native language clustering rules into English. In Spanish, for example, the clusters [sp], [st], [sk], and [str] are all allowed within words but only after an initial vowel (e.g., *español, este, escuela, estrecho,* etc.) and not at the very beginning of a word. The natural tendency of speakers of these languages, then, is to add a vowel before the consonant cluster.
- In contrast, an initial [s] followed by a vowel is allowed in Spanish. In fact, it is very common and easy to pronounce (e.g., *sí, sombrero,* etc.).
- To overcome this difficulty, practice by **focusing on the initial [s]** and consciously, dramatically **lengthening it** before pronouncing the other consonant(s) in the cluster. For example, say "Ssssssssss-mart ssssssssssspouses . . . " Then, gradually shorten the initial [s] sound until it becomes natural in length.

Final [ŋ]-[ŋk], CC6

- Many English learners who are native speakers of Germanic or Slavic languages tend to add a [k] sound after [ŋ] at the end of words like *sing*. The result is confusion with words like *sink*.
- The proper pronunciation of [ŋ] is important because the *-ing* ending is very common in English. It is used on all progressive tense verbs (e.g., *He is going, We have been working*) as well as on participles (e.g., *the crying baby*) and gerunds (e.g., *Collecting coins is my hobby*).
- The first step in overcoming the mispronunciation of *-ng* as [ŋk] is to realize that the [ŋ] sound represented by the two letters *ng* is **not really a consonant cluster** at all. In speech, it is a **single consonant** much like [k] or [g] but nasalized. Do not attempt to pronounce the final *g* as a separate sound.
- In English, [ŋ] never comes at the **start** of a word. It occurs only in the middle and at the end of words.
- To produce [ŋ] correctly, after saying whatever sound precedes it, **bunch (arch) the back of your tongue upward** and press it against the back of the roof of your mouth (Hint 1).

- **Lower the back of the roof of your mouth** (technically called the "soft palate" or "velum") to meet the back of your tongue. If you open your mouth a little and use a mirror (Hint 4), you can see this happen. Lowering the velum this way blocks the air flow through your mouth and opens the nasal passageway at the back of your mouth.
- Make your vocal chords vibrate (Hints 7 and 8). This consonant is **voiced.**
- Let air flow through your **nose** (nasal passage) in a **smooth, steady stream.**
- Because [ŋ] is a **nasal,** no air should come out of your mouth when you are saying it, even though your jaw and lips remain open (Hints 11 and 12).
- **Do not build up air pressure** in your throat behind your tongue. The [ŋ] sound can be sustained for a long time until you run out of breath.
- At the end of the [ŋ] sound, **do not release** it by dropping your arched tongue suddenly. Doing so may result in the [k] or [g] that you are trying to avoid.
- Instead, **keep your tongue pressed against your palate until after you stop the air flow.** Then you can lower your tongue **without making the puff of air** that is part of the [k] and [g] sounds.
- Following the above steps should help you leave the [k] sound off the end of [ŋ] in words like *thing* and *sing.*
- Practice by **gradually building up** consonant clusters. For example, begin by saying [θɪŋ] *(thing)*. Then add the [k] sound at the end and say [θɪŋk] *(think)*. If you want to try a three-consonant cluster, add an [s] and say [θɪŋks] *(thinks)*. Then **go backward,** removing the final consonants one at a time until you are back to [θɪŋ] *(thing)* again.

Final [C + t]-[C + d]-[C + s]-[C + z], CC7/8/9/10/11
- Many final consonant clusters are created in English by the addition of the **plural/possessive/present-tense ending -s** (usually pronounced [s] or [z]) or the **past-tense ending -ed** (usually pronounced [t] or [d]) to words that already end in a consonant. In addition, **reduction and blending** of words like *is* and *did* often create similar clusters of consonants.
- When they occur in word-final position, the consonants [t], [d], [s], and [z] are often **unreleased** (see descriptions for [t], [d], [s], [z], and similar consonants in the "Phonological Explanations for Consonants" part of this section of *Pronunciation Matters*). When these unreleased sounds occur in clusters, they are especially difficult for many nonnative learners of English to hear and/or produce.

- An important step toward correctly hearing and producing the clusters in which unreleased consonants occur (as in Units CC7 and CC9) is to **practice and master this unreleased pronunciation.**
- A common but mistaken tendency is to ignore these final consonants when listening or leave them off the ends of words when speaking.
- Simplifying these clusters by **leaving off the final consonant should not be done.** It is not natural or proper in English. The final consonants in these clusters carry important grammatical signals, such as tense and plurals. If they are ignored or left out, the communication of meaning will suffer.
- Native speakers of English often **simplify final consonant clusters in other ways.** For example, a final cluster of three or more consonants, as in [fækts] *(facts),* can be pronounced as a cluster of only two consonants [fæks]. Likewise, [lɪfts] *(lifts)* can become [lɪfs]. Notice, however, that in these simplifications the **middle consonant is left out.** The important **final consonant is never left off.**
- Another way that native speakers of English deal with complex consonant clusters at the end of words is "**phonetic syllabication.**" It is a very common and natural process, but it can be done only under certain conditions.
  1. The word following the word that ends in the consonant cluster must **start with a vowel sound** and
  2. The two words must be **closely related and/or in the same "thought group"** (e.g., a verb and its object).
- When these two conditions are met, you can **shift the final consonant of the first word over to the first syllable of the following word.** For example, in Unit CC8 pronounce *passed every* as [pæs dɛvriy].
- Using this process, you can often simplify complex three-consonant clusters into easier two-consonant clusters and simplify two-consonant clusters into simpler single consonants.
- When phonetic syllabication or other processes cannot be used to simplify clusters (as in Units CC7, CC9, CC10, and CC11), you will simply have to **pronounce each consonant carefully, in sequence.** Use unreleased pronunciation when appropriate but do not leave out important consonants.

Final [d]-[ld], CC12

- The [l] sound is common in **final** consonant clusters in English. The possible **two-consonant** clusters that contain [l] and occur in word-final position in English are the following: [lb], [ld], [lf], [lk], [rl], [ln], [lp], [ls], [lt], [lθ], [lv], and [lz]. Final **three-consonant** clusters with [l] include [lbd], [rld], [lmd], [lnd], [lvd], [lfs], [lks], and many others.

- As you can see from these examples, [l] is usually the **first consonant** in these final clusters. For this reason, it comes immediately **after the vowel(s)** in the word.
- When [l] occurs in final clusters, many learners of English simply leave it out, so that [kɑld] *(called)* becomes [kɑd].
- Many speakers of Brazilian Portuguese substitute an [ow] or [u] vowel for the [l] so that [kɑld] *(called)* becomes [kɑud] and [kowld] *(cold)* becomes [kowd].
- Leaving out or changing the [l] in this way can result in important or confusing changes in meaning. For instance, instead of sounding like the past tense of *call*, *called* may end up sounding like a type of fish *(cod)* or the sound made by a crow *(cawed)*.
- A step-by-step explanation of the pronunciation of [l] is provided on page 341. As you go through that explanation, pay special attention to the part that explains how **word-final** [l] is often **unreleased**—especially when it is followed by another consonant. To make it unreleased, end the [l] sound with your tongue touching your gum ridge. Hold it there until you begin making the next consonant sound.

[CC]-[CəC], CC13

- A quick, **unstressed vowel between two consonants** can make a big **difference in meaning.** For example, [browk] and [bərowk] differ only in the [ə] sound, but the difference in meaning between *broke* and *baroque* is great.
- When they encounter consonant clusters that are hard for them to pronounce, many learners of English break up the clusters by inserting a vowel between the consonants. This insertion can be a useful step in a pronunciation practice activity, but it may cause comprehension problems if it is done in normal speech.
- As noted above (in the explanation for "Final [C + t]-[C + d]-[C + s]-[C + z] CC7/8/9/10/11" on pp. 350–51), **native speakers of English use various techniques** (such as "phonetic syllabication" or leaving out the middle consonant in a final three-consonant cluster) for dealing with complex consonant clusters. Inserting vowels between consonants, however, is **not** one of these techniques.
- When you pronounce a consonant cluster, **move quickly** from one consonant to the next in order to avoid inserting a vowel. **Do not pause** between consonants.
- For practice, try saying a word like [təreyn] *(terrain)* slowly and carefully. Then quickly say its counterpart without the [ə]—[treyn] *(train)*.
- Another practice activity is to alternate saying two English words

that differ only in the [ə] inserted between consonants in a cluster. For example, practice saying, "Support, sport, support, sport" and so forth until you can clearly distinguish between them.

- Other possible word pairs for such practice include *broke / baroque, scum / succumb, finely / finally, form / forum, Clyde / collide, plight / polite, crowed / corrode, bray / beret, dried / deride,* and *claps / collapse.*

- In natural, informal speech, some of the [CəC] syllables in words in the story in Unit CC13-A may be reduced to [CC] consonant clusters with no change in meaning. For example, *history* can be pronounced [hɪstriy] *(histry)*. However, doing the opposite (inserting a [ə] sound between two consonants) with the [CC] syllables makes the pronunciation unnatural and/or may change the meaning entirely. For example, adding a [ə] sound between the first two consonants in *broke* results in *baroque*. The same thing happens with *sport* and *support.*

Phonological Explanations for Reduction and Blending (Section 5)

- In **natural, normal, casual speech,** speakers of English often reduce sounds or blend them together.

- **Reduction** occurs when **vowels** such as [u] and [ow] become [ə] because they are in **unstressed** syllables or words (e.g., compare the vowels in *phótograph* and *photógrapher*).

- **Blending** happens when **two sounds next to each other** (such as [t] at the end of *don't* and [y] at the start of *you*) **combine into a new one** (like the [tʃ] in "donchu"). In another form of blending, **sounds drop out** when other sounds are next to each other, such as in the contractions *don't* and *it's.*

- Reduction and blending are typical of normal, relaxed speech, but they **do not always occur.** Sometimes English speakers avoid contractions and reductions and use unblended forms. There are several **reasons for not blending.**
  1. To **compensate for perception difficulties,** such as those experienced when speaking with a person who is hard of hearing, in a noisy room, or with a person whose English skills are limited. In such cases, especially when repeating something that was not heard well the first time, English speakers often use a nonblended, nonreduced pronunciation.
  2. To **be extra careful** in conveying a message. Be cautious, however, when using unblended speech for this purpose. Unblended, nonreduced pronunciation may come across as being **pretentious** or **affected.**
  3. To **show politeness at a formal function,** such as when giving a speech to a large audience.

4. To **show anger, irritation, or frustration.** When a person is reaching "the breaking point" he or she may use unblended pronunciation as a **warning signal.**

5. As a result of **sentence stress** patterns or **grammar.** For example, when a word or syllable is stressed to indicate contrast (see phonological explanation for Unit SS1 on p. 364 for details and examples), it is not normally reduced or blended. Likewise, words in sentence-final position are not reduced the way they are when they occur in the middle of a sentence. (For example, compare the pronunciation of *want to* in *I want to (wanna) do that* and *Who else wants to?*) Also, some expressions like *gonna* are used only before verbs (e.g., *I'm gonna leave*). When *going to* comes before a noun, the full form is used (e.g., *I'm going to town*).

6. To indicate a **foreign accent.** Since reduction and blending are a natural part of native English speech, people, such as actors, who are imitating nonnatives whose English is limited often use unblended, unreduced speech.

[h]-[ ] (Present—Dropped), RB1
- Dropping the [h] sound off the front of **pronouns** such as *him, his, her,* and *hers* is a common reduction when these pronouns come **after a verb or a preposition** and are **not stressed.**
- To produce this reduction, simply **drop (do not pronounce) the** [h] sound. This will indicate that you are in a **natural, relaxed state.**
- On the other hand, if you are trying to be **extra careful or clear** for your listener(s), pronounce the [h].
- Notice that pronouns like *he, his, her,* and *hers* are **not** normally reduced when they come at the **front** of a sentence.
- Also note that while this reduction is common in speech, it is not acceptable in most writing. The contractions *'er, 'is, 'im,* etc., are used **only in informal writing,** such as personal letters or comic strips.

Reduced [kən] *Can*—Unreduced [kænt] *Can't*, RB2
- In natural speech, the modal *can* is **normally reduced** (except when it is stressed) so that it is pronounced [kən], with a schwa sound.
- The vowel in the negative modal *can't* is different. *Can't* is normally pronounced [kænt].
- The [ə]-[æ] **vowel difference** is the major distinction between *can* and *can't* when they are spoken. Of course, *can't* also has a [t] sound at the end, but that [t] is often unreleased or pronounced lightly. Sometimes it even blends in with the beginning sound of the following word.

Unblended *It is*—Blended *It's*, RB3

- The contraction *it's* is **very common** in natural spoken English although the full form *it is* is also used.
- *It's* is **more casual** and relaxed than *it is* is.
- **Both** forms are also commonly used in **writing.**
- In speech, do the blending by simply **removing the** [ɪ] sound at the beginning of *is* and creating a final [ts] consonant cluster.
- Note that in the story in Unit RB3-A, the **innkeeper** uses unblended forms (and no contractions) for two possible reasons: (1) she is not a native speaker of English and (2) she is extremely polite. The story **narrator,** on the other hand, makes frequent use of blended forms.

Unblended—Blended *to* after verb, RB4

- A common reduction and blend in natural English affects the word *to* following words like *want* and *going*. The words ***wanna*** and ***gonna*** are the results of this process.
- With *going to,* the reduction and blending occur **only when the following word is a verb,** e.g., *I'm gonna go. Gonna* is not used when a noun (a destination) follows the *going to,* e.g., *I'm going to* (not *I'm gonna*) *New York.*
- With *want to,* the reduction and blending may occur **regardless** of whether the following word is a **noun or verb.** In other words, *I wanna go* and *I wanna cookie* are both possible.
- To produce these reductions/blends
   Drop the final consonant, [t], in *want.*
   Change the [ɪŋ] in *going* to simple [n].
   Reduce both the consonant and vowel in [tuw] to the neutral vowel [ə].
- In the story in Unit RB4-A, Jimmy changes from the normal, blended form *wanna* to the unnatural, unblended expression to show that he is **upset and frustrated.**
- In the story in RB4-B, Peter uses the unblended form when he is talking to his English teacher to show **respect,** as well as to try to **impress** her. Later, when he is talking with his friend casually, Peter uses the reduced and blended *gonna.* Ms. Ingles, on the other hand, uses the unblended form with Peter because she is maintaining her **professional image** as a cautious, educated English teacher. She also uses the more formal unblended form to keep a professional **distance** between herself and her student.
- In practice cards RB4-c, the full form *going to* must be used when it is followed by a **place** (Gallup, a city in New Mexico). The reduced and blended *gonna* may be used only when it is followed by the **verb** *gallop,* what a horse does.

Unblended *Don't know*—Blended *Dunno*, RB5

- The processes of reduction and blending that create the word *dunno* are similar to those that create *wanna* and *gonna* (see preceding explanation).
- To produce reduced and blended *dunno*
  Drop the final consonant, [t], in *don't* and
  Reduce the vowel [ow] to the neutral vowel [ə].
- The vowel in [now] *(know)* is not reduced to [ə] because that syllable is stressed.
- In the story in unit RB5-A, the students use blending when they **feel discouraged.** The more discouraged they get, the more they slur their speech. Later, when they perk up and change their attitude, they pronounce each word more distinctly to show some **enthusiasm.**
- There are also important **stress and intonation differences** between the contrasting sentences in Unit RB5-A.

Unblended *What do you*—Unblended *Whaddaya*, RB6

- Because the first word *(What)* is **strongly stressed,** the vowel in it is **not reduced.**
- The [t] at the end of *what* is **blended** into (assimilated by) the [d] sound at the start of the following word, *do.*
- To finish the reduction/blending process, the two [uw] vowels in unstressed *do* and *you* are **reduced** to the neutral schwa [ə].
- The words *whaddaya* and *whodaya* are **never used in formal writing.** In fact, they are extremely rare even in informal writing.
- When English speakers are being **careful** or **extra polite,** they often use unblended forms. Similar things happen when they are speaking to **people whose English is limited.** In the story in Unit RB6-A, Professor Jones uses the blended and reduced form at first because he is upset and not trying to be polite. When he finds out it was his student who was knocking and realizes that she might not know the culturally appropriate behavior, he switches to the more careful and polite unblended form.

Unblended [t + y] *Get you*—Blended [tʃ] *Getcha*, RB7

- In English, when a [t] sound is followed immediately by a [y] sound, they combine into a [tʃ] sound.
- This blending occurs **within words** such as *situation* where the final [t] of *sit-* combines with the [yuw] sound of the next syllable, resulting in the pronunciation [sɪtʃuweyʃən] *(not* [sɪtyuweyʃən]).
- It also happens **between words.** For example, *get you* ([gɛt yuw]) often becomes [gɛtʃuw] or [gɛtʃə] *(getcha).*
- In the case of ***what are you . . . ,*** the *are* is reduced so much that it drops out entirely. Then the final [t] of *what* combines with the initial [y] of *you* and becomes [tʃ] in ***whatcha.***

- The same thing can happen with **what do you . . .**, which can also become **whatcha** by dropping the *do* and blending the [t] and [y].
- The spellings *whatcha, don'tcha, getcha,* etc., are **not normally used in written English.** Except in the most informal situations, write unblended, full-word forms instead.
- In the story in Unit RB7-A, the boys use natural, blended forms when they are speaking normally. They change to unblended forms when **difficult conditions in the environment** (e.g., noise and distance) make it hard for them to hear each other.
- In the story in RB7-B, the narrator uses casual, blended forms with the members of the study group because they are **friends.** In contrast, the narrator uses full forms with the **guest** because *(a)* she is a stranger and *(b)* she is older. Also, in the question the narrator asks her, the word *you* is stressed because it is in contrast with *my friends* (see the units in SS1 for practice with contrastive stress). Words that carry stress are not usually reduced.

Unblended [d + y] *Did you*—Blended [dʒ] *Didja*, RB8

- In English, when a [d] sound is followed immediately by a [y] sound, they combine into a [dʒ] sound.
- This blending occurs **within words** such as *education* where the final [d] of *ed-* combines with the [yuw] sound of the next syllable, resulting in the pronunciation [ɛdʒuwkeyʃən] (*not* [ɛdyuwkeyʃən).
- It also happens **between words.** For example, *did you* ([dɪd yuw]) often becomes [dɪdʒuw] or [dɪdʒə] (*didja*).
- The spellings *didja* and *didn'tcha* are **not normally used in written English.** Except in the most informal situations, write the more orthodox forms *did you* and *didn't you* instead.
- In the story in Unit RB8-A, Jerry, who speaks normally, uses blended forms. Sid, who is **pretentious** about being educated, uses artificial-sounding full forms.

Unblended [s + y] *Guess you're*—Blended [ʃ] *Guesshur*, RB9

- In English, when an [s] sound is followed immediately by a [y] sound, they combine into a [ʃ] sound.
- This blending occurs **within words** such as *insurance* where the [s] of *ins-* combines with the following [yuw] sound, resulting in the pronunciation [ɪnʃurənts] (*not* [ɪnsyurənts).
- It also happens **between words.** For example, *miss you* ([mɪs yuw]) often becomes [mɪʃuw] and *guess you're* ([gɛs yowr]) becomes [gɛʃər].
- The spelling *guesshur* is **not used** in written English. Even though you say "guesshur," always write *guess you're.*
- Although it is not illustrated in a unit in this book, essentially the same thing happens when [z] is followed by [y], except that the combined sound is [ʒ], as in *treasure* or *is your . . . ?*

- In the story in Unit RB9-A, Yumi, a learner of English, has trouble understanding the blended phrase *guesshur* probably because she is not yet accustomed to naturally spoken English with reduction and blending. She experiences no difficulty when each word is pronounced distinctly.

Blended *will*, *would*, *have*, *had*, and *did*, RB10/11/12/13

- Except when they are stressed, function words like *will*, *would*, *have*, *had*, and *did* are often reduced and blended with the words that come before and after them.
- When *will*, *would*, *have*, *had*, and *did* are fully reduced and blended in with the preceding words, only their **final consonant sounds—[l], [d], and [v]**—remain. For example, [ðey wɪl] *(They will)* becomes [ðeyl].
- These final consonants are often **unreleased,** making them even more difficult to hear. (For more information on unreleased final consonants, see the [l], [d], and [v] explanations in the "Phonological Explanations for Consonants" on pp. 341, 339–40, and 337, respectively.)
- Final [l], [d], and [v] may also **blend in with the following consonant,** further reducing their prominence.
- When pronouncing contractions like *they'll*, *they'd*, *they've*, *where'd*, *where've*, and *where'll*, make sure you say the [l], [d], and [v] sounds **quickly** and **connect them** with the sounds that come before and after them. **Do not release a puff of air** at the end of [l], [d], and [v].
- The contractions *where'd*, *where've*, and *where'll* are acceptable in **informal written English only.** However, parallel forms with pronouns like *I*, *you*, *we*, *she*, and *he*, (i.e., *I'd*, *I've*, *I'll*, etc.) are more widely used and are acceptable in **even semiformal writing.** The contractions *they'll*, *they'd*, and *they've* are a bit informal, but they are **common in written English at most levels.** When writing becomes highly formal, however, they may not be appropriate.
- Unit RB10-A focuses on *will* and *would*. They are related words, but their meanings are quite different. When used in present-tense situations, *will* is used for referring to expected, **future** events. In present-tense situations, *would* is used in conditional constructions, where the activities are only **hypothetical, imaginary, or unlikely.** In this unit, listen carefully to the short but important sound after [ðey]. If it is [l], it represents *will*, and that means that the action is probable. If the sound is [d], it represents *would*, and that means that the action is possible but unlikely.
- Unit RB11-A focuses on *have* and *had*. These are also related words with distinct meanings. When used as an auxiliary to the main verb, *have* indicates **present** perfect tense and *had* indicates

past perfect tense. In this unit, listen carefully to the short but important sound after [ðey]. If it is [v], it represents *have,* and that means that the action took place at some indefinite time before the present. If the sound is [d], it represents *had,* and that means that the action took place sometime before another designated event in the past.

- In the contrasting sentences in Unit RB11-A, it is possible to use "phonetic syllabication" (explained under "Final [C + t]-[C + d]-[C + s]-[C + z], CC7/8/9/10/11" on p. 351). Simply **attach the final consonant, either [v] or [d], to the start of the following syllable.** The result will be either [ðey viytən] *(They veaten . . .)* or [ðey diytən] *(They deaten . . .).*

- Unit RB12-A focuses on *did* and *have.* Notice that *did* reduces to the same [d] sound that *had* reduces to. (You cannot tell whether [d] refers to *did* or *had* by the sound alone. You must look at the grammatical forms of other, related words in the sentence.) In this unit, listen carefully to the short but important sound after [wɛr]. If it is [d], it represents *did,* and that means that the action took place at a particular time in the past.

- Unit RB13-A focuses on *did* and *will.* In this unit, listen carefully to the short but important sound after [wɛr]. If it is [d], it represents *did,* and that means that the action took place at a particular time in the past. If the sound is [l], it represents *will,* and that means that the action is expected to take place at some future time.

Phonological Explanations for Word Stress (Section 6)

- Stress is the relative **strength or loudness** of a syllable compared to other syllables around it.

- English makes more use of differences in stress to communicate meaning than many other languages do.

- There are **three basic levels** of stress in English words—primary, secondary, and weak.

- **Primary** stress (the strongest, heaviest stress) is indicated in this book with a ´ mark (or LARGE CAPITAL letters).

- **Secondary** stress, or light stress, is marked with a ` symbol (or SMALL CAPITAL letters).

- **Weak** stress, or no stress, is left unmarked (or written in lowercase letters).

- In English, stress can fall on virtually **any syllable** in a word. The location of stress varies depending on the word's **origin** (i.e., what language the word came from originally) and on its **form** (e.g., noun, verb, etc.).

- In the phonetic representations in this book, the symbol [S] stands for any syllable.
- Stress is related to **pitch** or **intonation**. Normally (but not always) the pitch rises on a stressed syllable in English.

[S´-S]—[S-S´], Two-syllable words, WS1
- These units focus on stress in **two-syllable words.**
- In each word in the contrastive pairs, the **primary** stress is on either the **first syllable** (marked [S´-S]) or on the **second** one (marked [S-S´]).
- The other syllable is **not stressed.** The vowel in that syllable is typically **reduced** to either [ə] or [ɪ].
- This stress pattern is often used to make a distinction between **nouns** and **verbs** in pairs, like *récord* and *recórd, cónduct* and *condúct,* or *próject* and *projéct.*
- This stress pattern is also one of the key differences between **-teen numbers** (13, 14, 15, 16, 17, 18, and 19) and cardinal **numbers that are multiples of ten** (30, 40, 50, 60, 70, 80, and 90) in North American English.
- The **first** syllable of the numbers that are multiples of -ten is always stressed. For example, *nínety.*
- The **first** syllable of the -teen numbers is usually stressed when **counting** or when it **modifies a noun.** For example, *séventeen, éighteen, níneteen.*
- The **last** syllable of the -teen numbers is stressed when it comes at the **end of a phrase** or when a speaker is trying to **make the distinction** between the -ten and the -teen numbers. For example, *Not nínety. I said that I counted ninetéen, ninetéen new people at the meeting.*
- The **vowel sound** in the last syllable of the -teen numbers is also a little **longer** than the vowel of the last syllable of the -ten numbers.
- To practice hearing or producing the difference in stress patterns in these pairs of words, try **humming** or using a **kazoo** (Hint 14).
- For more practice, when you are saying the contrasting words, **clap your hands** or **tap on a table or desk** in time with the syllables (Hint 13). Make the first beat strong and the second one weak or vice versa.

[S´-S-S]—[S-S´-S], Three-syllable words, WS2
- These units focus on stress in **three-syllable words.**
- In each word in the contrastive pairs, the **primary** stress is on either the **first syllable** (marked [S´-S-S]) or on the **second** one (marked [S-S´-S]).
- The other syllables carry **weak or no stress.** The vowels in unstressed syllables may be **reduced** to either [ə] or [ɪ].

- To practice hearing or producing the difference in stress patterns in these pairs of words, try **humming** or using a **kazoo** (Hint 14).
- For more practice, when you are saying the contrasting words, **clap your hands** or **tap on a table or desk** in time with the syllables (Hint 13). Make the first beat strong and the second one weak or vice versa.

[ˋS-Sˊ]—[S-Sˊ], Verbs and nouns with prefixes, WS3

- The general pattern for **verbs** that begin with a **prefix** (such as *re-, un-,* or *dis-*) is that the first syllable of the **base** or root part of the word receives **strong** stress. In contrast, the **prefix** receives **light** or **no** stress. For example, *repéat, uncóver, discóurage.*
- When a word with a prefix functions as a **noun,** the pattern is generally the **opposite.** The **first syllable** (the prefix) receives the **strong** stress, and the **base** receives **light or no stress.** For example, *préfix, réfund, únderwear, fórearm.*
- In **special** cases, when the meaning emphasizes **doing something again or starting over,** there is a third pattern in which **both the prefix and the base** receive stress. For example, *rèconsíder,* meaning to consider again, or *rècondítion,* meaning to restore something to good condition. Normally, the base receives strong (primary) stress, and the prefix receives lighter (secondary) stress, although this pattern can be reversed to place even greater emphasis on the repetition.
- Sometimes this greater emphasis is **contrastive.** For example, "They just fueled the plane, and now they have to *réfùel* it."
- These dual-stress words are often rather unusual words that have been formed for a **special purpose** by adding *re-* to a verb that can stand alone. They may not be found in dictionaries, and they may be hyphenated to distinguish them from more normal counterparts with different meanings. For example, *re-lease* (to lease again), *re-form* (to form again).

[Sˊ-ˋS] Noun compound—[ˋS-Sˊ] Modifier + noun phrase, WS4

- In English there are many pairs of words that are similar except for the stress (and the intonation that follows the stress). The stress pattern makes a big difference in meaning.
- Sometimes these word pairs consist of a **modifier followed by a noun.** The meaning of this **modifier + noun phrase** is simply the combination of the meanings of the two individual words. For example, a *hot dog* is a dog that is hot, and a *green house* is a house that is green. Removing the modifier does not alter the basic meaning of the noun.
- Modifier + noun phrases are always written as **two words.**
- In these phrases, the **second** word (the noun) receives the **strongest** stress.

- The **first** word in the phrase carries **lighter,** secondary stress (e.g., hòt dóg).
- **Noun compounds** are quite different.
- Noun compounds may consist of a **modifier and a noun** (e.g., blackboard) or **two nouns** (e.g., sunglasses).
- Noun compounds may be written as **one word** or **two words** (e.g., tap dance). The two-word spelling is more common when either member of the compound has more than one syllable (e.g., rocking chair).
- A noun compound often has a **special, new meaning,** different from the meanings of the two parts individually. For example, a *blackboard* may not be black, and a *greenhouse* is not necessarily green. Removing the first word may radically alter the meaning.
- In noun compounds, the **first** word receives the **heavy,** primary stress.
- The **second** word in a noun compound receives **lighter,** secondary stress (e.g., hót dòg).
- Occasionally both stress patterns are used with the **same meaning,** as in *íce crèam* and *ìce créam,* but this is relatively rare.
- In different **dialects** of North American English, the stress patterns on some of these combinations also vary.

[S´-S] Noun compound (gerund)—[S-S´] Verbal object complement, WS5

- The **second** element in a noun compound noun may also be a **verb form,** such as a gerund, that refers to an activity (e.g., road racing, mountain climbing).
- These noun compounds are usually written as **two words** when the second (verbal) element of the compound has more than one syllable.
- The **first** word (the noun) is often the **object of the verb,** the second word in the compound (e.g., *I practiced mountain climbing* means that I climbed the mountain).
- In these noun compounds, the same as in those explained above (for Unit WS4), the **first** word receives the **heavy,** primary stress (e.g., fúnd ràising).
- The **second** word in a compound receives **lighter,** secondary stress.
- In contrast, other noun + verb combinations look and sound a lot like noun compounds, except for the stress (and intonation) pattern. These **noun + verb sequences** follow the same stress pattern as the modifier + noun phrases do. That is, in these sequences the **second** word (the verb) receives the **strongest** stress.
- The **first** word in the sequence (the noun) carries **lighter,** secondary stress.

- In contrast to the noun + verb compounds described above, in these noun + verb sequences the **first** word is the **doer** of the action described in the verb. (In grammatical terms, it is the verbal object complement.) For example, *I watched a man húnt* means that the man hunted.

Phonological Explanations for Sentence Stress (Section 7)

- The preceding section focused on stress differences within and between individual words. When these individual words are used in **sentences,** however, additional stress patterns must be considered.
- The most common modification of stress that occurs when individual words are used in sentences is the **dropping** of some of the stresses. It is not appropriate to place stress on every word in a sentence the way you might in a list of words.
- Normally, **content** words (nouns, main verbs, adjectives, etc.) that carry the **most information** are the ones that receive strong stress in a sentence.
- If a sentence contains an **interrogative** (such as *what, who, when,* or *why*), that word often receives strong stress.
- Another important consideration is the **spacing between strong stresses** in a sentence. In general, English speakers avoid placing these stresses close together.
- In spoken English, strong stresses tend to occur at **regular intervals of time,** no matter how many weak or unstressed syllables are between them. This pattern is what gives English its characteristic **stress-timed rhythm.**
- Although the intervals between heavy stresses in spoken English sentences are not precisely equal, there is a strong tendency to **reduce and blend the unstressed words between strong stresses** to shorten them, or to **pause briefly** if there are few or no unstressed words between stresses, in order to make these intervals more regular.
- In **songs** and **poetry** with a heavy beat this tendency is even stronger. In these cases, you can often clap or tap at equal intervals in time with the strong stresses (Hint 13).
- Aside from these basic sentence-stress considerations, there are a number of others that are less general but still important to the clear communication of your intended meaning. The units in this section focus on a couple of these considerations.

Strong stress on a key content word, SS1
- **Content** words are nouns, verbs, adjectives, adverbs, etc. They carry and communicate information.

- When particular content words in a sentence need to be **highlighted** in order for a **special meaning** to be communicated, those words receive a **stronger than usual stress.** (In other languages, special prominence may be achieved by changing the word order or by some other means.)
- Strong stress on content words in a sentence often indicates that they are conveying **new, important,** or **contrastive** information.
- When you are speaking, place this special stress on the syllable that normally carries the primary stress in the key word but make it even stronger.
- **Contrastive stress** normally involves two parallel things and emphasizes the key difference between them. The two contrasted words are often opposites, such as *high* and *low* or *new* and *old*. They may occur in two separate sentences or in the same one. One of them may not even be mentioned directly; it may only be implied.
- **Both** elements in a contrastive pair may receive strong stress, but the **strongest** stress normally goes on the **second** one (Hint 13).
- You can use this contrastive stress pattern to **correct, contradict,** or **argue** with what someone has just said.
- You also use this contrastive stress pattern in **closed-choice alternative questions** (see Units I6 and I7).
- In the stories in Units SS1-A and SS1-D, strong stress is used to **correct a misunderstanding or mistake** on the part of the butler and the restaurant worker. Before being corrected, the butler thinks that Mr. Smythe (not Mrs. Smythe) was the one that Mrs. Johnson spoke with. At first, the restaurant worker makes a mistake with the number of items ordered. Later, the worker makes a mistake with the type of food ordered.
- When **something unexpected** or **surprising** occurs, then that information receives primary emphasis through strong sentence stress. In the story in Unit SS1-B, Sally and Bob are first surprised that Mr. Webb rides a bike because he is so old. The word *Wébb,* therefore, receives the primary stress in the sentence. Later, they are surprised that such an old man still goes to work every day, so the word *wórk* receives the strongest stress.
- In the story in Unit SS1-C, Jennifer **emphasizes** that she wants ice cream, not mousse, by adding extra stress on *ice cream.* Later she strongly stresses the word *chocolate* to emphasize that she wants that flavor and not vanilla.
- In the story in Unit SS1-E, Jack **argues** that the bag belongs to him, not the woman, by placing strong stress on the word *mine.* Arguing back, she does the same. Later, when talking with the security guard, Jack communicates a very different meaning (that he is not absolutely certain the bag belongs to him) by stressing the

word *think* (in contrast with the word *know* in the guard's question).

Strong stress on a key function word, SS2

- **Function** words are articles, auxiliary verbs, prepositions, conjunctions, etc. They signal grammatical relationships.
- When particular function words in a sentence need to be **highlighted** in order for a **special meaning** to be communicated, those words receive a **stronger than usual stress.** (In other languages, special prominence may be achieved by changing the word order or by some other means.)
- Strong stress on function words in a sentence often indicates that they are conveying **new, important,** or **contrastive** information (see the preceding explanation). However, strong stress may also indicate **affirmation.**
- To affirm means to **declare positively and firmly,** often in response to some sort of opposition. An affirmation is **stronger than a simple statement of fact.** It communicates conviction.
- In the story in Unit SS2-A, for example, Sam stresses the word *had* when **defending** Bert. The strong stress on this function word (instead of on the main verb *studied*) expresses Sam's **conviction** that Bert really did study.
- In the story in Unit SS2-B, Zina needed someone who would **affirm** her capabilities and give her confidence. When you tell this story and say the sentence *You can do it, and you will* put extra stress on the function words *can* and *will* (Hints 13 and 14).
- In the story in Unit SS2-C, Rick uses strong stress on the function word *do* in his sentence *I really do* to emphasize and reaffirm the point made in his previous sentence, *I love this food!* Later, he stresses the function word *are* (which in a normal statement might be unstressed and reduced) in the sentence *These microwave dinners are pretty good* to emphasize his surprising degree of agreement with Joe.

Phonological Explanations for Intonation
(Section 8)

- **Intonation** is the **melody** of language, the rising and falling of the **pitch of the voice.** English has a complicated intonation system that is important to meaning.
- Because it is not represented by letters of the alphabet in writing, intonation may seem less important or less real than vowels and consonants. The reality is that intonation is both **real and important.**
- Intonation is used in every spoken English utterance. It is **un-**

Phonological Explanations

366

avoidable. Every time you speak English you use intonation, whether you are aware of it or not.

- Using the intonation patterns of your native language when you speak English can result in a strong **foreign accent,** even if you pronounce all the vowels and consonants correctly. Incorrect intonation may also be **misleading** or **confusing** to people who listen to you.

- Intonation signals the **grammatical function** of an utterance (e.g., statement or question), as well as the speaker's **attitude, emotion,** and/or degree of **certainty.**

- In some languages (like Chinese), individual words have tones that go up and down. In English, each **"thought group"** or **intonation unit** (a group of several words) has its own intonation contour or pitch pattern.

- There are basically **three levels** of pitch in English intonation. (A fourth, extrahigh level is also possible for showing extreme emotion.) In this book, these three basic levels are indicated by the numbers 1, 2, and 3. They are also shown on horizontal lines, similar to those in a musical staff.

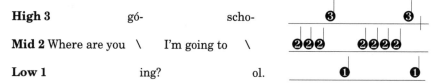

High 3	gó-	scho-
Mid 2 Where are you \	I'm going to \	
Low 1	ing?	ol.

- These levels are **relative** to each other within the range of each individual's voice. Some people have deep voices, and some people have high ones, so the actual tone will vary from speaker to speaker.

- In most cases, an English intonation contour **begins on the neutral level 2** and then rises or falls from there.

- Pitch changes up or down may occur as **steps** (a jump from one level to another between syllables) or as **glides** (a smooth change within a single syllable).

- An intonation contour may end in a **rising or falling glide** in which the voice rises or falls even further. In this book these glides are indicated by arrows [↗] or [↘].

- Pitch changes in an intonation contour are closely related to the **strongly stressed syllables.** Normally, the pitch reaches its highest level on the stressed syllable of the most prominent word in an intonation unit. Any following syllables in the phrase are pronounced at a lower pitch level.

- **Pausing** and intonation are also closely related. In writing, there are various ways to indicate the pausing that occurs in speech. This book uses vertical bars in the phonetic representations. A single bar [|] indicates a brief pause. A double bar [||] indicates a longer pause. Pausing is the focus of the next section.

- For many meanings, the intonation pattern that occurs at the **end** of a sentence is the most crucial. The contour occurs relative to the **last strongly stressed syllable** in the sentence.
- A good way to focus on the rise and fall of intonation when you are practicing a sentence is to close your lips and **hum** or use a kazoo (Hint 14).
- Another trick to make your intonation more obvious when you are practicing is to hold your hand in front of you and then move it up or down to match the rising or falling intonation of the sentences you say (Hint 15).

[231(↘)]—[23↗], Statements and questions, I1

- The **[231(↘)] final-falling intonation contour** (which may end in either a falling glide or a level pitch) is for **neutral, declarative statements,** as well as for *wh-* **(information seeking) questions** and **commands or directives.**
- With neutral statements there is usually no special emphasis in the meaning of the sentence other than that expressed by the individual words.
- To produce this intonation contour, **start on pitch level 2,** raise the pitch of your voice to **level 3 on the last strongly stressed syllable** in the intonation unit or sentence, and then go **down to pitch level 1** for the rest of the sentence (Hints 14 and 15).
- Whether your voice goes down to level 1 in a **step** or a **glide** depends on what comes after the last strongly stressed syllable. If the last strongly stressed syllable is also the last syllable in the intonation unit, then you will need to **glide down quickly,** perhaps lengthening the vowel in that syllable. If there are other syllables after the last strongly stressed one, you can probably **step down** to them and then keep your voice pitch low. In this case, you may add a small **final falling glide** on the **last syllable** and drop the pitch even lower.
- In contrast, the **[23↗] final-rising intonation contour** changes a statement into a *yes/no* **question,** even when there is no change in word order.
- In addition, the rising intonation adds an additional meaning of **surprise** to the sentence. For example, the sentence *It's dark already?* expresses the speaker's surprise at the lateness of the hour.
- This pattern may also have the function of expressing **amazement** or **disbelief** and asking for a **confirmation** that the information just expressed is really correct.
- A common discourse pattern is for [231↘] statements and [23↗] questions to occur in a sequence. One speaker makes a neutral statement, and a second speaker expresses surprise in a way that asks for confirmation. (For an example, see the story in Unit I1-A.)

- The [23↗] final rising intonation pattern also changes a *wh-* (information seeking) question into **an echo question** (a repetition of a previously asked question that is spoken by a listener before answering the question—for example, Speaker A: "Where are you going?" Speaker B: "Where am I going? I'm going home").
- To produce this intonation contour, **start on pitch level 2,** then rise to **level 3 on the last strongly stressed syllable** in the intonation unit or sentence and **stay at that level** for the rest of the sentence (Hints 14 and 15). You may raise the pitch even higher on the **last syllable** by adding a small **final rising glide.**

Follow-up *wh-* question, [31↘] Requesting more information—[23↗] Requesting repetition, I2

- The one-word question "**What?**" (as well as "Who?" "When?" etc.) said in response to an utterance and with a **falling** intonation calls for a substantially different answer than "What?" said with a **rising** pitch.
- The **falling [31↘]** intonation makes the question into one that **requests additional information.** In other words, it is much like a normal *wh-* question. For example, in the story in Unit I2-A, the second "What?" question (asked by Eric's father) means "What is the title of the book?"
- To produce this **[31↘]** contour, **start at pitch level 3.** Then, lengthening the vowel in the *wh-* word, quickly **glide down to level 1.** As the word ends, you may let your voice pitch drop even lower (Hints 14 and 15).
- In contrast, the **rising [23↗]** intonation *wh-* question asks for **repetition** of the preceding utterance—either because it was **not heard correctly** or because it was **hard to believe.**
- To produce this **[23↗]** contour, **start at pitch level 2.** Then, lengthening the vowel in the *wh-* word, quickly **glide up to level 3.** As the word ends, you may let your voice pitch rise even higher (Hints 14 and 15).
- A **high but fairly level [33↗]** intonation indicates a similar meaning but is used less commonly.
- To produce this **[33↗]** contour, **start at pitch level 3.** Then, lengthening the vowel in the *wh-* word, **keep your voice at level 3.** As the word ends, raise the pitch of your voice **even higher** (Hints 14 and 15).
- For showing **extreme emotion** (such as complete amazement), a [34], [24], or even [14] intonation, with a long, dramatic glide, is possible.
- *What?* is the question used most commonly with this intonation pattern, but *Who, When, Why,* and other *wh-* words are also possible.

Tag question, [23 ↗] Signaling uncertainty—[31] Requesting confirmation, I3

- A **tag question** is a short question that is attached to the end of a statement. The question checks on the truth of the statement. For details on how to form tag questions, you will have to consult a grammar book. Here, only the intonation of tag questions will be explained.

- There are **two main intonation contours** for tag questions. One goes up, and the other goes down. The choice depends on the **speaker's degree of uncertainty** about the statement that precedes the question. In both cases, the speaker is not absolutely certain about the statement, and the listener is expected to respond. However, the degree of uncertainty and the expected response are quite different in each case.

- The **[23 ↗] rising intonation** signals a **considerable amount of uncertainty** on the part of the speaker. Although the speaker wants or expects the response to be affirmative, the tag question is a **real inquiry.** Both *yes* and *no* responses are probable, and if the response from the listener is negative, the speaker will not be very surprised.

- To produce this **[23 ↗]** contour, **start at pitch level 2.** Then, after the strongly stressed word in the tag question **step up to level 3.** As the question ends, you may let your voice pitch rise even higher (Hints 14 and 15).

- For signaling even greater uncertainty, a **higher [33 ↗]** intonation is also possible although it is less common.

- To produce this **[33 ↗]** contour, **start at pitch level 3.** Then, **keep your voice at level 3.** As the question ends, raise the pitch of your voice **even higher** (Hints 14 and 15).

- On the other hand, the **[31] falling intonation** is used when the speaker's degree of uncertainty is low. In other words, the speaker has a **fairly high degree of certainty** and is reasonably sure that the listener will agree. The speaker is really just requesting confirmation or agreement. If the response to this type of tag question is negative, the speaker will probably be surprised.

- Tag questions with [31] falling intonation are often just "conversation questions." They keep the conversation moving by ensuring that the listener is involved in the conversation.

- To produce this **[31]** contour, **start at pitch level 3.** Then, after the strongly stressed word in the tag question **step down to level 1.** As the word ends, you may let your voice pitch drop even lower (Hints 14 and 15).

[231‖23↗]*Wh-* question + continuation—[231‖231(↘)] *Wh-*question and response, I4

- When English speakers use ***wh-* questions to ask for information,** they usually use [231(↘)] intonation (see the explanation for Unit I1) and wait for an answer. The **answer** typically takes the form of a neutral statement using the same [231(↘)] contour or a [31(↘)] contour if the first syllable of the response carries the primary stress.

- To produce this [231(↘)] contour, **start on pitch level 2,** raise the pitch of your voice to **level 3 on the last strongly stressed syllable,** and then go **down to pitch level 1** for the rest of the intonation unit (Hints 14 and 15). You may add a small **final falling glide** on the last syllable and drop the pitch even lower. (For additional details, see the explanation for Unit I1 on p. 367.)

- Sometimes, however, before an answer can be given, English speakers follow up their questions with **tentative guesses that use [23↗] intonation.** These guesses consist of information that the questioners hope is accurate, but they **require *yes/no* confirmation** from the listener. In other words, by the addition of a guess and the changing of the intonation, the *wh-* question is changed to one that calls for a *yes/no* response.

- This **[231‖23↗]** intonation contour is used when the answer to a question is **obvious but very surprising** (astonishing or unbelievable) to the speaker. For example, in the story in Unit I4-A, Art is surprised to see Sam studying at 3 A.M. He can hardly believe his own eyes.

- To produce the **first** part of this [231‖23↗] contour, **start on pitch level 2,** raise the pitch of your voice to **level 3 on the last strongly stressed syllable,** and then go **down to pitch level 1** for the rest of this part of the question. You may add a small **final falling glide** on the last syllable and drop the pitch even lower (Hints 14 and 15).

- Before continuing, **pause slightly.** In this book, this pausing is indicated by vertical bars [‖].

- For the **second** part of the [231‖23↗] contour, the tentative guess, **start at pitch level 2.** Then, on the strongly stressed syllable **glide or step up to level 3.** As the question ends, you may raise your voice pitch even higher (Hints 14 and 15).

- In the story in Unit I4-A, Art is surprised to see Sam studying at 3 A.M., so he uses the [231‖23↗] question and continuation pattern. Sam, on the other hand is not surprised to see Art and uses a simple [231] *wh-* question pattern, although with contrastive stress on the *you.* Art replies with a one-word [31] statement.

- In the story in Unit I4-B, when the young students question Mr. Park about the ostriches, they think they know they are birds but are not 100 percent sure. Therefore, they use the [231‖23↗] question and continuation pattern, and Mr. Park answers, "Yes." In contrast, in his responses to their [231↘] *wh-* questions, Mr. Park employs a simple [231↘] statement intonation.

- The contrasting sentences in Unit I4-C do not follow exactly the same grammatical pattern as those in the previous two units do. In the second one, *tomorrow* is part of the *wh-* question, not a response. However, the contrasting sentences still follow the same intonation contours that were used in the previous two units.

Items in a series, [23↗] Unfinished (continuing)—[231↘] Finished (or compound), I5

- All **items in a series** typically have **rising [23↗] intonation** except for the **final item**, which has a **[231↘] rising-then-falling intonation.**
- To produce the [23↗] intonation contour, **start at pitch level 2.** Then, after the strongly stressed syllable **glide or step up to level 3 and stay there** for the remaining syllables of the item, possibly gliding even a little higher at the end (Hints 14 and 15).
- Usually, you will **pause slightly between items** in a series. In this book, this pausing is indicated by vertical bars [‖].
- An alternative, less commonly used intonation for items in a series is [323↗]. Although this contour starts high (on pitch level 3) and then drops (to level 2), it still rises at the end and is followed by a brief pause (Hints 14 and 15).
- To signal the end of a series, the **final item** normally uses a [231(↘)] contour.
- To produce this [231(↘)] contour, **start on pitch level 2,** raise the pitch of your voice to **level 3 on the last strongly stressed syllable** in the item, and then go **down to pitch level 1** for the rest. You may add a small **final falling glide** on the last syllable and drop the pitch even lower (Hints 14 and 15).
- In Unit I5-A, in addition to the series intonation, notice the contrastive stress (see Unit SS1) when Mr. Allred says, "You made mé wait; now I'm going to make yóu wait."
- In Unit I5-B, the compound word *houseboat* has falling [31] intonation. However, because it is in the middle of a series, the intonation rises slightly again after reaching level 1. The result is a [231↗] intonation contour.

Alternative questions, [23↗‖231] Closed-choice—[23↗] Open-choice (*yes/no*), I6

- There are two types of alternative questions: closed choice and open choice.
- In a **closed-choice alternative question** the listener is expected

to **choose one of the options given.** No other choices are available.

- For example, in the story in Unit I6-C, after the Stevens' mobile home was destroyed and they decided not to drive, their friends asked them a closed-choice question about their transportation because they knew that the Stevens were not free to choose other means of travel. In this case the Stevens needed to choose from a limited number of options.

- In a closed-choice alternative question, **normal series intonation** (see the preceding explanation) is used for the options. Each option except the last one has a [23↗] intonation contour, and [231] intonation is used for the last option.

- To produce the **[23↗]** intonation contour, **start at pitch level 2.** Then, after the strongly stressed syllable **glide or step up to level 3 and stay there** for the remaining syllables of the item, possibly gliding even a little higher at the end (Hints 14 and 15). Then **pause briefly.**

- Use this same [23↗] contour for each option except the last one.

- For the last option, just as for the last item in a series, use a [231(↘)] contour.

- To produce this **[231(↘)]** contour, **start on pitch level 2,** raise the pitch of your voice to **level 3 on the last strongly stressed syllable,** and then go **down to pitch level 1** for the rest. You may add a small **final falling glide** on the last syllable and drop the pitch even lower (Hints 14 and 15).

- In the closed-choice alternative question in the contrasting sentences for Unit I6-A, the appropriate intonation contour looks like this.

```
3                pen,↗ ‖      pen-

2 Should I use a        or a        ↘

1                                cil?
```

- In contrast, in an **open-choice alternative question** the listener is **not limited to the particular options given.** In fact, the options may only be examples of a more general type or category. Other options of that same type may be available, and the listener may accept or reject all of the alternatives as a group. In this way, an open-choice alternative question is very similar to a *yes/no* question.

- For example, in the story in Unit I6-C, when the Stevens were first asked an open choice question about how they were traveling, they were not limited to one of the options (train or plane). People just assumed that they would be using some common type of long-distance transportation. In fact, their response was that they traveled by mobile home—an option not mentioned in the question.

- In an open-choice alternative question, a **single [23↗] intonation unit is used for all the options as a group.** This intonation is identical to the intonation used in simple *yes / no* questions.

- To produce the **[23↗]** intonation contour, **start at pitch level 2.** Then, **on the strongly stressed syllable of the first option** glide or step up to **level 3 and stay there** for the remaining options, possibly gliding even a little higher at the end (Hints 14 and 15).

- In the open-choice alternative question in the contrasting sentences for Unit I6-A, the appropriate intonation contour looks like this.

3   pen or a pencil? ↗

2 Should I use a

1

[23↗ ‖231] Closed-choice alternative—[23↗] Modifier + noun at end of *yes/no* question, I7

- Some **closed-choice alternative phrases** sound very similar to some **modifier + noun combinations.** For example, because of reduction and blending, an alternative phrase such as *big or little* [bɪɡərlɪtl] may be easily confused with the adjective + noun phrase *bigger little* [bɪɡərlɪtl]. (Of course, the phrase *bigger little* does not make sense, but that only makes it more confusing.)

- The main difference between these two types of phrases is in the intonation.

- **Closed-choice alternatives** use the same **[23↗ ‖231]** intonation contour explained in the preceding phonological explanation (for Unit I6).

- To produce the **[23↗ ‖231]** contour, **start at pitch level 2.** Then, after the strongly stressed syllable **glide or step up to level 3 and stay there** for any remaining syllables of the first noun. **Pause briefly.** Then, for the conjunction and second noun, **start on pitch level 2,** raise the pitch of your voice to **level 3 on the last strongly stressed syllable,** and go **down to pitch level 1** for the rest (Hints 14 and 15). (For more details on how to produce this intonation, see the preceding explanation for alternative questions, I6.)

- In contrast, when they are in final position in *yes / no* questions, **modifier + noun combinations** use a **[23↗]** intonation contour identical to the one used by open-choice alternative questions.

- To produce the [23↗] intonation contour, **start at pitch level 2.** Then, **on the last strongly stressed syllable** of the intonation unit, glide or step up to **level 3 and stay there** for the remaining syllables, possibly gliding even a little higher at the end (Hints 14 and 15).

- In the story in Unit I7-A, when the server uses [23↗∥231] intonation with [suwpərsæləd], she is asking Paul and Lisa to make a choice between two items, soup or salad, and to select one or the other. On the other hand, when the server uses [23↗] intonation, she is treating [suwpərsæləd] as a single unit, "Super Salad," and merely asking a *yes/no* question.

[23↗∣231] Compound noun phrase—[231] Modifier + noun at end of statement, I8

- Some **compound noun phrases** (two nouns joined by a conjunction) sound very similar to some **modifier + noun combinations.** For example, because of reduction and blending, a compound noun phrase such as *gold and jewelry* (pronounced [gowldndʒuwlriy] because the *and* is often reduced to syllabic *'n'* in normal speech) may be easily confused with the adjective + noun phrase *golden jewelry* (also pronounced [gowldndʒuwlriy]).

- The main difference between these two types of phrases is in the intonation.

- **Compound noun phrases** use the [23↗∣231] intonation contour, which is also used by closed-choice alternatives. (For more details on how to produce this intonation, see the explanation for alternative questions, I6, on p. 000.)

- To produce the [23↗∣231] contour, **start at pitch level 2.** Then, after the strongly stressed syllable **glide or step up to level 3 and stay there** for any remaining syllables of the first noun. **Pause very briefly.** Then, for the conjunction and second noun, **start on pitch level 2,** raise the pitch of your voice to **level 3 on the last strongly stressed syllable of the noun,** and then go **down to pitch level 1** for any remaining syllables (Hints 14 and 15). (For more details on the production of this intonation, see the phonological explanation for Unit I6 on pp. 371–73.)

- This [23↗∣231] intonation often works with other types of compound phrases (such as compound verbs) also.

- In contrast, **modifier + noun combinations** (such as *golden jéwelry*) at the end of statements follow a simple **[231]** intonation contour. The entire modifier + noun combination is treated as **one unit.**

- To produce this intonation contour, **start on pitch level 2,** raise the pitch of your voice to **level 3 on the strongly stressed syllable of the noun,** and then go **down to pitch level 1** for any remaining syllables (Hints 14 and 15).

Phonological Explanations for Segmentation
(Section 9)

- Dividing what you say into appropriate **"thought groups" or segments** is crucial for clear communication.
- A thought group is not simply a sentence. While a short sentence may consist of only one thought group, a longer sentence may have several.
- Often segmentation is based on the **grammatical functions** of various sentence parts. Other times, groupings depend on the **special emphasis** that a speaker wants to create.
- In written English, some (but not all) of the boundaries between sentence segments are marked with commas or other punctuation marks.
- In spoken English, segmentation is indicated primarily by **pauses** that occur at the boundaries between segments and by the **intonation contour** of each segment.
- Sometimes, more than one grouping arrangement is possible in a sentence, and the meaning of the sentence changes according to the pausing/intonation used.
- Section 8 of *Pronunciation Matters* focuses on intonation. Section 9 focuses on contrasts where the primary distinction between two utterances is made by pausing. In reality, of course, pausing cannot be separated from intonation. Intonation contours go hand in hand with the units marked by pauses. In fact, **stress, intonation, and pausing** are all closely **interrelated** in spoken English.
- This book uses **vertical bars** to indicate pauses in speech. A single bar [|] represents a brief pause. A double bar [||] represents a longer pause.
- The intonation contour of segments is indicated with numbers and arrows, as was explained in the preceding part of these phonological explanations. When necessary, stress is marked using the same system used in the word-stress and sentence-stress explanations.

Quotation, [231 ↗ ||1 ↗ ||231] Interrupted —[231 ↗ |231] Uninterrupted, S1

- For the **interrupted quotation,** use **normal [231] statement intonation** for the **first part,** but when the pitch of your voice drops to level 1 at the end, **glide back up** quickly. In some cases, your voice pitch might not drop below level 2 at all (Hints 14 and 15).
- If the quotation starts with a strongly stressed syllable (e.g., "Máry") then begin your intonation contour on level 3, instead of level 2.
- At the end of the first part of the quotation, **pause briefly.**

- For the **identifying tag** (the "said" part of the sentence), **drop to level 1 and glide up at the end.**
- **Pause briefly** again.
- When you **continue the quotation, start at level 2** (unless there is some special stress on the first word).
- Raise the pitch of your voice to **level 3 on the strongly stressed syllable(s)** and then drop it down to **level 1 at the end** (Hints 14 and 15).
- In contrast, in the **uninterrupted quotation, use [231] intonation for the identifying tag.** You may end the tag with a quick **upward glide [↗]. Pause very briefly.**
- For the quotation itself, use **normal [231] statement intonation** (see explanation for Unit I1). Of course, if the quotation is a question, you should use the intonation appropriate to the question type.

Statement, [232‖12] With parenthetical expression at end— [231] With object, S2

- **Parenthetical expressions** are words or groups of words added to the main body of a sentence. They add information that is not necessary to the main meaning of the sentence. In other words, this information can be removed without changing the meaning of the sentence itself.
- In written English, parenthetical expressions are usually set off from the rest of a sentence with **parentheses, dashes, or commas.**
- The **name and/or title of the person being spoken to** (*Janet, Mr. Ramirez, doctor,* etc., often called "**direct address**") is one type of parenthetical expression. Other common parenthetical expressions include **expressions showing politeness** *(please, thank you),* **adverbials** (words that explain when, how, or why something was done, e.g., *the next week, luckily,* or *because he was angry*), and inserted **expressions of opinion or emotion** (e.g., He is, *I believe,* the best president in our country's history).
- When you use a parenthetical expression at the **start** of a sentence, you may employ a **[23 ↗ ‖]** rising intonation or a **[232 ↗ ‖]** falling intonation. Either should be followed by a **brief pause.**
- When you insert a parenthetical expression in the **middle** or at the **end** of a sentence, **stop the main sentence on pitch level 2** and **pause briefly.**
- Then, for the parenthetical expression, use a **[12] low-rising intonation.** After the pause, speak on pitch **level 1,** and on the **final syllable** raise your voice **to level 2,** possibly gliding up a little more at the end (Hints 14 and 15).
- When using a parenthetical expression in the **middle** of a sen-

tence, **pause briefly** at the end of the expression before going on.

- A similar [∥121∥] pausing/intonation pattern is used for **appositives** (e.g., "George, my best friend, works . . . ") and **nonrestrictive clauses** (e.g., "Canada, which in land size is the largest country in the Western Hemisphere, has . . . "), which are spoken as **asides.**

- If appropriate pausing/intonation is not used, parenthetical expressions may be confused with other sentence parts and the meaning may change dramatically. For instance, in the stories in Units S2-A and B, except for the pausing/intonation, the sentence-final parenthetical expressions are similar to direct objects and objects of prepositions.

Yes/no question, [23|3 ↗] With parenthetical expression at end—[23] With object, S3

- **Parenthetical expressions** added to the end of *yes/no* questions (which have a [23] intonation) serve the same functions as parenthetical expressions do in sentences with [231] intonation (described in the preceding explanation). However, the pausing and intonation are different.

- The **pause** before a parenthetical expression in a *yes/no* question is **very brief.** For this reason, it is indicated by a single vertical bar instead of a double one in the phonetic representation.

- Parenthetical expressions in *yes/no* questions (which end on pitch level 3) have a **[3 ↗] high-rising intonation.** (In contrast, parenthetical expression in sentences with [231] intonation use a [∥12∥] low-rising intonation.)

- To pronounce a parenthetical expression after a *yes/no* question properly, **pause very briefly** at the end of the question, **keep the pitch of your voice high** (on level 3), and then **glide it even higher** at the end (Hints 14 and 15).

- In contrast, to produce the proper intonation at the end of a **simple *yes/no* question** (with no parenthetical expression), go up to **level 3 on the last strongly stressed syllable and stay there.** Do **not pause** until the end of the sentence.

[231 ↗ ∥231] Number groupings, S4

- Grouping is important in **mathematics** also. For instance, different groupings produce different results in arithmetic problems. For example: (2 + 4) 3 = 18, and 2 + (4 x 3) = 14.

- When arithmetic problems are written, **parentheses** are often used to indicate the groupings.

- When groups of numbers are spoken, **pausing and intonation** show the beginning and ending of each group.

- In the S4 units, as you say the numbers in each arithmetic problem, **pause briefly at each boundary between groups.**

- Treat each group within the problem as a **separate [231] intonation unit.**
- As you do with all normal [231] statements and *wh-* questions, when you say these spoken arithmetic questions **start on pitch level 2** and then **move up to level 3 on the strongly stressed syllable of the first number in the group.**
- On the **last stressed syllable** in each group, **drop or glide down to pitch level 1** (Hints 14 and 15).
- When a group is **not the last** in the series or problem, immediately **glide the pitch of your voice back up** to show that the series is not finished (see explanations for Unit I5).
- **Pause briefly** before going on.
- At the end of the **final group** in the series or problem, **keep your voice on pitch level 1.** Do not let it rise.
- When a group consists of **only one number,** the intonation is usually shortened to a **quick [31 ↗] or [1 ↗] glide.**
- Several other **variations** on the intonation within number groups are possible. However, they are all characterized by a brief pause between groups and a nonfinal rising (or final falling) glide at the end of each group.

Index to Key Words
and Phrases Used in
Pronunciation Matters Units

This index may help you find a story or unit based on the key words or phrases contrasted in it. The number of the *Pronunciation Matters* instructional unit that uses each key word or phrase listed below is given to the right of it.